VANISHING SPECIES

Saving the Fish,

VANISHING SPECIES

Sacrificing the Fisherman

Susan R. Playfair

University Press of New England
HANOVER AND LONDON

University Press of New England, 37 Lafayette St., Lebanon, NH 03766

5 4 3 2 1

LIBRARY OF CONGRESS CATALOGING-IN-PUBLICATION DATA

Playfair, Susan R.

Vanishing species : saving the fish, sacrificing the fisherman /

Susan R. Playfair.

  p. cm.

Includes bibliographical references and index.

ISBN 1–58465–318–3 (cloth : alk. paper)

1. Lobster fishers—Maine. 2. Lobster fisheries—Maine. 3. Lobster

industry—Maine. I. Title

  HD8039.F66 U536 2003

  338.3'727'0974—dc21

2002153373

For Charles Butman, Jr.,

and all the other men and women who go to sea to feed

those who stay ashore

Out on the water, I discovered, everything is what it is. The life is too hard and too dangerous for it to be any different. That is why people who go to sea fall in love with it. Because what you do is who you are.

 —Paul Watkins, *The Story of My Disappearance*, Random House

They sincerely loved something, . . . lived for a myth about themselves and the idea of adventure, were convinced that certain things were really worth dying for, believed that they could make their lives into whatever they dreamed.

 —Susan Orlean, *The Orchid Thief*, Picador USA

Contents

Preface

The year was 1969, May or possibly June. Three of us were sailing an Alden yawl from its berth at Boston's Lewis Wharf south along the coast of Massachusetts, through the Cape Cod Canal, and on into Buzzards Bay.

All three sails were taut. The boat was slicing through the water at a speed averaging six knots. Wind was freshening to fifteen to twenty knots. It was close to nine in the evening. Visibility was clear, but clouds covered the moon. I was at the helm while the owner and my other friend were fixing coffee below.

As I bent to adjust a line to the jib, I saw streaks of white flowing from the hull of the boat. *Noctiluca* (commonly called phosphorescence), the tiny amoebic organisms that glow at night when agitated, illuminated our path through the water. We were several miles off Duxbury Beach and too far from Plymouth to see lights on the shore. The only light was the luminescence on the water as the *noctiluca* slid off our hull, and rolled in our wake.

Then I looked again. All down the length of the boat, silver streaks were swimming away from both sides of the hull. Mackerel. We were sailing through a seemingly endless school of mackerel, their bodies aglow as they swam through the *noctiluca*. For three more hours, the silver bodies of mackerel lit by the *noctiluca* outlined our path through the water. Cape Cod Bay was a sea of silver mackerel, and not just on the surface. For the rest of our passage, the motion of our hull activated the glow from layers of silver-streaked mackerel.

I grew up sailing on this bay, and had helped deliver boats from Maine to Cape May, New Jersey, but never before or since had the conditions allowed me to see so many fish. At that time, I was struck not by the number of mackerel as much as by the beauty of the *noctiluca* illuminating their bodies as they swam. Today, I would be more amazed to see that many fish in Cape Cod Bay.

Fish had bought the boat I was sailing. The owner was the son of one of the largest fishing-boat owners and processors on the Boston Fish Pier. In the 1960s and early 70s, that could buy a lot. Less than a decade later, the Magnuson Fishery Management and Conservation Act passed, including a provision for the formation of regional councils to preserve fish stocks. Canada and the United States set the first TAC (total allowable catch) regulations. And the first fishery management plan for harvesting groundfish in the Northeast was established. Conditions for the fish and the fisherman would be drastically altered.

In 1996, Amendment 7 to the Northeast Multispecies Fisheries Management Plan was enacted. It closed traditional fishing grounds to the fisherman, set minimum size limits for the fish a fisherman caught, specified target TACs for different species of groundfish, determined the goals for fishing mortality, and required that the fishing effort be reduced by 50 percent within two years. That same year, I had the privilege to meet Charlie Butman, a retired fisherman whose love of fishing and whose love of life were inseparable. Through Charlie, I met his oldest son Bobby, who had grown up fishing with his father, and in 1996 fished with three partners on the 87-foot dragger F/V (fishing vessel) *Captain Sam*, berthed in Boston. Bobby began to describe to me the conditions fishermen fish under today—a time when the freedoms his father described so vividly had been replaced by regulations severe enough to end traditional fishing in New England. I asked why no one was telling the fishermen's story. Bobby said that no one would want to hear it, but if I would tell it, he and his father would introduce me to a way of life in danger of disappearing.

Many recent articles and books have been written warning of the loss of fish in the sea. Carl Safina, for example, wrote *Song for the Blue Ocean*, in which he documents his travels around the planet to ascertain the loss of various species. In each of these books and articles, and in much of the press, the commercial fisherman is seen as either the cause of the problem or at best a scapegoat for those who profess to hold loftier ideals.

The men and women who earn their livelihoods fishing have been saying for some time that no one listens to them, even though they would seem the most likely source for understanding how best to save the fish from extinction. And who but the fisherman has a better reason to be concerned? If there are no more fish, his whole way of life disappears, and he becomes a vanishing species along with the fish.

The late Dr. Richard Schultes, a pioneer in studying cultures in transition, points out in the introduction to Mark Plotkin's *Tales of a Shaman's Apprentice*, "he is the student and they are the teachers." In writing *Vanishing Species*, I have tried to be the student hoping to learn from the fishermen. I have also tried to learn, through listening to men and women in the industry, why the fish have been disappearing, and what can be done to change the curve and help rebuild the fish stocks while permitting fishing communities to continue to exist and thrive.

The locale of the book is limited to New England for two reasons. First, I know it well and can relate to the area in a way that lets me best tell the story. Second, New England is closest to what have traditionally been the richest fishing grounds in the world. Because of this proximity, it has a strong tradition of commercial fishing and fishing lore.

Vanishing Species is not about fishing for swordfish or tuna, the giants of the food chain. At least three fine books have already been written on that topic: *The Perfect Storm, The Hungry Ocean,* and *Giant Blue Fin.* Instead, it is about the men and sometimes women who go to sea with gill nets, hook lines, and on trawlers forty to one hundred feet in length to fish for the flounder, mackerel, and cod that will be served to you at your favorite seafood restaurant. It is about the fishermen's wives, who are trying to get legislation passed to permit their men to continue to work in the only way they have known for generations. And it is about the fishermen's fathers, who fished for halibut and gray sole in the days when being a fisherman meant you could buy a new Cadillac and put food on the table for your children.

It is a story of groundfishing and "groundfish," that category of fish comprising the bulk of the commercially valuable marine fish stocks. This group of fish includes flatfish such as various flounders, halibut, sole, dabs, and plaice plus fish such as cod, hake, haddock, and pollock. These fish spawn and live on relatively shallow geological shelves, in most cases within a hundred miles of the shoreline, shelves with names such as Georges Bank, Stellwagen Bank, Grand Bank, and Jeffries Ledge.

In chapters that rely on creating a mood for what is happening in the story, such as chapters 1 and 2, where the reader is taken aboard a fishing vessel, I have followed the action. In other chapters, which deal with one or more issues, I have tried to present the material in the form of a collage, with different voices pasted together to give the most comprehensive impression of the whole.

When I have several voices addressing a fishing issue, it does not necessarily mean that the speakers are in the same room. I found that the men and women I interviewed spoke more freely and openly when I met with them on an individual basis than when they were in a crowd, confronted with people of differing views. Then they tended to become self-conscious and deferential. From their conversations with me, I have tried to create a forum where the different angles of a discussion could meet on the pages of this book. Conservation of both groundfish and the fisheries is a highly complex issue. In order to best acquaint the reader with the subject and still remain fair to the different viewpoints,

I have tried to include the views of a wide range of people most closely involved.

Vanishing Species is the story of Charlie, Mike, Steve, Jim, and Bobby . . . of Lois, Jody, Irene, and Sandy . . . of Harriet, Ellen, Judy, and their husbands . . . of Kevin, Rodney, Bill, Jim, Frank, and Paul. Theirs is a way of life that has existed since man was first able to devise a hook or snare in order to catch a fish. It is a way of life that is disappearing as you read these pages.

It is their story, and they are able to tell it best. I have tried to let the words come out of their mouths, and merely act as the one to draw out the story and assemble it on the following pages. Any material in quotes does not necessarily express my opinion, but rather is the opinion of the speaker. Originally, I had thought to confine the story to two generations of fishermen in one family, but I began to realize that, for a fisherman, the family includes other fishermen. A fisherman is not whole without his community of other fishing families. And one of the strengths of the New England fishing community is its ethnic diversity. The fishing history of many of the men and women who make up this story begins in Norway, Italy, Portugal, or Poland.

Vanishing Species is also the story of the flounder, the haddock, the gray sole—and of the men and women who have been working to keep them from extinction. Ultimately, it becomes the story of the men and women involved in preparing and serving fish in some of the restaurants where a beautiful, fresh fish is treated with the honor it deserves.

A few friends ask me why I am writing about fishermen. They have posed the question, "Why should we treat the present-day fishermen differently from farmers or cowboys in this country? Progress requires change." I happen to believe that society benefits from allowing the small farmer to produce specialty crops. But there is a significant difference I see that separates the cowboy and the farmer from the fisherman. The small farmer, the local greengrocer, and the small purveyor of meats in a suburban village have disappeared in large part due to competition in the marketplace. The small fisherman is disappearing due to government intervention. And that is something we should acknowledge. As a matter of national morality, we should at least inquire about the relationship between that purporting to be the common good and those it displaces. By creating a vehicle for the fishermen's stories, perhaps *Vanishing Species* can help prevent one part of our history from disappearing without our even understanding what we have lost.

S.R.P.

Vanishing Species

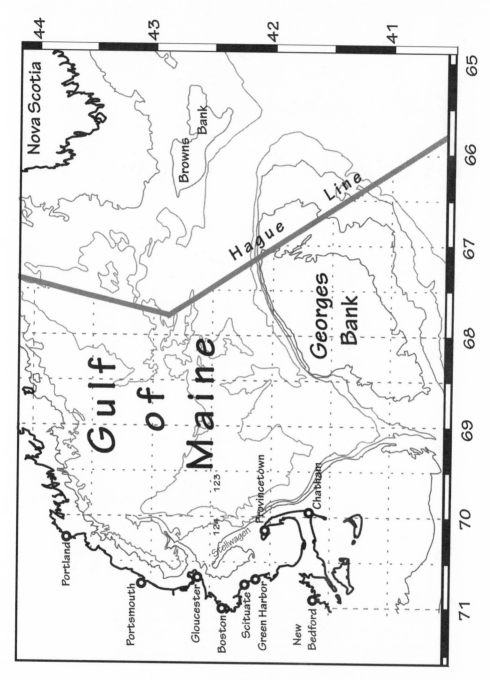

R. J. O'Connell

1

NEW ENGLAND GROUNDFISHING: TRADITION AND REALITY

You know this place they call Georges Bank? God made this place,
way back. The fish come from God knows where—from the eastern
waters, from the deep waters of around the western bank, from Nova
Scotia. That fish comes there every spring, just like clockwork.

—Frank Parsons, fisherman, quoted by Lynn Maxwell and Rebecca
Cole in *Spinner* 3: 1984.

At dusk, the headlights of a black 940 Volvo illumi-
nate the closed and shuttered industrial doors of
Ideal Seafood, Great Eastern Seafood, Atlantic Coast Seafoods, and the
other wholesale fish dealers still located on the Boston Fish Pier. The car
reaches the end of the pier and stops at the imposing three-story building
with a carved figure of Neptune over the door. A driver gets out and
opens the rear door for a woman in a simple black dress and high heels.
She takes the offered hand and emerges from the car. As she stands, she
wrinkles her nose and sniffs the air for a hint of the expected and un-
pleasant smell of rotting fish. Only then does she ascend the granite steps
to the building.

Once inside, she hears the notes of a harp playing and senses the
number of people gathered beyond the vestibule. She does not realize
that the harpist in the Great Hall is positioned where fishermen used to

stand in their wet rubber boots to hear what price they would receive for their days and nights spent at sea. Tonight, a Georgia carpet company is displaying samples of its newest nylon carpet designs where the fish auctioneer's table used to sit.

Waiters in the customary black jacket, white shirt, and black trousers fill and refill wineglasses as they move among the chatting guests. A young woman in a black skirt and white shirt appears and reappears with silver trays of hors d'oeuvres—wild mushroom pâté on tarragon croustades, radish roses filled with steak tartare, tiny pieces of harpooned swordfish marinated and rolled in a Thai sauce.

The harpist's long hair hangs over her shoulder as she plucks the strings of her instrument. Dulcet sounds of the harp mingle with bits of cocktail conversation to fill the space where Danny Bramante's voice used to call out the bids for flounder, gray sole, halibut, and cod.

This is the New England Fish Exchange, now named the Exchange Conference Center. It is the same building that was the destination for generations of fishermen who risked their lives in an attempt to be first at the dock, and thus to command the highest price for the fish in their boat's hold.

Today, it is the domain of Massport, a quasi-public organization that operates and manages Logan Airport, the Conley International Cargo Port, Boston's World Trade Center, the rest of the Fish Pier, plus most other facilities associated with commercial transportation into and out of Boston. It is an organization beholden to no one other than the legislature of the Commonwealth of Massachusetts, which is content to hand Massport the profits from all these holdings in return for peace of mind—a chimera exposed on September 11, 2001.

This building is ripe with the history of Boston as a working port, yet, with the exception of photographs placed in upstairs conference rooms, Massport has chosen to obliterate any trace of the building's past. Instead, it has created offices for its executives in one of the most beautiful examples of Georgian architecture in the city.

When Charlie Butman tied up at the Fish Pier to pick up bait in the 1930s, 140 fishing vessels of all sizes and rigs would be tied four deep on all three sides of the pier, and extending down the peninsula toward what is now the Conley Cargo Terminal. And they would all be waiting to be unloaded. "I used to plan to get there before two in the afternoon to beat the boats coming in from Georges Bank with a boatload of fish," he remembers. "Otherwise, I could spend the night there, tied up to three other boats, waiting for them to be unloaded."

Today, fewer than a dozen fishing vessels remain tied up here on the 277 or more days each year when they are not permitted to be at sea.

Captain Sam (the vessel owned by the Barry brothers and Charlie's son Bob Butman) used to have the first berth at the pier alongside the New England Fish Exchange Building. Now, F/V (fishing vessel) *Captain Mano* (a 97-foot dragger previously belonging to Judy and Herminio Ramos of New Bedford), the F/V *Navigator*, F/V *Jenasara*, F/V *Ripper*, F/V *Tripolina*, and another boat belonging to the Bramante family are among the few boats left at the dock.

Marie Geraldine Frattollilo, known as Gerry, has been president of the New England Fish Exchange since 1983. She started working on the Fish Pier as a secretary for a company housed in the building. When a position opened as switchboard operator for the Exchange, Gerry moved across the corridor. Then the Exchange president's secretary left, and Gerry moved into that job. When some of the Exchange bookkeepers left, Gerry added their responsibilities to her job. No one was ever hired to replace the people who left, so Gerry just kept taking on more work until she was the only Exchange employee other than the president.

"It was a good experience for me," Gerry explains, "because I got to learn the whole thing of it, the selling, the bookkeeping and all of it. Then one day, my boss—Bob Dunn—the president at that time, had a heart attack, a stroke. He was out, and the directors made me the acting president until they could find a man.

"They kept looking and interviewing. Six months went by, and then I called for a meeting of the board of directors. I said, 'Look, you've been looking and looking for someone to do the job I'm doing.' I told them that this is a place where you have to know everyone's move. You have to know these men. You just can't bring a stranger off the street to work with them.

"I told the directors I thought I had just as much balls as any guy they were searching for." Gerry laughs. This was in 1983. Gerry was made president and has been reelected by the stockholders of the Exchange every year since.

In 1994, Gerry received a letter from the director of Massport announcing that Massport had decided to move the New England Fish Exchange out of the New England Fish Exchange Building, the building that had originally been built to house the Exchange. The letter explained that the space was needed to "promote the resources of Boston Harbor." What the letter did not explain was that Massport had already contacted an architectural firm to provide preliminary plans for moving Massport's executive offices into the Exchange Building to replace the Fish Exchange.

From Gerry's perspective, "We didn't have a choice. I was here every day from five-thirty until seven at night, trying to get someone to listen to me. I wrote to every representative, every congressman, the governor, the mayor. Weld was the governor; Menino was the mayor."

At that time, the building was dilapidated. The windows would leak in a northeaster storm. Many of the support firms to the fishing industry such as customs, documentation, and insurance companies that had offices in the building had moved out because Massport had claimed it could not afford to repair the building. And, Massport controlled the rent. It could easily squeeze out a tenant if it had a long-term plan to occupy the building. By the time Gerry received the letter, the New England Fish Exchange was the only remaining tenant.

Construction costs to convert the Exchange Building to the Exchange Conference Center exceeded seven million dollars. One can only wonder what fraction of that number it might have cost to upgrade the building in order to retain its original intent and to preserve office space on the Fish Pier for the ancillary support operations of the fishing industry. Instead, Ideal Seafood, Great Eastern, Atlantic Coast Seafoods, and the other fish processors that the black Volvo passed have been asked to vacate their spaces by the year 2004 as part of a plan referred to as the "Seaport district."[1]

In January of 1999, when Boston's mayor Thomas Menino unveiled the master plan for the South Boston waterfront, the site of the Fish Pier was marked in green as "open space." All the buildings housing fish-related businesses on the east side of the Fish Pier, including the building presently housing what remains of the New England Fish Exchange, had been removed from the plan. The only buildings to remain on the Fish Pier were Massport's offices at the Exchange Conference Center and office space on the west side of the pier. To many, the message was clear: what was once a billion-dollar industry was being phased out in favor of the lure of tourism.

Cooper Robertson & Partners—the consultants hired to create the master plan—grouped Boston's World Trade Center on the neighboring pier with the Fish Pier under the heading "The Piers." Another area farther east was referred to as "the Working Port." This area, presently called the Marine Industrial Park, includes both a cargo-loading operation and one of the state's largest fish-processing operations, which purchases the bulk of its fish from outside the country, then skins, filets, and trims and packages the fish before distributing it to restaurants and supermarkets in New England.

In 1908, when the fish dealers and brokers previously located on Boston's T Wharf formed the New England Fish Exchange, their intent was to provide a fair market for the produce harvested from local waters.

The Exchange operates on much the same principle as the New York Stock Exchange or the Chicago Commodity Exchange, with a few unique rules dictated by the perishable nature of the commodity being auctioned. Supply and demand rule the trading.

When the Boston Fish Pier opened for business in 1914, the New England Fish Exchange Building occupied the prime site at the end of the pier. Three-storied rows of stores, processing warehouses, and offices for the fish dealers and brokers lined either side of the pier. On the back side of the dealers' spaces was room for the fishing boats to tie up plus room for the trucks to load the fish purchased at the auction. Romanesque arches between the buildings permitted the trucks direct access to the fishing vessels, as is the case today. On the top of the buildings lining either side of the pier, a train track ferried ice the length of the pier so that it could be dropped down chutes into the holds of the fishing boats.

In 1916, the dealers on the Fish Pier joined forces to create two firms: the Bay State Fishing Company and the Boston Fish Pier Company. For ten years, Exchange members had been able to purchase fish at a lower price than could nonmembers. Then in 1918, the U.S. government found the New England Fish Exchange, the Bay State Fishing Company, and the Boston Fish Pier Company guilty of restraint of trade under the terms of the Sherman and Clayton Antitrust Acts. New rules required that the New England Fish Exchange permit any wholesale or retail dealers to purchase fish on terms as favorable as those enjoyed by Exchange members.

Now any reputable fish market bonded for $50,000 is eligible to become a member of the New England Fish Exchange. Membership dues, which support the operations of the Exchange, are about $1,000 per year. In addition, any market or dealer not a tenant of Massport must pay an additional $750 per year to bring its truck onto the pier and to permit its owners or representatives to participate directly in the auction process. Each member of the Exchange must agree to assign someone to pick up the fish for that particular operation. A small market might purchase only one or two hundred pounds of fish per day and thus would be last in line at the boats. The cost plus the time involved would make it impractical for such a small market to join the Exchange. Also, the dealers' markup is only five to ten cents per pound, so it is worth it for all but the largest operations to purchase from the dealers on the pier. They, in turn, purchase at the auction.

Today is February 23, 1998, the Monday before Ash Wednesday, starting the week that traditionally brings the highest fish prices at auction. Tied up at the Fish Pier and waiting to unload are most of the boats that fish out of Boston. The F/V *Jenasara*, a 62-foot stern trawler, is tied up behind the F/V *Ripper* and F/V *Nobska*. The F/V *Tripolina*, a 90-foot stern trawler, owned by the Bramante brothers, is tied up behind the F/V *Jenasara*.

Jimmy Bramante is at the Boston Fish Pier auction, where he watches and listens to the prices being bid. Gray sole will come up for bid soon, and one of Jimmy's two boats has on board 600 pounds of large gray sole, 2,200 pounds of medium gray sole, and 11,000 pounds of small gray sole. Gray sole should fetch more than any other fish this week at auction. And Jimmy's boat is the only boat with large gray sole in the hold.

To a commercial fisherman, large gray sole are the jewels of the groundfish. Few know how to catch them or where and when to look for them.

"You have to be very delicate to catch them," Jimmy explains. "You don't want to disturb them, or they'll swim away. They like a silt bottom, and if you drag a net along the silt, the net causes the mud to cloud up, and scares them. You just have to skim the bottom," he adds. "You have to know what you're doing as far as knowing where the bottom is so that you place the net not too high and not too low so that it doesn't quite touch the bottom.

"The net used is your required six-inch mesh net, but it's rigged special. I've personally trained my skippers to catch sole the way my father taught me to catch them. If you disturb an area where the gray sole live, you have to get out of that area and leave it alone for four or five days for the fish to return. If you see another boat fishing an area where you expect to catch gray sole, you just go right by, and save it for another trip."

Jimmy is from a Sicilian family of thirteen siblings. His father immigrated to the United States in 1906 from Augusta, the Sicilian town that produced the fathers, grandfathers, and great-grandfathers of about half the Italian fishermen in Boston. Jimmy's father fished on the F/V *Caracara*, a 100-foot World War II minesweeper that used to be tied up at Tea Wharf until it burned outside Boston Harbor in 1966. After that, he fished from the steel-hulled F/V *San Andrea*. The decks of the *San Andrea* were the training ground for Jimmy and his brothers, until the boat ran aground in a storm off Nova Scotia.

Five of Jimmy's brothers are in the fish industry. Two brothers, Danny and Bernie, are the auctioneers at the New England Fish Exchange. Danny is presently standing behind the original auctioneer's desk, the one item remaining from the Exchange Building. It takes up almost half the length of the tiny twenty-by-thirty-six-foot room where the auction is taking place. Exchange members, balanced on plastic folding chairs with tablet arms, line the sides of the room. Each man has access to a telephone. As the bidding progresses, telephones ring throughout the room; the buyers alternate between holding their phone to their ear and signaling to Danny to register a bid. On the other end of the line are the restaurants, markets, and other customers who are instructing the buyers how high they are willing to bid, and how much of each species they are willing to take at a given price.

"I've got four open at one twenty-two," Danny calls out. He's taking bids to open at $1.22 per pound on four thousand pounds of medium-size hake.

A telephone rings in the hands of Sal Patania, the buyer for Ideal Seafood, one of the wholesale fish dealers on the Fish Pier. Sal picks up the telephone, listens, and calls to Danny, "One twenty-five for four."

"One is five, six, seven, eight, nine, ten, eleven and there is one open at one twenty-five," Danny replies.

Another buyer, with a telephone at his ear, raises the bid to $1.26.

"One twenty-six for four thousand, and one is five. At one-twenty-six, I've got fifty-five hundred under open. One twenty-six," Danny repeats. "Fifty-five hundred open at one twenty-six."

No reply.

The buyers are on the telephones receiving instructions. Each buyer has entered the auction with buy orders from his customers or his store. As the price rises, each customer may decide to lower the amount of an order or increase the "not to exceed" figure he had originally placed with the buyer.

Arthur Kloack, then chief buyer for Legal Sea Foods, responds, "One twenty-seven."

Many buyers prefer to purchase from a particular boat. That way their wharfman will not have to move from boat to boat to haul the fish. The buyers know which boats have been out the shortest time, and they prefer to purchase the fish most recently swimming. Also, loyalty exists between the buyers and the fishermen. In order to pick up a small amount of a particular species from a particular boat, a small fish market will often pay a few cents more instead of trying to enter the bidding and possibly ending up with too much or nothing.

"All the boats that land here usually have the number one top-quality fish," Gerry says. A seller can refuse to sell at a particular price, similar to the minimum-bid rules of any auction. If the captain of a vessel feels the bids are too low, he can "scratch" his fish off the board and sell the next day with hopes of getting a higher price. Of course, by then the fish are one day older, so there's a risk of receiving an even lower price.

"We've got one thirty-one on the *Jenasara*," Danny calls out. "So, now we can reopen the bidding." Then he calls out a new number, thus changing the bidding. "One thirty-two. Now we can't reopen."

If a four-cent spread exists between the price for a particular species on one boat and the same species on another boat, and at least a thousand pounds have been sold at the higher price, the condition is referred to as a "sellover." That is what Danny is referring to when he says he can "reopen." The other boats then have the option to reopen the bidding to try to reach the price that was to be paid to the boat with the higher price. If the difference is less than four cents, the bidding cannot be reopened, as is the case when Danny takes a bid for "one thirty-two." Competition is keen. If a buyer chooses, he may submit a bid for less than the four-cent spread in order to stop the bidding from reopening.

"One thirty-five on the *Ripper*."

"I've got one thirty-three on *Jenasara*. One thirty-three, one thirty-five, and one twenty-six," Danny continues. "Do we have a thousand at one thirty-three?"

A review of the bidding ensues. The buyer for Atlantic Coast Seafood, run by Jimmy's nephew Tory, bids for an additional two thousand pounds at $1.33.

"O.K., we've got three thousand at one thirty-three. Are we set?"

Two telephones ring simultaneously. The bidding continues, then moves on to redfish.

"One fifteen, half or all," Danny's voice announces.

"One twenty for seven hundred," a buyer answers.

"Are we set at one twenty for reds?"

"One twenty-one."

The bid jumps to $1.35. Two buyers slouch in their chairs. Each is seemingly oblivious to the other and engaged in conversation on the telephone. Jimmy points out, "See those two guys bidding? They'll bid the redfish up because they know their Portuguese customers love redfish, and once that Portuguese market owner is in the store, he'll also buy hake, dabs (a flatfish similar to flounder), whatever other fish is available." He laughs and shakes his head. "They don't want to make their competitiveness too obvious."

The bidding opens for gray sole. Jimmy's attention focuses on the buyers and their bids. He knows the fluctuations of gray sole prices by heart. "Once we got six seventy-six per pound for gray sole three years ago. The *QE2* [the ocean liner *Queen Elizabeth II*] was in town and they wanted to serve gray sole for dinner on board that evening. They bought all the gray sole we caught that trip." Jimmy points out that the price for large gray sole reached $7.35 per pound this winter.

Danny opens the bidding at $3.75. "I've got six hundred open at three seventy-five."

Sal at Ideal calls out, "Three seventy-five for two."

Another buyer raises, "Four for two."

Danny confirms, "I've got two open at four. . . ." The bidding continues.

Final prices come in at $4.27 per pound for the large gray sole, $3.51 for the medium gray sole, and $1.66 for the small gray sole. At a local fish market, medium gray sole filets are selling for $12.99 per pound, but those just sold at the Boston Fish Pier will go through many hands and many means of transportation before they reach the retail market— even more by the time they are served.

Frank Mirarchi, fishing out of Scituate, thinks the consumer should not have to pay more than the price to the boat adjusted for yield loss (the ratio of the edible to the inedible portions of a fish) plus two or three dollars a pound to cover profit margin and the various values added such as labor, packaging, and transportation. More than that he thinks is a rip-off. "But, given the price volatility in today's market, the consumer has absolutely no way of ascertaining whether it's a fair price, or not a fair price, because the boat price can change by fifty percent in three days."

Most money transactions at the Fish Pier are funneled through Gerry and the New England Fish Exchange. When a fishing boat ties up at the dock, the captain must first report to an inspector, who arrives to ascertain how long the boat has been at sea and the sizes, amounts, and number of species in the hold. Only after the boat has been cleared is the captain permitted to list his catch at the auction, where it is then posted on the auction board. When the fish are sold, "lumpers" arrive to unload the boat, or move the different species from the hold up to the dock. Meanwhile, the buyers go out to the boats or send their wharfmen to haul the fish to their processing plants, or into their trucks heading for their stores.

At that point, the captain or owner will go upstairs at the Exchange to settle accounts. Danny or Bernie will send Gerry an accounting in the form of slips showing the boat's name, the person who bought the fish, what he or she bought, and for how much. Gerry and her assistant then consolidate the information to produce a settlement sheet for each boat. The boat owner receives a check for the net amount, consisting of the total amount sold, minus Massport's docking fee, minus the fee for selling the fish through the Exchange, minus the fee for hiring lumpers, and minus any other expenses the trip may have occasioned, such as water, fuel, and ice charged on that particular boat's account. The Exchange then bills the buyers for their purchases, and they have twenty-four hours in which to pay the Exchange.

As Gerry is explaining the procedures governing the "settlement," the telephone keeps interrupting. One of the drivers of a refrigeration truck filled with fresh fish just purchased at auction tells her that neither he nor any of the other truck drivers can get off the dock because a small Massport mail truck is blocking the archway.

Gerry telephones Massport management. She explains that the trucks have a short window of time to deliver these fish to their stores in time for them to be served in restaurants that evening. "Your delivery truck is blocking a fire lane, again," she says, hoping to elicit acknowledgment of a need to comply with safety regulations.

She is told that they have permission to be there.

"Can't they park the truck twenty feet around the corner so that my trucks can get off the pier in the mornings?"

She is told that it is more convenient for them to park in the archway while they make deliveries. Three more calls come in from exasperated drivers of refrigeration trucks. After ten minutes, the Massport employee finally returns from dropping off his package and moves the van.

Government employees of one sort or another have replaced the fishermen on the Fish Pier. When people complain about government intrusion into the economy, most have not even begun to comprehend the extent to which this is possible. Let them try to operate a fishing vessel in U.S. waters, where marine law (basically unchanged since the sixteenth century) supersedes the rights to privacy protected by the Fourth Amendment.

Imagine, for example, arriving at the Fish Pier one morning as Jimmy Bramante did, to be told drug enforcement agents were on his boat. Jimmy climbed on board and started to get it ready for the next trip while leaving the agents alone to conduct their search.

"Who are you?" one of the fully armed agents asked, emerging from the galley, where he had been hunting for drugs.

"I'm the owner," Jimmy replied.

"Get off this boat!" the agent ordered.

"What?" Jimmy asked, incredulously.

"Get off this boat!" the agent again demanded.

"I own this boat," Jimmy explained.

"Oh, so we have a wise guy here."

"You don't have a wise guy here. You've got an owner here."

This exchange went on for ten minutes, getting more heated until the man's boss came out of the engine room. "We've got a wise guy here," the agent announced to his boss. Turning to Jimmy, he asked, "Do you know who I am?"

"You're either drug enforcement or customs or something like that," Jimmy replied. "But I don't know you personally."

"Well, I can see you like trouble," the agent continued.

Then the agent's boss spoke to Jimmy in a calmer voice. "You know, we have a difficult job"—and he began to explain to Jimmy the problems of policing the boats on the waterfront.

Jimmy Bramante is a soft-spoken man whose demeanor is that of a gentleman, not a bully. Despite his five-foot-four-inch height, he has a presence that asserts itself through his rational approach to most matters. "I know you have a hard job," Jimmy reasoned, "but I'm going to tell you the first thing you did wrong was when you told me to go away. Because if I was smuggling drugs, wouldn't you want me to be the guy you grab instead of telling me to go away? If I'm willing to present myself as the owner of the boat, you should want me around. If I had run away, you'd be asking, 'Where's the owner?' "

"That sounds reasonable," the agent in charge agreed.

After recounting this story, Jimmy laughingly admits, "Of course, fishermen are known liars. If one of my boats was hauling in a good catch, do you think the captain would get on the radio and let the other boats out there know where he was fishing and how much he was bringing in?

"They say that all these haddock were caught around here years ago." Jimmy smiles knowingly before adding, "Well, no they weren't. Up to the time we began to keep logbooks, it was all word of mouth." That was when Amendment 5 came in, requiring that each captain keep a log in part to substantiate each vessel's days at sea (DAS). Jimmy says that nothing was done for conservation until five years ago. "Before that, they used to have these guys come down to the dock to take statistics. At least they thought they were keeping statistics." Jimmy laughs and shakes his head as he reminisces. "You know the government has eighty-seven thousand holidays, so if a boat came in during one of their 'holidays,' well the catch was just never recorded because there was no one here to record it.

"When they were here, they'd ask us how long we'd sailed." Jimmy's voice takes on a singsong tone to indicate how unimportant it all seemed then. "If a boat came from the other side of Nova Scotia, the Western Bank, the captain would lie and tell them he'd just come from the channel which is out here off of Nantucket, in this area." Jimmy gestures out the window to the south. "That way, he'd automatically get three cents more for his fish," he explains. "You know, when you're talking seven-cent fish or nine-cent fish, three cents more is a lot of money when you're talking a hundred thousand pounds." He looks at the photograph of the F/V *Caracara*, his father's boat, hanging on the wall of his office. "If you wasn't in this circle, no one down here was going to tell you what went on."

Jimmy mentions Keith Robertson, an agent in the law enforcement department of the Massachusetts Division of Marine Fisheries. "The guys who are actually here all the time, like Keith, know and understand us. They know us personally. Then you get two or three guys who are just hired because the government changed or something. You know the type. They'll come down here, they won't know the first thing about what they're doing, and they'll treat you like you're an oaf.

"Someone like Keith isn't going to bother you in the middle of a trip, and say, 'I want to see your license' that someone just saw the trip before. Now if I had my license the trip before, where else am I going to go? This is all I do is fishing, right?

"Keith knows me personally," Jimmy adds. "That's the best way. I've stressed that to the government a few times. I've said, 'You know, most law enforcement relies on getting to know the people, building up trust. You guys come along, the Coast Guard comes on the boat like we're guilty right away. The Coast Guard who come on the boat who personally know us don't act like nitwits," he says. "Like yesterday you knew us; today you don't?"

It's hard to imagine a lawyer or stockbroker tolerating drug enforcement agents regularly invading his or her workplace. The prevalence of drug use around the docks is increasing as regulations are putting more and more fishermen out of work, but the focus of drug searches on the few fishermen like Jimmy Bramante who are still in business seems to be missing the point.

Jimmy Bramante has never been arrested. He has been married to his wife for many years, and is the father of a fifteen-year-old daughter. He is part owner of a family business that includes a restaurant, and also a fish-processing company that ships monkfish to France, where it appears as *lotte* on the menus of the most prestigious Parisian restaurants. Jimmy is president of Bramante Fisheries, Inc., which owns and operates two fishing vessels of eighty-five to ninety feet in length. By most standards, he is the epitome of a successful family man and businessman. Yet because he is a fisherman, and because he does business on the Fish Pier, he is subject to search and seize operations that appear to circumvent Amendment IV of the Bill of Rights and various laws set up to protect the rights of even the most dangerous of criminals.

Why does the fisherman put up with this treatment? Other than the obvious answer that he has no choice, it may be that the fisherman is so used to seeing himself as being apart from society that he may have learned a greater degree of tolerance. But he also may be easily victimized because he speaks the language of the sea, and is unfamiliar with the language of committees.

Alongside the Boston Fish Pier, and one week prior to the auction described, Mike Barry turns his head to the right to make sure the docking lines are free, then slowly engages the engine on the 87-foot trawler, the F/V *Captain Sam*. A space opens between the boat and the pier's pilings.

Mike is seated in the worn leather swivel seat in the center of the pilothouse. He adjusts the knob on the depth finder with his right hand while his left hand rests on the wheel. The varnish on the thirty-inch mahogany wheel has long ago lost its luster, and pencil line cracks show in the grain of the wood. Mike's weathered hands know this wheel better than they know the feel of anything else. Together, those hands and this wheel have supported his family and brought him and his crew back to land through gale winds and white waves where one false move could have plunged the ship into a trough so cold and so dark that nothing could have saved them.

With his left hand moving the wheel, he reaches into the right pocket of his jeans to touch the letter with the seal of the U.S. Department of Commerce. Still there. It makes him think of the twenty-six years, more than half his life, that he has been heading out of harbors, looking for the groundfish that have made a few Boston family fortunes and been the death of many a fisherman.

Has he made the right decision? Many of the boats the size of *Captain Sam* have disappeared from the waterfront. Fishermen in yellow foul-weather gear have been replaced by the men and women in brown uniforms, green uniforms, blue uniforms, and black uniforms—all bearing insignias of some regulatory arm of the U.S. government, and all paid to monitor the activities of fishermen. Mike has filled out papers twice before to sell *Captain Sam* as part of the government buyback program. Both times he changed his mind after his application was accepted and the boat was about to be sold.

Down a set of metal steps from the pilothouse, Bob Butman and Mike's brother, Steve, have stowed their gear and headed for their bunks in hopes of a few hours sleep while *Captain Sam* heads for the fishing grounds. In the galley, next to the bunk room, Salvio Licata is refrigerating ten pounds of T-bone steak, carrots, broccoli, garlic, onions, three dozen eggs, three pounds of bacon, and three cartons of milk to put on breakfast cereal. He carefully unpacks tomatoes, lettuce, and a new tin of olive oil for the meals he plans to prepare while they are at sea.

Mike heads *Captain Sam* out the main channel past a barge filled with home heating oil, anchored and waiting for permission to enter the harbor. Long Island Bridge is on one side; Boston's Logan Airport on the other. Mike heads toward red buoy No. 2, encrusted with ice and snow. It's Sunday, February 15, 1998, sunny and clear. The temperature is 34 degrees Fahrenheit. The stone blocks of Fort Warren, built during the Revolutionary War, glow in the afternoon sun. Farther on, Nix's Mate, a black triangular marker, looms to remind anyone entering or leaving that Boston can be unforgiving to seamen. In the eighteenth century, skeletons of hanging victims were left here to blow in the winds of the outer harbor as a reminder to seamen of the fate of pirates and mutineers. The marker is named after a crew member accused and convicted of murdering Captain Nix. The nameless crew member proclaimed his innocence to the end, and in the last minutes of his life he prophesied that if the executioner hanged him, the island where the gallows was located would disappear in protest of the hanging of an innocent man. Today, the island is underwater at high tide.

The gray granite of Graves Light passes astern as the skyscrapers of Boston's Financial District begin to disappear from view. A conversation between two vessels, one named *Socciadoro*, interrupts the silence: ". . . been icing up all night," Mike hears. He notices that the barometer is rising—a good sign. It is now 1:05 in the afternoon. The speed is 10.2 knots. The radar shows a ship about three and two-thirds miles ahead. "Probably a tanker," Mike figures. He spots another fishing vessel off the Cohasset coast. By 2:20, he can read the fishing vessel's name— *Navigator*—as it passes. "Heading for the barn," Mike muses.

Mike has *Captain Sam* on a course heading of 147 degrees southeast from Boston. By 3:10, the wind is blowing from the northwest. Seas are still relatively calm. Wispy clouds are building on the horizon ahead. "Might be able to sleep yet today," Mike says to himself. A barge towed by a red tugboat heading for the Cape Cod Canal is visible ahead. Mike checks the various gauges. All look good. Oil pressure fine. Same for water pressure. Voltmeter reading O.K.

Despite the extra weight, a well-stocked fishing boat is equipped with every aid to navigation that could possibly help save an injured crew member. The gear used to catch fish has taken many a man's arm off at the elbow or dragged him into a freezing sea. Help could be several hundred miles away. To compensate for a possible malfunction where time might save a life, the F/V *Captain Sam* has duplicates of

a storm warning in effect for Georges Bank, near *Captain Sam*'s location. Gale winds are expected to reach forty knots shifting to the northwest. Fog and snow are still predicted that evening. At 3:15 in the afternoon, after haulback number nine, Mike turns away from the levers controlling the winches and cranes. As he sits in his seat at the wheel of the boat, he scans the radar to his right, then slowly turns the wheel to head *Captain Sam* back to port. A school of porpoises races the boat through the waves. Mike wonders if they know a storm is coming. He suspects they do. By 11:15, he picks up Graves Light on the radar screen. Pretty soon the lights of Boston give a red glow against the dark night sky. Eventually Mike picks out the No. 10 channel marker in the outer harbor, then the lights of the Boston Harbor Hotel beyond the Fish Pier, and at 6:10 in the morning, Mike positions *Captain Sam* at its berth alongside the old New England Fish Exchange building.

Mike is forty-three years old. When he was seventeen, he signed on as cook on a swordfishing boat out of Scituate, a fishing town south of Boston. Until November 1998, fishing was his way of life.

He fished for swordfish for three summers, and in the winters he fished on Charlie Butman's F/V *Orca* with Charlie's son Bob. Today, Bob Butman is the engineer and co-owner of *Captain Sam*.

In 1977, five years later, Mike decided to give up swordfishing in the summer and try groundfishing year-round. "It was big money back then," he explains. "Or it seemed like big money. All the old guys at the dock discouraged me. They all said, 'No, don't do it. Don't come fishing.' They were sixty or sixty-five years old at that time, and that was all they knew. They didn't want to stop. A couple of the men I knew died at sea."

Mike vowed he would quit by the time he was forty-five. "I wasn't going to be one of those guys in my sixties who had no choice but fishing—you know, going down the harbor saying, 'I don't want to be on this boat any longer.' They'd show up at the boat and they'd all be drunk. It was sad.

". . . Remember, when those men started off, it was a week's work . . . plus you got to bring free fish home, and sometimes that was worth more than the money. They'd go out and they'd fill the boat with fish and at the end of the week they'd get twenty dollars, maybe forty dollars.

"They'd bring in two hundred . . . two hundred fifty thousand pounds of fish, and no money—but, they'd get to bring fish home. And that was the Depression, the twenties and thirties. When I started in the early seventies, a regular crew man could go out and make fifty . . . sixty thousand dollars a year—easy. Those men who were in their sixties saw both ends of it."

Despite the admonitions of older fishermen, Mike signed on as cook on the F/V *Old Colony*, a 130-foot-long side trawler owned by J. M. Fulham and Sons and fishing out of Boston. The first trip for the boat and for Mike was in late December 1977. "We steamed out to Georges Bank, where I had swordfished in the summer," Mike explains. "But this was different."

On a commercial fishing boat, when the captain eats, the cook drives the boat. Mike went up to the pilothouse so the captain could eat, and as he describes it, "I'd never before seen anything like it. It was the end of December, about three-thirty in the afternoon and just getting dark. I looked out the windows and the waves were thirty feet high. The wind was blowing fifty miles an hour. And we were still fishing! I called down to the captain to tell him it was pretty rough. He called up, 'Yeah, yeah, just keep it going.' It was terrible! But, that was the norm for the *Old Colony*."

In 1979, Jimmy Bramante commissioned the F/V *Captain Sam* to be built in Pascagoula, Mississippi, and he put together a team to deliver the vessel to Boston. Bill Hallsen, who had served as first mate on one of the largest fishing vessels out of Boston, was captain, Franny St. Croix was mate, and the engineer was Clark Duncan. Mike was the cook.

The trip north was an inauspicious beginning for a new fishing vessel. Bill Hallsen motored along the West Coast of Florida in calm seas. When the *Captain Sam* came around the tip of Florida, it hit the Gulf Stream. And it was rough. Diesel fuel suddenly started shooting out of the vents. The whole asphalt deck melted. It did not go away. It just melted and stayed there. The men did not know that when the boat was fueled for the trip, too much fuel had been pumped on board. By the time they got to New Bedford, they had to strip the deck and pull the asphalt decking up. Each person on the boat had to wrap his shoes in aluminum foil before going out on deck so that his shoes would not stick to the boat.

Back in Boston, Mike signed on as crew for the maiden voyage on the F/V *Captain Joe*, a 70-foot-long stern trawler, berthed at the Boston Fish Pier. He was the only one on board who had grown up speaking English.

"I had never before encountered illiteracy," Mike explains. "One trip, I brought in a joke I had cut out of the paper for one of the men on board. And I handed it to him to read. I was laughing as he looked at it, and I didn't understand why he wasn't laughing with me. Then I looked at the question in his eyes, and I understood."

In 1984, Jimmy Bramante and his brother Salvy decided to commission a new, slightly larger boat. It was completed in 1985, and Mike captained it for one year before shifting over to the F/V *Captain Sam* to serve as captain. Steve Barry became first mate, Bob Butman the engineer, and Jim Barry (Mike and Steve's brother) the cook.

"The *Captain Sam* ushered in a new era when it came on the water. It's a stern trawler, you see, and up to then, the fishermen around here were fishing with side trawlers," Jimmy Bramante explains. The side trawler, referred to as an "eastern rig," is still believed by some to be a better boat in heavy seas than the stern trawler, or "western rig." The main difference is that the side trawler, with its aft pilothouse, is designed for nets and dredges to be hauled over the side as the boat lies broadside to the wind. The stern trawler, where the wheelhouse is forward, is rigged with a spindle at the back of the boat for rolling the net up over the stern. In seas, the boat jogs into the wind during the haulback, and the crew are protected from the wind and sea by the pilothouse. A crew of three is all it takes to operate a stern trawler; a side trawler requires seven men to operate efficiently.

"I took a risk introducing that boat at that time," Jimmy says. "Fishing had died down in the seventies. You couldn't support a family or make any kind of living, because the factory ships were coming over here and cleaning out the fish.

"But after I saw those men working on the *Captain Sam*, I felt better. I said, ' . . . all these men will captain their own boat someday.' There was a little competition to learn all there was to learn about the boat faster than the other man. No one wanted to sleep when he wasn't on watch. And each of those men loved his job, loved being on the water."

In 1986, the Bramantes indicated an interest in selling *Captain Sam*. Mike spoke to Bobby and his brothers about their buying *Captain Sam* together. The deal went through, and they have fished for groundfish as owner-operators for twelve years, during a period when fishing stocks dwindled almost to extinction and the number of government workers hired to protect the species increased inversely to the fish and the number of fishermen.

Sunday, February 21, 1998—the boat heads out again. Tomorrow is Steve's birthday, and his twins are turning eight the same day. Steve does not want to go on this trip. But of all the trips he has been on, he knows he cannot miss this particular one.

They reach the fishing grounds at 10:20 in the morning and pay out the net. Alongside *Captain Sam*, black wing tips tucked under a long white body identify a gannet, a seabird that winters on the Atlantic

Ocean and now sits on the surface, where it rises and falls with the swells. Its lean silhouette and seventy-inch wingspan permit it to dive from a height of fifty feet straight down underwater to catch a fish. This one calmly waits for breakfast as the net pays out. Mike sees the bird as a good omen. "At least we're not alone."

When the net is reeled in at 12:45, it is almost too full to haul up. Mike estimates a catch of 5,100 pounds: 3,200 of haddock, 500 of scrod, and the rest cod, monkfish, flounder—all marketable species. Steve raises his arms to heaven and clowns by falling spread-eagle onto a whole bin of haddock. Bob and Sal laugh as they help him up out of the fish bin.

"That's Steven's birthday present right there," Mike beams. Everyone is fresh after a couple of nights onshore.

At 2:50 in the afternoon, they begin haul number two. Sal readies the chains. The nets produce 1,500 to 1,600 pounds of scrod and haddock. Mike heads north to search for flounder and cod. Again the weather report predicts ". . . gale winds, with visibility lowering to less than one mile in fog and freezing rain."

Haulbacks number three and four are also good. The last is mostly redfish, as planned, with a couple of lobsters, large cod, and pollock. The men decide to get a few hours of sleep, and the boat trawls for four and a half hours. At the next haul, the net comes in slack, as are the faces of the crew. No fish! Bob discovers a hole in the net that he and Steve have to repair before they can trawl again. They head for the boat's forepeak, where a triangular room lined with shelves holds all the tools needed to repair anything from the engine to the winches to the net. Sets of sockets, wrenches, screwdrivers, pliers, saws, and hammers fill cubbies built into the frame of the hull.

This room, together with the engine room and the gear on deck, is Bob's domain; the galley is Sal's, and the deck and hold are under Steve's supervision. Together the three men feed out the nets, haul in the nets, and separate and gut the fish before placing them in the hold. Aside from those shared duties, each has his special area of expertise together with a portion of the ship where he is in charge. When the mix of personalities is properly balanced, as in this vessel, it creates an operation whose level of efficiency would be the envy of most corporations. Nothing is wasted, including time; the boat goes to sea, harvests fish, and returns with the catch in as short a time as possible.

Haul number six makes up for the previous haul. It reveals a large bag of fish, similar to haul number one—Mike estimates between 4,000 and 5,000 pounds of pollock, monkfish, dabs, skates, some dogfish.

If this were a regular trip, *Captain Sam* would be allowed to catch only 1,000 pounds of haddock per day. Due to the significance of this trip, however, Mike has negotiated permission to use up his annual government allowance. As he calculates the amount of the catch, he feels good about his decision.

The National Marine Weather Service is still issuing a winter weather advisory with snow, gale winds, freezing rain, and heavy seas. Mike figures *Captain Sam* is about eight and a half hours from Boston Light, and can just get into the harbor by about 2:30 in the morning if they head home now. At 6:02 P.M., Mike adjusts the course for home, hands the wheel to Steve, and goes below to check on Sal's preparations for their last supper on board—dinner at eight.

As Mike descends the stairs to the galley, Sal proudly shows him the T-bone steak he is preparing with peppers and onions, and of course Sal's garlic bread. "Nice salad over there," Sal says proudly between missing front teeth. "Sal's special dressing for the captain?"

"You bet!" Mike replies. "With cheese?"

"Sure, you think I'd leave off the cheese?"

The table is set for four with folded napkins and wrapped bread inside a basket. Across from the galley is the bunk room where Bob and Steve have stowed their gear in the customary bins: Steve's bunk on top, Bob's below, Sal's bunk four feet across the room.

Mike tries not to look in the room at the familiar pattern of each man's clothing defining his customary space. If he does, he fears it will make him lose his resolve.

At 4:40 A.M., more than two hours past the expected time of arrival, *Captain Sam* is ten miles outside the harbor. The wind is blowing thirty-five miles per hour from the northeast. Sleet and freezing rain are pelting the windshield. Mike can barely make out the lighted channel markers. Waves are breaking through the scuppers and onto the deck, constantly cleaning it of debris. The boat is surfing along with the seas. At 6:25, Mike expertly maneuvers *Captain Sam* alongside the Boston Fish Pier.

This is the last trip Mike, Bob, and Steve will ever make as fishermen, at least on *Captain Sam*. Jim Barry, the fourth partner, stopped fishing in 1995. And this is the last time the F/V *Captain Sam* will ever be permitted to haul fish. When the vessel's lines are secured at the Boston Fish Pier at the end of this trip, *Captain Sam*'s license to operate will be confiscated and never renewed. The boat will belong to the U.S. government. Unless the present owners can find a nonprofit organization to purchase this specialized hunting machine, it will be ground up for scrap metal.

A $25 million government buyout program was put into effect in 1995 to reduce the harvesting of groundfish and give some relief to fishermen. The National Oceanic and Atmospheric Administration (NOAA) estimates that the boats acquired in the program account for 20 percent of the $85.7 million annual groundfish catch.[3] Mike, Steve, Bob, and Jim are being paid $517,000. After they pay the bank loan on their new engine, the four owners will divide $357,000, not including all expenses and outstanding invoices.

Theirs is the seventy-ninth and next-to-last sanctioned government buyout of a commercial fishing boat in New England. Depending on the weather, the price of fish, whether you are on the dock, at home, or fishing for groundfish on a commercial fishing boat, you may or may not consider them to be the lucky ones.

"It's the end of an era," Charlie Butman says in a flat voice. He is sitting in his favorite chair while recuperating from an operation for colon cancer. And he has just read about the buyout of *Captain Sam*. "Of course, I'm the last to know what goes on in this family," he grouses. "But, I can't say I'm happy about this."

At seventy-three, Charlie Butman, Bobby's father, is 305 pounds of muscle, bone, and stainless steel—the latter from two knee replacements and one hip replacement. His weight may be quantifiable, but his love of life and fishing knows no limit. Charlie may be the last of the old-time fishermen using wooden-hulled vessels who was not affected by conservation regulations. If health had permitted, he would still be fishing, but his stories of the heyday of fishing would be tainted as a result.

"When I was a boy," he muses, "I used to go to the Paul Pratt Library [in Cohasset, Massachusetts] and lug home these two huge books all about fishing records and history. I remember my library card number was eight hundred seventy-eight, and I kept taking those books out, one and then th' other. But what amazed me is that no other library card numbers were stamped in those books, only eight hundred seventy-eight. I was the only one taking them out. And I knew everything in them by heart.

"My mother thought I was crazy, reading those books instead of playing with the other kids. Of course, I grew up quahogging and mossing and fishing, but I wanted to know how the real fishermen did it."

Charlie looks out the window, across the snow toward the 250-year-old house where his great-grandparents used to live, where his father and mother used to live, and where his son Bobby and Bobby's family now live.

"This is a fishing family," Charlie adds. "I fished for forty-eight years of my life, and Bobby has fished for seventeen years. He grew up fishing as a boy." The previously robust voice now lacks purpose.

"Just to say we can't fish. There's something wrong with that. For seven generations . . . ," Charlie emphasizes his point by clearing his throat, "this family has had connections to the sea. It started with three brothers who were sea captains in Scotland. Their name was Stewart. One brother came to this country and married an Indian woman who bore him twelve children—all born at sea. And now Bobby has carried on that link to the sea. He started lobstering with me when he was six or seven years old.

"The ocean gets ahold of you and you can't let go."

Charlie's home is beside a ledge in Cohasset, a town whose history is shaped by the sea. He was born there and, except for four years as an infantryman during World War II, has always lived there and on the surrounding ocean. The weathervane atop the Paul Pratt Memorial Library, where Charlie first read about fishing, is in the shape of a gold-leafed mackerel. Cohasset was the training ground for Henry Bigelow, coauthor of *Fishes of the Gulf of Maine*, the book still used today by the National Marine Fisheries Service as the source for fish behavior and the foundation for fisheries regulations.

Up until 1840, Cohasset built and manned many of the fishing schooners that sailed for the codfishing grounds of the Grand Bank and Georges Bank. Fishing was the primary source of income for the town where the men would often be at sea from April through September. Out of a population of 1,200, at least 300 were actual fishermen, while an additional 20 or more boys were employed to pack the fish, and many more labored in cooper shops, saltworks, and shipyards.[4]

When the men from Cohasset, Gloucester, and other seaport towns returned from fighting in the Civil War, they turned to finding ways to "modernize" fishing. The purse seine, a purse-shaped net capable of entrapping a whole school of fish, replaced the handline. Commercial fishing before the war consisted of twelve or so men lining the rail of a fishing schooner while each man held in his hands four lines with hooks meant to snare codfish, mackerel, or halibut as they swam fifty feet below the bottom of the boat. Purse seines permitted the crew of a fishing schooner to haul in a school of fish instead of pulling one at a time over the side.

At least one fisherman expressed concern over what he perceived as the "devastating and destructive" method of seine netting. Captain Sylvanus Smith, writing at the age of eighty-six, described how plentiful halibut had been along the coast of Cape Ann. As Captain Smith saw it, fish did not bite a hook during spawning season, and as a result "countless millions of young were left to mature and become themselves producers in nature's marine farm, the ocean."[5] With the advent of seining and later steam trawling, Captain Smith reported seeing vessels catch vast tonnages of spawning-age fish during spawning season, with "thousands of barrels of smaller fish destroyed, the vessels saving only the best."[6] Seines indiscriminately trapped menhaden and other small fish that had previously provided food for mackerel, cod, pollock, and dogfish or sand sharks. Captain Smith contended that in the absence of menhaden, the dogfish turned to eating the mackerel, cod, and pollock.[7] *Fishes of the Gulf of Maine*, published in 1953, attests to Captain Smith's assertion. Despite both scientific and observed knowledge that dogfish eat commercial groundfish when bait fish such as menhaden are not available, a moratorium on catching dogfish exists in the Gulf of Maine in the year 2001, and menhaden are ground up for fertilizer. The debate continues.

Purse seining soon gave way to dory trawling, a move inherent with danger for the fisherman. A schooner now went to sea with six or eight double-ended open rowing skiffs or dories. Each was about fifteen feet in length, high-sided, and looked as if it could not possibly stay afloat on its flat bottom, a fraction of its overall volume. Dory trawling knew no season. It could leave two men adrift in a fog, out of sight of home and ship, with the possibility of freezing snow and ice barring their way back to the mother vessel.

Despite its first impression when out of water, the dory remains even today one of the fastest rowboat designs on the water. In the late 1800s, after sailing to the fishing grounds, a fishing schooner would lower the dory or dories into the sea. Each dory, holding two men and a tub of hooks and line, would be rowed a mile or so to the likeliest spot for fish. The men would then send a barrel buoy over the side and feed out approximately a mile of fishing line, supporting thousands of ganging lines from which hung individual baited hooks. Once the fishermen payed out the contents of the tub, they would drop another anchor and buoy over the side to mark the farthest end of the "trawl," or line linking it all together. The men would then row back to the fishing schooner to warm up with a "mug up" of coffee while the then-plentiful fish literally "bit the hooks."

After coffee, it was back to the trawl, where the fishermen could expect to haul in a ton or so of halibut or cod. Then back to the schooner, where they would send the fish up over the rail to their shipmates, and then up and over the side themselves to spend the day or night cleaning and salting the catch.

The haul from that one dory would probably have taken a vessel of handliners a week or more to catch. Multiply that by eight for the number of dories on board, and the first signs emerge that man might tip the balance between supply and demand from the sea. But at that time, cod stocks were perceived as inexhaustible.

Until the middle of the nineteenth century, only cod was harvested in large quantities. In 1880 gillnetting was introduced from Norway. Gillnetting caught flatfish with gills, such as flounder, in a fence of netting as they swam through the water. Fishermen began to claim a portion of the ocean for the nets attached to weighted buoys and left in place until the boat returned the next day to reel in the catch. Fish swimming closer to shore were now more easily harvested as they swam into the fixed nets, and people began to devise recipes for species other than cod. Mackerel became a principal food fish, later followed by herring, haddock, and halibut (previously fed only to slaves). The category of fish caught commercially was expanding, as was the number of men involved in catching them. In 1880, the New England states listed 29,838 men registered as commercial fishermen, more than half from Massachusetts.[8]

The fish still had man's susceptibility to weather on their side. As demand for fish grew, so did the demand for high-speed vessels. Boat owners paid their designers and shipbuilders to "lay on more sail." Fishing schooners became more "clipperlike." Masts 110 feet tall, supporting combined sail areas of more than eight thousand square feet of canvas, drove bowsprits into the sea and swept men from the decks, promoting the nickname "widowmakers." Any sailor knows that increasing sail area not only increases speed but also increases risk. A fishing schooner that could now sail faster could also sail farther from shore, and when a "nor'easter" would blow up without warning on Georges Bank, a boat could be a long way from port with a load of fish to get to market. In the twenty-five years between 1866 and 1890, the town of Gloucester alone lost 382 schooners and 2,454 fishermen, nearly 10 percent of Massachusetts' fishing population.[9] One hundred fifty-nine Gloucester men were lost in a single gale in February of 1879.[10]

Finally, in 1882, Captain Joseph Collins, a Gloucester skipper working for the U.S. Fish Commission in Washington, D.C., began to publish letters and articles highlighting the dangers inherent in the design of the Gloucester fishing schooners. Captain Collins was aware that owners of fishing vessels resisted building deep-draft boats because they wanted their vessels to move easily over the shallow waters of both Georges Bank and Gloucester's inner harbor, no matter what the tide. At Collins's urging, the Fish Commission financed the design and building of the research schooner *Grampus* by the East Boston yard of Dennison J. Lawlor. *Grampus*, believed to have been designed by Lawlor though credited to Collins, had a deep hold (over a foot and half deeper than existing schooners) and a low center of gravity so that it could naturally right itself when blown over.[11]

The *Grampus* introduced innovations to a line of elegant fishing schooners that culminated in the launching of the *Gertrude L. Thebaud* in 1930. Considered by many to represent the pinnacle of the fishing schooners, the *Thebaud* was 132 feet long at the waterline with a sail area as large as a standard tennis court. From its launching until October 1938, when the Depression finally put a stop to the glorious days of the competition between the Canadian schooner *Bluenose* and the *Thebaud*, the *Thebaud* was the pride of the fleet. It was also the last full-rigged Essex fishing vessel.

The April 1998 issue of the *National Fisherman* includes an interview with Captain Frank Mitchell, one of the last surviving captains of a sail-driven fishing schooner. Captain Mitchell relates the story of being caught offshore on board the 122-foot schooner *Adventure* during the great hurricane of 1938, which had winds that were clocked at 183 miles per hour.

Adventure, with 140,000 pounds of fish on board, was heading to Boston's Fish Pier from Emerald Bank south of Halifax when a crew member picked up a report of the storm on the ship's radio receiver. The schooner was too far out to sea to seek safety. Mitchell ordered the sails to be furled, and all deck gear to be lashed to the deck. He commanded his crew to go below, then told them, "There's a bad one coming up the coast. Not much we can do. Mother Nature's going to take care of herself. We'll just have to ride it out."[12]

Mitchell recalled, "When that wind struck, she [*Adventure*] laid right over until half her cabin house was in the water, and the spars nearly touched the water."[13] Time and again the wind would subside and the schooner would partly right itself, only to be blown over again.

Later, Captain Mitchell would describe *Adventure* being "tossed around like a ball." He firmly believed the weight of the load of fish they were carrying saved them from going under. Whatever the reason, the storm passed, and the *Adventure* returned to port with all men on board. Not all crews were so lucky. In that same storm, six hundred people lost their lives, more than two thousand were injured, and fishing vessels that went to the bottom showed up, plank by plank, as driftwood on the rocky shores of Maine and on down the coast to Gloucester.

In 1905, the F/V *Spray*, the first American steam trawler, was commissioned by a group of Boston investors who called themselves the Bay State Fishery Group. The *Spray* was the first American fishing vessel outfitted with an otter trawl.[14] Wooden doors weighing upwards of

1,500 pounds held open a large baglike net, closed at one end (the cod end) and dragged along the bottom five hundred to six hundred feet behind *Spray* to scoop into the closed or cod end whatever fish were in its path. The otter doors on *Captain Sam* are not very different from those on *Spray*. Otter trawls, together with man's ability to fish without relying on the wind to push sails, augured that the seemingly inexhaustible fish stocks could conceivably be fished out.

Dory fishermen, still fishing with hook and line, feared that the otter trawl would be a threat to the fish stocks, and they petitioned their Massachusetts legislators to ban the new gear or to restrict its use. The older fishermen pointed out that their hooks caught only mature fish, while immature fish caught in error could be returned live to sea to reproduce and ensure a healthy stock. They contrasted their methods of fishing with those of the steam-powered trawler, whose otter doors caught everything in the trawler's path and where the fish were all dead by the time they were brought on board. Captain Smith raised the same question ten years after the introduction of the otter trawl: "In sweeping over the banks, these great trawlers overturned clams, mussels and other seafood which attracted fish in great numbers—but has fish been found in great quantities since?"[15] Eighty-five years later, Paul Parker and other members of the Cape Cod Hook Fishermen's Association are still voicing the same concerns and still waiting for legislative action.

Boats driven by steam power, then by diesel power, replaced the schooners. In the year 1900, fifty traditional fishing schooners sailed out of Gloucester. By 1940 there were only two. The rest were powered by engines.[16]

"Gawd, I love to read about those old fishing schooners!" Charlie Butman slaps the flat of his hand against his thigh in exclamation.

"I used to build boats with the same details I imagined were in those schooners."

Charlie's first boat was the *Bulldog*, which he bought for five dollars and sold for fifty. *Bulldog* was a 20-foot double-ended English steam lifeboat with no engine, and as Charlie describes it, "not much in between the top and the bottom." Charlie installed an old five-horsepower Lathrop engine he bought for five dollars. He made a new sheave for steering from wood cut on the property managed by his uncle Arthur. Then he changed the name to the *Lois J.*, after the lady who would become Lois Butman. And he was on the water.

He was fourteen years old. The year was 1939. His father was working for two dollars a day digging trenches to feed the family. Charlie remembers that in winter months, when he could not quahog or fish, his father would give him exactly two bullets and tell him to go hunt for dinner. He learned to be a good shot, and most evenings the family ate squirrel, either fricasseed or stewed.

When he decided he needed a larger boat, the same inventiveness born of necessity caused him to cut the *Lois J.* in half and add a four-foot section between the two halves. He then bought a four-cylinder Willys engine out of a Jeep, and went lobstering. Four years later, when Charlie returned from fighting in Guam, he sold the *Lois J.* and borrowed $650 from a friend to buy the boat of a local fisherman. The original caulking between the planks turned out to be made of silk stockings. Charlie bought the boat in the winter, and when the ice around the silk stockings melted, the garboards holding the engine in the boat sagged, and the engine fell out. Undaunted, Charlie found a six-cylinder Ford flathead engine from a car wreck to replace the old engine. "I just wanted to be on the sea. Bobby is the same. We're a vanishing species," Charlie laments, his blue eyes looking out toward the sea beneath the black brim on his long-billed red cap, the same type of red cap that immediately identifies him to everyone on the waterfront.

The spirit and enticement of fishing continued to lure young men such as Charlie to the water, but it would be the larger harbors of Boston, Gloucester, and New Bedford that provided a base and a market for their labors. By the time Charlie was fishing out of Scituate in his 73-foot trawler, painted the red of his hat, the confluence of several factors provided conditions more favorable for the New England fisherman than had existed before, or have been seen since.

In the mid-1960s, factory trawler fleets from distant countries such as the Soviet Union, Spain, and Iceland arrived to fish on the Grand Bank, Flemish Cap, and Georges Bank, previously the fishing grounds for mainly Canadian and New England fishermen. The hope was that the Canadian and U.S. fishermen could somehow continue to fish alongside the nomadic giants, whose size and degree of industrialization far outstripped the traditional methods of the shore-based fishing fleets.[17]

While the factory trawlers combed the outer banks, Charlie Butman was fishing out of Scituate on a 150-ton wooden stern trawler. He had a roller net for hard-bottom fishing and a disc, or chain net, for sandy-bottom fishing. He made all his own reels. He painted his boat the same red as his cap and named it *Orca*. His main catch was codfish.

"One day, I caught a hundred-thirty-five-pound codfish with several soft-shell lobsters in its belly. They'll swallow a three-pound lobster with a new shell just like nothing," Charlie recounts. "Course they've got a mouth that big." Charlie holds his hands out, palms about ten inches apart. "They'll take fish, herring, whiting, anything . . . and whiting have sharp teeth, but they'll swallow them things whole, cause you cut 'em open, and those fish come out whole, just about ready to eat.

"We used to get codfish—big codfish—when we were in shrimp country. Those cod were swimming along, eating the shrimp at the same time as we were catching them . . . probably eating 'em in the net. And the shrimp that came out of them were about as fresh as you could get. We'd cut the bellies open, dump the shrimp out into a tank of water to wash 'em, take 'em home, and eat 'em," Charlie laughs appreciatively. "I used to take home about three or four big bread bags of shrimp after a fishing trip, and Lois and I would sit at the table with old Jasper, our dog we had then. And every broken one went to Jasper. Oh, he loved them.

"I miss all that stuff, you know, 'cause I lived on it," he reminisces.

When Charlie was in his thirties and fishing out of Scituate, Frank Mirarchi was in his early twenties and had just purchased his first fishing boat. Today, Frank is fifty-five, and still fishing out of Scituate on the F/V *Christopher Andrew*, a 60-foot stern trawler he owns jointly with his son Andrew.

"Charlie used to fix my boat for me, and I would mend his nets," Frank reminisces. "We were competitors, but we were collaborators too. And that spirit is what is the most important part of fishing to me. When I started fishing in the summers, while I was in college, it was the most wonderful life you could possibly imagine. All the people cooperated to help each other."

As a young boy growing up in Scituate, Frank fished from a pleasure boat his family kept in the harbor. Later, in college, he got a summer job on the F/V *Frances Elizabeth*, a 60-foot side trawler owned at the time by Captain Dan Arnold, and still fishing today out of Plymouth, Massachusetts, captained by Dan's son, David.

"I loved boats, loved the water, and always loved to go fishing," Frank recounts. "When I found that fishing for three months in the summers could pay my college tuition and still leave me some spending money, I said, 'This is great! This is the kind of thing I like to do, and I can make a lot of money doing it.' "

The year was 1963. As Frank tells the story, "Nobody had been fishing these inshore waters, and it just got better and better"—until 1968 or 1970, when the foreign fleets began to arrive on Georges Bank and then along in toward Cape Cod Bay.

At the time, only two fishing vessels hailed out of Scituate. One was Charlie's *Orca*, the other the *Frances Elizabeth*. An American fishing presence was well established in the waters east of Provincetown, but it hailed from the ports of Gloucester, New Bedford, and Boston. The inshore grounds between Georges Bank and Scituate, inside Cape Cod Bay, were virtually untapped. All species of groundfish were abundant, waiting to be brought to market. After Frank graduated from college with a major in geology, he looked at the choice of being a geologist or going fishing. Given the favorable fishing conditions, there was no contest. He fished for two years while living at home, and was able to save enough money to buy his own boat.

From 1965 to 1969, the peak harvest years, the U.S. fishing fleet landed an estimated 723,000 metric tons of cod, haddock, and yellowtail flounder from the fishing grounds of Georges Bank, southern New England, and the Gulf of Maine.[18] The foreign fleets caught and processed almost sixteen times that amount from the same waters. New England landings for these same species soon began to decline. In New Bedford, where yellowtail flounder and scallops made up the bulk of the catch, yellowtail flounder landings fell from 34,700 metric tons in 1965 to 17,000 metric tons in 1976.[19] The percentage of haddock landed from Georges Bank by U.S. fishermen dropped from 90 percent in 1960 to slightly more than 10 percent in 1972. The rest was taken by foreign vessels. Gulf of Maine cod landings dropped from 92 million pounds to 41 million pounds.[20]

Fishermen called on the government to help, and Congress responded by passing legislation to extend the Exclusive Economic Zone from three nautical miles off the coast to two hundred miles, effectively prohibiting most foreign trawlers from fishing inside the two-hundred-mile limit. Congressman Gerry Studds from Massachusetts and Representative Warren Magnuson from the state of Washington sponsored what was originally called the Fishery Management and Conservation Act. Renamed the Magnuson-Stevens Fishery Conservation and Management Act twenty years later, it was originally crafted as a plan to develop—more than conserve—the fisheries.

Plans to produce more revenue from the ocean dovetailed with the introduction of more sophisticated electronics for finding and harvesting fish. Raytheon and other manufacturers of marine electronics ran full-page ads in the classified section of *National Fisherman* with the words "Lets you see every fish in the ocean," or "Nowhere to Hide." In the year 1999, Roger Berkowitz, president of Legal Sea Foods, a chain of seafood restaurants, would comment, "it's good that we became more efficient, but to become efficient on the one hand while not managing the stock at the same time created the problems we see today."

Charlie's approach at the time was, "you had to know mathematics to figure out how to operate loran, sonar, and then GPS and SATNAV.

I wanted to teach myself, but when I didn't understand anything, I turned to Frank because he thrived on all of that. Frank was a very intelligent kid. He always was and he always will be."

Frank has owned multispecies licenses for squid, whiting, and everything in between to groundfish, which he harvests today. From the F/V *Christopher Andrew*'s launching until 1991, the boat fished with a crew of three to four, and would be out from one to three days at a time. Today, Frank and his son Andrew constitute the full crew, and the boat makes only day trips. Even with the present crew of two, Andrew is the only one getting paid. Frank just runs the boat.

"It's not so much the money, though that's obviously the fuel that makes the whole thing run, but it's the community spirit inherent in fishing which I think is so important, because this is where I came from," Frank comments.

Frank cites Scituate's "Irish mossing" as an example of what he means by community spirit. "It embraces community life, the value of hard work, and putting young people on the water in this wonderful, helpful environment. It's just fantastic." For as long as anyone can remember, a white seaweed has rolled into Scituate Harbor on the waves and clung to the rocks beyond the lighthouse. When raked and dried in the sun, it was used in refining beer, and as an ingredient in cough syrup, puddings, toothpaste, and chocolate milk. More recently, it was harvested for its medicinal values and sold to pharmaceutical companies.

Called carrageen, it is also found on the West Coast of Ireland, and is credited with bringing an Irish community to Scituate to harvest "moss" 150 years ago. More recently, high school students were hired every summer to row out in dories and harvest the seaweed from two hours before low tide until two hours after low tide. Charlie mossed when he was in high school. "Everybody loved the mossers," Frank says. "They were bronze, strong, and they could make a pretty good living . . . twenty, thirty, forty dollars a day. For a high school kid, it was a heck of a lot better than working at McDonald's. And a lot of those young people then went into fishing or lobstering, and that's what breeds a solid community.

"And today it's dead," Frank laments. "The market disappeared. The product now comes from the Philippines, because they'll work for about one-tenth what we'll work for. It's terrible." The summer of 1997 was the last year for the Scituate mossers. Marine Colloids, the primary buyer of Scituate moss, then shifted its buying to the Philippines, where the company can purchase moss for less money.

Charlie also equates mossing with his youth and with the spirit of fishing as it used to be. After hearing of the removal of the business to another country, he comments, "Everyone takes for granted that fishing is easy, that anyone can hop on a fishing boat and catch fish. Well let me tell you, a fisherman today has to be a smart, flexible person or he can't exist."

After removing the foreign fishing fleets from New England waters, Congress was under the misapprehension that the United States "possessed" a valuable commodity, and thus focused attention on how best to manage it.

Whatever expectations fishermen had for the closing of the fishing grounds to foreign trawlers were more than realized after the two-hundred-mile limit went into effect in March of 1977. The reported U.S. landings of groundfish rose approximately 34 percent that year. The share for an average crew member of an offshore trawler leapt to $25,000, a 25 percent increase, bringing a fishing crewmember's earnings to about twice those of the average worker in a manufacturing job.[21]

Suddenly, offshore groundfishing was seen as a lucrative business. Fishermen already in the business decided to capitalize on their new prospects by purchasing new or additional boats. And the government abetted their decision by making low-cost loans available to the fishing community.

While handing out money, the U.S. government, with the best of intentions, was also tying the hands of the fisherman so that he would be debt-ridden if he accepted the offer. Few fishermen new to the industry realized this until it was too late. "There were a lot of people who came to this country around that time," Jimmy Bramante, *Captain Sam*'s original owner, explains. "They got government grants to fish, then went out of business and went back to their own countries, leaving debts and a bad image for the fisherman."

The fishing towns of Gloucester and New Bedford were bankrupted partly as a result of the irresponsible policies forged in Congress and sold as being beneficial to the economy. Roger Berkowitz, whose Boston-based seafood chain serves an average of fourteen tons of fresh seafood per day, sees this period as the crux of the problems now facing the fishing industry: "Unfortunately, when the two-hundred-mile limit came into effect, the government made a tactical error. Without having a science in place, it encouraged too many people to enter the fishing industry by offering them tax advantages and financial loopholes."

The Fishery Management and Conservation Act (referred to as the Magnuson Act) established areas designated as those where fish populations would be managed, and it set up the original means to manage those fish stocks. The act introduced the concept of "optimum yield," or the maximum amount of fish that should be harvested for each managed stock. The act also stipulated that regional fishery management councils be formed to act as stewards to protect the fishing grounds. As a result, in 1977 the New England Fishery Management Council was created. By the end of 1978, a plan had been put in place to set a minimum mesh size for fishing of five and one-eighth inches, to establish the rules for mandatory reporting by each vessel, and to establish the quotas allowed for the catch of each species per vessel per trip.

"For years, it's been apparent that we couldn't [continue to] have the effort out there that we had," fisherman Rodney Avila recounts as he points in the direction of New Bedford harbor. "It [the number of boats and fishermen] exploded after the two-hundred-mile limit was set." "Remember," he adds. "In the sixties and seventies, we had only twelve hundred boats on the whole East Coast. Suddenly, the government said, 'This is our new frontier.' They encouraged exploitation by giving government-guaranteed loans to buy boats, with ten percent down. Previous to that, you had to put fifty percent down . . . or have a good backer go to the bank with you and guarantee your loan."

Rodney was born into a New Bedford family that had fished for five generations, three of them off the coast of Portugal in the Azores. His great-grandfather came to the United States in the 1890s at the age of fourteen, and began fishing in Provincetown before moving to New Bedford. Seven of his uncles fish today; he cannot even say for sure how many cousins of his are fishermen; and a son is captain of one of Rodney's two boats. Rodney first began fishing with his father in the summers, when he was thirteen.

In 1996 the Magnuson-Stevens Fishery Conservation and Management Act, known as the Sustainable Fisheries Act, replaced what was commonly called the Magnuson Act. The SFA, as it became known, requires that stocks of each species be built, within a preordained time period, to a level determined by the National Marine Fisheries Service. Today, many people both outside and within the fishing communities believe that requirement to be unreasonably harsh on the fishing communities.

Fishermen began to comprehend what they were facing in August of 1994, just as Rodney, age fifty-one, replaced Frank Mirarchi on the New England Fishery Management Council as Frank's term was ending. Amendment 5 had been implemented in May. It limited the number of vessels fishing for groundfish and reduced the days at sea (DAS) by 10 percent per year over a five-year period to half of the 176 days previously allowed, with the goal of achieving a 50 percent reduction by 1999. Mesh size was increased to permit smaller, spawning-age fish to swim through the nets, and Areas I and II on Georges Bank, traditionally the most fertile fishing grounds in the world, were closed to fishing. Frank recalls that council meeting as "the worst I have ever attended."

While the new regulations were being implemented, Amendment 7 was being formulated. By 1996, before anyone had a chance to see if Amendments 5 and 6 were working, the timetable for reducing fishermen's days at sea was reduced to two years. Then portions of the Gulf of Maine were closed to fishermen in order to protect porpoises, and the total allowable catch (TAC) for cod in the Gulf of Maine was limited to 6.1 million pounds (more than an 80 percent reduction from the catch recorded only six years earlier). Additional frameworks to Amendment 7 further limited the cod and haddock allowed to be landed per trip, and reduced the 6.1 million pounds of Gulf of Maine cod landings to 5.7 million pounds. In 1998, the year following Rodney's service as a council member, Framework 25 was enacted. This framework limited the catch per trip to 700 pounds in May, then to 400 pounds per trip once half of the 1998 total limit of 3.9 million pounds had been reached. Jeffreys Ledge was closed, and portions of the inshore section of the western Gulf of Maine were closed from March to June. Since the 1980s, six thousand square miles of fishing grounds have been closed, and catch limits in the Gulf of Maine are so low that it is effectively closed. Fishermen, whose livelihood was being destroyed by the regulations, began to appear at council meetings ready to do battle.

Rodney's three-year term on the council ended in August of 1997. Today he jokes, "I aged ten years in the three years I served as a council member." He presently serves as an "approved adviser" to the council and is director of the New Bedford program to retrain fishermen and their families for alternative careers.

Council members, other than state directors, may remain on the council for three consecutive terms (a total of nine years). State directors remain on the council for the duration of their appointments. Rodney would still be on the council if he had not felt he had a conflict of interest. He was in the midst of a divorce, and he did not think it was right for him to serve on the committee if he could not devote all his energies to it.

Rodney does not hold with those in the fishing industry who fault the fairness of the council. "You have to realize, this is one of the last industries to be regulated," he states. "Years ago, our forefathers used to walk around with six-guns on their hips, go into a bar, and if they didn't like someone, shoot him. You can't do that anymore." He laughs, "I mean, it's being done, but you can't legally walk around with guns anymore. There was an era when it was acceptable, but it's not acceptable anymore. And it was the same thing when a lot of these men started fishing. There were no rules and anything was acceptable because as long as it made a dollar on the other end, it was O.K."

Rodney's Jeep Cherokee sports a bumper sticker stating, "I love my country; it's the government I'm afraid of." He keeps computers on each of his boats to keep the skippers abreast of the latest changes in the fisheries management rulings, by which the fisherman has to abide or risk substantial fines. Council rulings are arcane and change frequently. At a recent council meeting, Coast Guard Rear Admiral Richard Larrabee (the man charged with enforcing the regulations) twice rose from his seat to appeal to the council for simplification of the regulations, stating that he had neither the budget nor the manpower to enforce them as they were written. "Even with the increased manpower, which we have just been granted, we would be unable to check for compliance, given the complexity of the rulings."

Most fishing boats do not have scales on board with the capability to weigh several thousand pounds of fish. The fisherman is required to know how many pounds of each species he has on board, and he must know which areas are closed even though they are not roped off and resemble the rest of the seemingly endless sea. The regulations he must comply with change regularly and are so convoluted that a random telephone call to council headquarters to request a copy of the Magnuson-Stevens Fishery Conservation and Management Act elicited the response, "There are so many amendments and rulings, I don't know which you are looking for."

Yet the fishermen do comply. They estimate what weight of each species they have on board. They give a wide berth to the areas marked as closed on their charts, even though this may sometimes create a danger to them and their crew. And they keep logs recording all the data required by the government-appointed enforcement bodies.

"My Dad always taught me, 'You keep good records 'cause you'll forget,' and I thank him every day for it," Rodney says. "What he taught me was to keep good records because someday someone was going to question me. And he was right."

In 1984, in a decision whose outcome today elicits finger-pointing and intimations of political machinations, the United Nations World Court established the Hague Line marking part of the Gulf of Maine and much of the Northeast Peak of Georges Bank as Canadian territory. New England's offshore fishing fleet moved inshore to waters where fish stocks were already under pressure from the inshore fleet, which had burgeoned as a result of the low-interest government loans available for the purchase of fishing vessels. As the number of boats fishing inside the

Hague Line increased, the fish stocks decreased, causing governmental regulations on the fishermen to increase. The result: even more areas inside the Hague Line were closed to fishing.

Rodney previously harpooned swordfish in the areas of the Northeast Peak, Corsair Canyon, and Browns Bank—all now off-limits to the American fishing fleet. After the rules of the Hague Line were put into effect, and the grounds where he harpooned were closed to him, Rodney and the owners of ten other boats turned to drift netting large swordfish using a 22½-inch mesh. The National Marine Fisheries Service decided to base that year's quota for the eleven boats on the previous year's landings. Rodney and the other ten boat owners received notice that the fleet of eleven boats had landed 60,000 pounds of swordfish. Rodney went back to his records and discovered that his boat alone had landed 85,700 pounds of swordfish that year. He called Congressman Gerry Studds, who arranged a hearing before Senators Kerry and Kennedy, and representatives from the National Marine Fisheries Service.

Richard Shaffer, director of the National Marine Fisheries Service at that time, rose to speak. After pointing out that he had known Rodney and his family for a long time, he said, "Maybe Mr. Avila did catch 85,700 pounds, but the records don't show it. Maybe he didn't turn in his landing slips, or maybe he sold his fish to a restaurant here or there and pocketed the money, as fishermen have a habit of doing. . . ."

Rodney was furious. "Luckily I had my landing slips," Rodney recounts. "I said, well Mr. Shaffer, maybe some fishermen do what you describe, but this fisherman doesn't. And this fisherman has his records on NOAA slips . . . which means a copy went to you, a copy stayed with the buyer, and I have a copy. This means I landed 85,700 pounds of fish; I sold 85,700 pounds of fish; and I paid taxes on the sale of 85,700 pounds of fish. So, if you insist that despite my records, I only landed a fraction of that, I would like you to walk over to the IRS with me, because I've got a big refund check coming back."

Today, when Rodney says he has data to back up a statement, no one questions him. But the incident underscores that even a fisherman who has been a council member is guilty until he proves his innocence. Rodney is taking no chances. He cannot afford to. Each of his boats is equipped with a computer. Each computer is programmed to show the closed quadrants with an overlay of where the boat is fishing. Each computer program is continually updated to show the latest regulations for each of the species targeted by that boat.

Not everyone can afford to purchase this type of software or the hardware to go with it. Yet a man or woman fishing today, with the complexity of regulations, almost cannot afford to go to sea without some fairly sophisticated electronic equipment on board to safeguard the vessel from straying into a recently closed area. Rodney pulls up a chart showing an area of Narragansett Bay where his boats fish. "This program costs me about five hundred bucks." He adds that after each of his boats comes ashore from a fishing trip, the captain brings Rodney a computer printout of exactly where he has fished, in case anyone questions him later.

Now that he is fishing less, Rodney has refined his love of fishing to invent new ways to fish within the rules. His computer enables him to stay on the water even when he is in his office. Recently, he and a friend developed a spreadsheet to show how many days each of his boats was at sea relative to how many days they were allowed to be at sea for the fiscal year May 1 to April 30. Rodney is in front of his computer in the meeting room of the Family Assistance Center, his job location, where he pushes buttons to bring up information on the screen. "Let's pick a year. Nineteen eighty-nine. See what I mean? Look at the different fish we caught that year. Angler, cod, summer flounder, winter flounder, lobster, hake, pollock, yellowtail, swordfish, angler tuna, shark . . . we never fished for just one thing."

He shifts back in time. "When I bought a boat, I had to put up equity. The bank wasn't going to loan me money because it liked me. It's a lending institution. It needed equity.

"Boats were always considered a bad risk 'cause they sink, you don't take care of them, you let 'em go, you walk away from them. Before 1976, who wanted a fishing boat? Fishing wasn't big money. It was a living, but not big money. Big money came after the government stepped in and they made fishing valuable. The government wanted to develop the fishing grounds, so it threw money at the fisherman.

"I know one guy personally who wanted to get a new boat. He had an old wooden boat and he wanted to get a newer boat—not brand new," Rodney emphasizes. "So he went to whatever the office for government loans was called at that time, and he told them that he needed eighty thousand dollars to purchase the boat he wanted. The government spokesman said, 'No, we won't give you eighty thousand dollars but we'll give you one hundred eighty thousand.' My friend said he only needed eighty thousand. He was told, 'We don't write out small loans.'

"So my friend bought two boats. Didn't want two boats, but he had two boats. He ran one boat and hired a captain to run the other one. He only had to put ten percent, or eighteen thousand dollars, down, and he had just sold his boat for twenty-one thousand, so he now owned two boats, and was three thousand dollars ahead.

"Or so it seemed."

Before low-interest government loans were available, a fishing boat might have cost between $30,000 and $60,000. A new boat could be built and outfitted for $100,000. Rodney points to a picture of one of the two boats he owns. "See this boat? This boat was built for ninety-seven thousand dollars in 1969. Everyone used to ask me, 'Rodney, why don't you buy a new boat?' I bought each of my boats secondhand and fixed 'em up." He points to a picture of his other boat, the F/V *Seven Seas*, a 76-foot stern trawler featured as Boat of the Month in the July 1998 issue of *National Fisherman*. At the time of the article Rodney and his skipper and partner had recently converted the *Seven Seas* from a side trawler to a stern trawler, with the capability of becoming a research vessel in the future. Rodney points out that *Seven Seas* was built for about $100,000 in 1965. Each of those two boats today is appraised for $750,000.

"As soon as the government got involved, the shipyards escalated the price of the boats," he explains. "It's government money, they all said. They forget that we're the government. We're paying this. Our taxes are paying this, but people think it's free money.

"My father always told me, 'Rodney, only buy what you can pay for. Don't overextend yourself. What you can afford, what you pay for, that's what you do.'

"I know a lot of people who got into fishing when it was very good. They got out of high school, fished for a year, and they bought a Jaguar. You take a twenty-year-old kid who's only crewed on a fishing boat, and suddenly he's riding around in a Jaguar. He goes to the high school to pick up his girlfriend, and all the guys in school who see that say, 'Hey, he just got out of school. I'm going fishing next year when I get out. I'm not going to work for ten dollars an hour. I'm going fishing.' They'd ask their friend if he could get them a job, and he'd say, 'Sure, I'll get you a job.' And that's how it started.

"Some of those guys made eighty thousand to ninety thousand dollars on deck during those years," Rodney adds. "When I started fishing, I made five thousand two hundred dollars. And I looked at it and said, 'That's good. That's a hundred dollars a week. That's what I would do working anywhere else.' And I loved fishing. I always wanted to go fishing.

"When the government stepped in, there was a lot of fish around, 'cause we got the foreigners out, and Georges Bank hadn't been closed. Then what happened is people like me who had more than one boat, we would hire the best person as mate, then break in another mate for the second boat. As the fish started to deplete, the people in it the longest knew their gear. They knew how to make their gear work best, knew the tides and how to work with the tides and not against the tides, and knew how to play the market so that you fished when you could get the most money for your fish.

"For instance," Rodney explains, "Fourth of July weekend, Labor Day weekend, fish are not worth money. I say, why waste my time when I can take my Fourth of July and spend it with my family, and then go out right after the Fourth? These guys are coming in for the Fourth, selling their fish before the Fourth. They're getting lousy prices. Then they're discussing, 'Well, I'm taking a few extra days off. I'm not going back out there 'cause the prices are so lousy.' So in the meantime, you come back in and the price is up. They rush out again."

Rodney laughs and shakes his head as he says, "I mean it's a strategy thing. The people who could figure this out, who knew the trends of fishing, who know that you catch a lot of fish in April, May, and June— the people who know when the fish are getting together to spawn, those are the people who are still in the business. Lots of time, there may be a lot of fish, but they're not worth money. Those are the times when you should be doing your boat maintenance. I'll do my maintenance when the rest of the fleet is sailing. It's a good time to paint, to get hauled out. Nobody is around. It takes three weeks to a month of work to maintain a fishing boat each year. The smart fisherman is going to be doing that work during the least optimum periods for selling fish.

"I fish, but I don't fish for fish, I fish for dollars. Dollars are the end result.

"What's the good of coming in, beating your chest, and saying, 'I got a boatload of fish but I only made a hundred dollars,' when I can come in and say, 'I didn't catch much fish, but I took home two hundred bucks.' You work less; it's less wear and tear on the gear, and you're making more money.

"So these were the people who had the edge on everybody. And a lot of people knew this because they'd been around. They'd played the game for a long time. The new fella, the guy you broke in just to take your other boat, or some of the companies like the Deco Company, a bunch of investors run by a con man, they got way behind on their taxes. And that's when the trouble started."

Unlike some of the commercial boat owners, Rodney deducts all taxes from his crews' pay. He is proud to say, "On my boat everyone is current with the IRS. My crews have families, homes, and they don't owe money to the IRS. Their bills are paid and they don't have a problem.

"I had a good teacher—my dad," Rodney fondly relates. "When my brother and I started fishing, my father would look at our paychecks and say, 'This much has got to go into the bank; this has to go for room and board; and this is what you can spend. No more than that.'

"At the time, we thought it was horrible." Rodney imitates a teenager's incredulity. " 'I have to pay to live here?' I asked my father. I thought I had the worst father in the world—until the day I got married, and my father came to me with a bankbook, and said, 'You know all that room and board you had to pay? Well, it's all right here, and it's yours.' Then he gave me that bankbook."

2

The Regulations versus the Regulated

They're closing the grounds where we make a living, during the most productive times of the year. If they keep this up, there won't be any future generations to fish.

—Mark Carroll, fisherman, Rockport, Mass., quoted in *National Fisherman*, March 1998

Three orange dories rise and fall with the swells on the water side of a stark white building fronting Gloucester's outer harbor. Less than five hundred yards down a rock-strewn beach is the oft-depicted *Fisherman* statue, dedicated to the men who "go down to the sea in ships."

The building is Gloucester's Tavern on the Harbor, where today—Thursday, September 24, 1999—the New England Fishery Management Council has convened for a two-day meeting to discuss and determine, among other items:

- Management measures for the Atlantic Herring Fishery Management Plan (FMP)
- Northeast Multispecies FMP Amendment 9 for groundfish (description of measures, draft proposed rule, summary of impacts)
- Scallop Fishery Management Plan (FMP) Amendment 7

According to the announcement for the meeting, "Interested persons are invited to attend."

Discussion on the first item, herring—including the final decisions on management measures for the Atlantic herring fishery—was slated to begin yesterday. Today is the second and last day of the meeting.

At 1:00 P.M., the hour designated for the beginning of the groundfish committee report, the room is empty except for two Coast Guard recruits stationed in Gloucester. Both men have taken the time to attend the meeting to try to learn about the newest rules they will be mandated to enforce, and also to try to get a sense of how complex these rules are and how difficult it may be for a fisherman to comply with them.

Around two o'clock, council members, together with the various lawyers representing the many organizations who have brought suit against the council, begin to filter back into the room to a horseshoe-shaped table equipped with a microphone at each member's place. Two stenographers assume their positions before computers.

Brass chandeliers hang over the speakers' table, but the room's main light comes from the glass wall on the water side of the room. Outside, the sky is the cloudless blue of a perfect fall day in New England. The sun sparkles off ripples in the harbor and enlivens the red of the tile roof adjacent to Beauport, nineteenth-century interior decorator Henry Davis Sleeper's turn-of-the-century "cottage." Once a magnet for art collector Isabella Stewart Gardner and other idealistic and offbeat intellectuals, the house is now the property of the Society for the Preservation of New England Antiquities. The marked contrast between mankind's loftiest aims and reality was perhaps no greater during the heyday of Beauport than in this room where the meeting resumes—still on herring.

In recent years herring have come to figure heavily in Gloucester's future. Many of the port's larger vessels used to fish for species other than herring off the Grand Banks and Georges Bank, but they are no longer fishing. Their fishing grounds have been closed, and the boats have either been sunk or remain at the dock because the owners cannot afford to take them out for ten-day trips when the permitted days at sea are so few, and the catch is so limited.

Herring, which is shipped overseas, is at the moment more plentiful than other species. And herring can be harvested within a day's voyage of Gloucester. Thus they can be caught by smaller boats requiring smaller crews and less maintenance. What remains of fish-related support industries to the fishing vessels is now serving herring boats almost exclusively. If the rules decided on to monitor herring are too restrictive, they will exert a heavy economic pressure on a significant segment of the Gloucester population. If the rules are too lax, the already diminishing stocks of the species that rely on herring for food will be further depleted.

David Borden, the chairman of the committee to decide the amended rules for catching herring, is asked to clarify what the motion about to be voted on is all about. "Trust me," he answers. "We're the government." The support column blocking him from the audience's view makes it impossible to tell whether he is joking or not. He adds that the "staff made an error in typing the wording." Other members of the committee ask for clarification. Each disagrees on the meaning of the wording on the issue on which they are about to vote.

In addition to the months of meetings preceding this meeting, the council has been discussing this same issue for one and a half days. James O'Malley, who seconded the motion, asks, "Then we're not actually voting on this issue?"

The motion is passed, though it is unclear what passed.

Eric Anderson, a New Hampshire fisherman who sits on the council, recommends five points he would like to see included in the amendment to help the fishermen who traditionally fish for this species. Another council member opposes on the basis that Anderson is not following procedures by making his recommendation.

"At present, July fifteenth to October first is all that is allotted to this species," Anderson adds. "Then part of that period is set aside for spawning."

John Nelson, chief of the Marine Division of the New Hampshire Fish and Game Department, moves that "it" be sent to a committee to be restudied before the next meeting. It is unclear whether "it" is the amendment or the recommendation.

A council member reminds Mr. Nelson and the other members, "What remains of the council's budget may not allow for another meeting."

David Pierce, senior biologist with the Massachusetts Division of Marine Fisheries and a council member, turns the discussion to the issue of replacing restricted spawning area Option B with Option A. Another member points out that Dr. Pierce seems to have confused A and B.

John Nelson says he needs to have the whole matter presented again to refresh his memory before he can vote on it. "The motion was originally presented in the morning," he reminds the council.

Barbara Stevenson, an owner of fishing vessels in Maine and a council member, expresses her concern with the overcapitalization of this fishery, and the fact that overcapitalization has not been as much of an issue as she feels it should be. She lists several provisions she would like to see included. Then she says, "but I can't see how logistically this could work."

As the members of the council continue to discuss the matter on which they have already voted, a lean man in jeans and a worn corduroy jacket over a blue shirt waits patiently at the microphone reserved for audience participation. During a pause in the discussion, several members look toward the microphone where he stands, and he takes the opportunity to introduce himself as "Bill Crossen, fisherman."

He explains to the council that he has not been able to fish, and will not be allowed to resume fishing, until the council makes a decision as to when or how many days at sea he is permitted. He adds that he uses a traditional raised foot rope trawl for fishing, and needs to know whether otter trawl boats such as his are permitted to use a two-inch mesh. "I captain my own boat, and I have no means of earning a living while I am prohibited from fishing."

Joseph Brancaleone, council chairman and a former fisherman, answers, "I don't have the answers for you. I wish I did."

Mr. Crossen's voice rises as he asks, "What good is this system? I've been speaking to my representatives for two years, and now you say—"

William Amaru, one of the two active fishermen on the council, interrupts to ask, "Isn't this a whiting issue?"

Chairman Brancaleone follows by telling Bill Crossen, "Sir, you must find out when the next meeting is to discuss rules for harvesting whiting."

Another council member adds, "Your opportunity is to attend the meetings."

Bill Crossen leaves the microphone. And, in disgust, he leaves the meeting.

Discussions on the rules to limit herring catches, to place quotas on herring, to monitor or reduce herring bycatch (those herring caught and required to be discarded when fishermen are fishing for other species), and to close some areas to the harvesting of herring began at 8:30 A.M. the previous morning, and are only now coming to a close. David Borden, chairman of the herring committee, turns the discussion to a request from two foreign fishing ventures, one from Estonia and one from Lithuania, seeking permission to process herring and mackerel. With no discussion, the council approves the requests immediately and unanimously.

Mr. Borden applauds the fine work done by all on the committee. Various council members congratulate Mr. Borden for a job well done. The council members then congratulate each other and the council in general for their accomplishments.

can, and as fast as they can. If they were truly working to save the fish stocks, no fisherman would complain. But they're sending us a message saying they want us out of business."

Phil Coates, then director of the Massachusetts Division of Marine Fisheries and chairman of the groundfish committee for the New England Fishery Management Council, is of the opinion that Paul's views may not "be totally driven by paranoia." He chooses his words carefully: "If you were a manager sitting on high, and you said 'Gee, you've got eight hundred of them little boats running around. They're tough to keep track of; they're tough to force regulations on; they're always having problems; we have to go out and rescue 'em; they come at you in droves; and they're just a pain in the neck. Wouldn't it be nice if we just had a few big boats catching all those resources?' Now I'm not saying that those discussions are taking place. I think they're usually couched in language such as 'Let's just let the market forces work and see how these guys survive when they're not artificially propped up with the various things the New England council has done for them."

Paul believes that the U.S. Congress would like to see five factory trawlers offshore, and the first twenty-five to fifty miles of water from land reserved for lobstermen, charter party boats, and sportfishermen. "And that's not right. The sportfishermen can wipe out fish stocks just as fast as we can." He talks about a hypothetical situation where a fisherman from Arkansas comes to New England to fish. The vacationer catches a lot of fish and returns to tell his friends. They all make plans to return in five years. "Well, guess what. When they return, there are no more fish because the charter boats before them have caught them all. What's left is a lot of regulations that didn't work.

"If those areas were just closed to save the fish, no one," Paul emphasizes, "*no one* would be allowed in there to fish. Where you're allowing certain sectors to go in, you're now saying on the one hand you want to conserve fish, and on the other hand you want to let charter boats fish—even though they're taking fish out of what is claimed to be a spawning area.

"Codfish hadn't been seen on Stellwagen Bank [an area closed to commercial fishermen but not to fishing charter boats] for years. Then, all of a sudden, the sand eels showed up, and suddenly all the codfish showed up right behind them."

The position of the council is that there might be a lot of cod, but the juvenile, spawning-age cod need to be saved. Dan McKiernan, who coordinates state regulations for the Massachusetts Division of Marine Fisheries, defends this line of action on the basis of recent trawl surveys together with relevant material in a book written in 1953 that lists the spawning grounds for codfish as the southern end of the Gulf of Maine, including Cape Cod Bay, for the period of February, March, and April.

A map in the 1953 source book, *Fishes of the Gulf of Maine,* indicates that the chief spawning grounds of cod in the western side of the Gulf of Maine are well inshore of Stellwagen Bank.[1] Paul and the other fishermen who fish for flounder on the edges of the bank cannot argue about the presence of juvenile or undersize cod, because the size of mesh they use permits the small fish to swim through it. "We can't fight 'em, because we don't see small fish," Paul concludes.

"When the Magnuson-Stevens Act put the regional councils together to manage the fisheries, they should have insisted that they give each ruling enough time to see if it worked. It's bang, today this law, and two days later they add a new law on top of that law, so they don't know what's working and what isn't." Paul illustrates his point by referring to the decision made by the National Marine Fisheries Service to require groundfishermen to use six-inch mesh. "The problem is that at the same time, they also increased the size of the fish we are allowed to land."

Paul explains that some undersize fish always get caught in a net. "I think that if they had only changed the mesh size, the amount of discarded fish would be reduced. But instead both the mesh size and the fish size increased, so the percent of discard stayed the same, but you are now discarding bigger fish."

Phil Coates agrees. "That's true. We haven't had a chance in many instances to evaluate the outcome of previous regulations before we're suddenly facing more restrictive regulations." Phil attributes the inevitability of the overlaying of regulations to "the dynamics of the 1996 Sustainable Fisheries Act, which is still being implemented."

He allows, "It's very confusing for the fisherman to deal with the old plan and the new plan, and the new definitions and the new restrictions. The old plan of management under the Magnuson-Stevens Act allowed us to continue a biomass of fish at a low abundance. It didn't mandate rebuilding to certain levels." Phil translates by pointing out that the council used to be able to keep the stock of haddock at a low level and keep the harvest rate for haddock at an equally low level. Now, under the Sustainable Fisheries Act, it is no longer enough to keep the harvest rate low. Instead, the act requires rebuilding fish stocks to higher levels than exist at present, "to levels of very high abundance, and within a certain time frame—within ten years. So that's a major change."

Paul counters with a sentiment shared by many commercial fishermen. "For the government to point the finger at us is easy. It's simple to say, 'There's no fish, because of the fisherman.' But they're not looking at pollution problems; they're not looking at all the outfall from the cities, all the chlorine being dumped in the harbors; and they're not looking at global warming." He tells the story of a program he saw on the Discovery Channel showing a coral reef destroyed within three months by a two-degree temperature increase due to El Niño. "The fishermen are now in trouble in that area, but no one in that country blames the fisherman, because they understand."

Fishes of the Gulf of Maine, the encyclopedia of fish and fish behavior in this area, points out, "Years ago many cod . . . spawned over a small area off Boston Lighthouse and thence northward toward Bakers Island. Few breeding fish have been reported there of late, however, probably because this general locality has been used as the dumping ground for the refuse from Boston."[2]

In November of 1988, scientists presented numbers to the New England Fishery Management Council that indicated cod stocks were at record lows. A number of fishermen in both Gloucester and New Bedford suggested that the grounds where cod were caught should be shut down for a few years to give the cod and other groundfish a chance to recover. New Bedford fisherman Rodney Avila and Paul were both proponents of this idea. The proposal was unique in that members of both the Gloucester and New Bedford fishing communities bought into it. The fishermen suggested that no one should be able to fish in the closed areas—neither sport nor commercial fishermen.

"We were told that we were saying that [in order] to draw attention to the plight of putting fishermen out of business, that we wanted to make an issue. No! I want to be able to fish tomorrow," Paul states.

"After that, a lot of propaganda went over the Internet from some council members saying the Gulf of Maine Alliance wants to put you out of business no matter what you fish for. And it's not true. I thought it was a good idea because I know that in Italy, Portugal, and Iceland, when their fisheries are in trouble, they shut them down. They subsidize the boats, but they say, 'This is our resource, and we want it to come back for our people, no one else, just our people.' Here it doesn't seem to work that way.

"After twenty years of regulations, every year it gets worse. They're pointing their finger at the fisherman saying, 'You're doing this wrong, and that wrong. It's your fault!' " Paul asks, "How is it that we're following their rules, and each year it gets worse when it's supposed to be getting better? They're the problem. This council right now is doing nothing to save the fish.

"Managing the fish shouldn't be as difficult as they're making it seem." Paul relates that his uncle, Tom Brancaleone, once proposed to the council that it permit each boat to catch a certain amount of fish based on the size of the boat. A larger boat would be allowed to catch more fish; a smaller boat, fewer fish. Once that limit was met, the boat would be required to head to port. "Instead, last spring, we saw boats coming from Georges [Bank] with sixty thousand to seventy thousand pounds of codfish, and we're only allowed to catch four hundred pounds of cod per day." Paul explains that any boat large enough to fish in the cod-exempted area south of 42 degrees 30 minutes latitude can take as much cod as it can catch.

Paul holds a pencil up. "See this pencil? The line between where you can catch as many cod as you want and where you can land only four hundred pounds a day is thinner than this pencil." Many of the inshore boats are manned by only one or two crew members. For these boats to get out beyond the closed areas and into the cod-exempted areas, they must steam for nine hours one way, fish in unpredictable conditions, and then steam back for another nine hours. Two men in a relatively small boat are no match for bad weather, and they would be too far from home to risk steaming for port in the winter months. "These closures were aimed at Gloucester, Scituate, and the small-boat fleet. We can't get outside the closed areas. For a two-man crew, it's not good.

"They're on this kick, where everyone says, 'We've got to reduce the fleet, we've got to reduce the fleet.' If it were 1980, I'd say, 'You've got a point.' But it's a far cry from the fleet we had in 1980. We used to tie the *Stella* down at the dock at St. Peter's Square, and come fiesta weekend, you could walk from the fort to the Gloucester House without leaving a boat."

Paul says that the fishermen his age realize they cannot fish the way they used to fish, or the way their fathers fished. They are trying to work within the rules. They have no choice if they want to fish. Paul and four other younger fishermen have filled out nomination papers in hopes that one of them will be appointed to the council. "We need more fishermen on the council, not politicians. We need to make a difference. And we can. The alliance is a young group, and we've come up with ideas. We have to have ideas that will work for everyone. Everyone has to be open-minded and work together."

Neither Paul nor any other fisherman with the alliance was appointed to a seat on the council.

On Wednesday, January 27, 1999, at 4:07 A.M., another Paul—Paul Gillis—pushes a 10-foot-long gray skiff away from the dinghy dock at the town pier in Scituate, Massachusetts, where Charlie used to berth his F/V *Orca*. Kevin Shea brings the skiff's motor to life and slowly puts the boat in reverse. "Well, at least today it started," Joey Blanchard, the third crew member, points out.

No reply. At this hour, each man would rather be back in bed instead of out here where the water is as black as the sky. The good news is that the National Marine Weather Service is predicting about as good a day as could be expected when you are planning to be twenty miles off the coast of New England in a 42-foot fishing boat named *Endeavor*.

Paul has been wondering for the past two weeks what he is doing here and how long he will have the opportunity to be here. His choices are limited. The first day of his senior year in high school, he was driving to school, skidded around a corner, and ended up in a helicopter on his way to emergency surgery at Massachusetts General Hospital. On the basis of vital functions, he died that morning. He was returned to life because an off-duty policeman was walking his dog, saw the accident, and stabbed the house key in his pocket through Paul's throat so he could blow life back into Paul's body.

Below the scar left by the key, and a disarming smile, Paul is the product of seven pounds of steel: three plates repairing head injuries, and pins holding bones together all down one side of his body. He was in a coma for three months and in the hospital for more than eight months. The possibility of a college education was spent on hospital bills. The motivation to continue schooling was exchanged for a life on the water.

Tomorrow is the monthly meeting of the New England Fishery Management Council. The expected outcome of the meeting is that the grounds the *Endeavor* crew fish will be closed—at least to them. Unless a Hollywood agent is waiting to discover him when he returns to port, Paul expects to be out of work again, and without a means to pay his rent.

When the wind shifts to the east on a summer workday, a lawyer or stockbroker walking out of Boston's International Place or Exchange Place may inhale deeply of the salt air coming in from the sea. And he or she may, for a moment, dream of the pleasures of hauling lobster pots or catching fish for a living. But, options abound. The moment will pass. For Paul Gillis, gillnetting is more than an option.

Kevin cuts the motor on the skiff as it coasts alongside *Endeavor*. The sodium lights on the dock silhouette Paul's profile as he grabs hold of *Endeavor* and hoists himself aboard. Kevin has been the owner and captain of *Endeavor* for two years. This is his third boat. He has been fishing these waters since he was thirteen and fished with a neighborhood pal in his friend's skiff. "I still love being on the water," he says, "but what can I do now? Unless a miracle takes place at the council meeting tomorrow, I'm out of business after Sunday."

The F/V *Endeavor* is a converted fiberglass lobster boat and shares more with a lobster boat than it does with the F/V *Captain Sam*. *Captain Sam* is basically a three-story fishing machine, designed to be offshore and to provide a home away from home for periods of four to ten days. *Endeavor* is designed for a captain and crew to fish for one day. Crew comfort, navigation, and the hauling, sorting, and storing of both fish and nets take place on one level, with a two-step drop to the galley and bunks.

The F/V *Endeavor* is a gillnetter. The F/V *Captain Sam*, the F/V *Captain Mano*, and most other boats fishing out of Boston are stern trawlers. The profile of each vessel portrays its method of fishing. *Captain Sam* lowers its gear into the sea and drags the net along the bottom as it trawls. After the haul, the net goes back into the sea, and the boat begins to trawl again. When *Captain Sam* returns to port, so does the rolled-in net. *Endeavor* plants its nets in specific places on the seabed, then comes back the next day to see how many fish swam into it, much as a lobster boat does with traps. *Endeavor* fishes for the flatfish found in relatively shallow water; *Captain Sam* may fish for flatfish, but usually fishes for the fish with swim bladders that live in deeper waters.

The National Marine Fisheries Service, in making regulations and creating rules for fishermen, often treats both boats alike. The same rule applies to the gillnetter as applies to the trawler.[3] Yet, by nature of its size and design, the trawler has far more options. This partly explains why the small-boat owners feel they are being unfairly regulated. It also may begin to explain why Greenpeace activist Niaz Dorry and other environmentalists consider the small-boat owner less of a threat to the ocean's resources.

After calling the prescribed contact at the National Marine Fisheries Service to report a planned day at sea, Kevin starts *Endeavor*'s engine. Paul goes forward to cast off the mooring. At 4:23 A.M., *Endeavor* heads out of the harbor. The only lights in the pilothouse are the green lights on the few digital display screens used for navigation. Kevin navigates mostly by a loran C moved from his previous boat. A worn depth sounder mounted on the far side of the steps to the galley and bunks and an early design Raytheon radar are what he uses to gauge what is above and below the surface of the water.

F/V *Endeavor* is motoring at 9.6 knots through the water. By six in the morning, green and yellow lines on the depth sounder begin to curve upward, indicating shallower water. At the same time, Kevin shines a light on one of many markers set out by lobstermen to permit them to find their traps in fog or inclement weather. "It's getting harder and harder to find a place to fish for flounder," he explains. "The lobstermen are turning this place into a fish sanctuary."

This is the western edge of Stellwagen Bank, commonly known as Middle Bank. It is also a favorite habitat for flounder, minke whales, right whales, and boats of all sizes and types either transporting tourists to watch the whales or transporting men and women to catch fish. On December 11, 1998, the New England Fishery Management Council devastated the fishermen in attendance by stipulating that as of February 1, 1999, the area where *Endeavor* is fishing will be closed to all fishing, with the exception of lobster boats, scallopers, harpooners, and a few others. This emergency measure was crafted to save a dwindling cod population. The gillnetters, who do not fish for cod, are not exempted from the provisions of what is labeled Framework Adjustment 26 to the Magnuson-Stevens Act.

Kevin has not hung cod gear for seven years. He fishes for yellowtail flounder and other flatfish such as American plaice and winter flounder. The net is made of thin, almost clear polyfilament, with a seven-inch mesh. This is a larger mesh size than that prescribed by the National Marine Fisheries Service, partly because the fishermen in Scituate do not want to be accused of catching cod, which can swim through this net, and partly because they do not want to contribute to the bycatch problem. Also, from a practical point of view, they can fish faster and more efficiently if they are not spending time dislodging fish of species other than flatfish from the nets.

By 6:10, the horizon is beginning to appear as a faint line to the east. *Endeavor* is still in forty-eight fathoms (288 feet) of water. Then, at 6:23, the green and yellow lines on the depth sounder make a more dramatic upward curve and straighten out at sixteen fathoms, with a few bumps in the line indicating a gravel bottom. At 6:30 Kevin puts *Endeavor* on automatic pilot and goes to wake up Paul and Joey, who have been catching up on lost sleep while *Endeavor* was steaming to Middle Bank.

The gray dawn light discloses a stick with yellow, green, and orange flags, one above the other, marking the spot where Kevin placed his net yesterday. He throttles down the engine and climbs out of the pilothouse onto the starboard deck of the boat, where he proceeds to oil a Crossley net lifter, *Endeavor*'s hauling mechanism for the nets. He returns the oilcan to the boat. Then he picks up the marker and hands the uppermost tip to Joey, who carefully carries it and its ballast back to the stern of the boat to be stored until the haul is completed and the nets go back in the water and back to work.

Kevin starts to winch in the net. First a white lead line comes up, then a length of black polypropylene attached to the lead line, and finally the southern end of the net. The sea is calm. The sun is beginning to show its first red edge above the horizon. As visibility increases, two trawlers appear, fishing at the edge of Middle Bank where the water is deeper. As if on cue, four seagulls appear from nowhere and settle in the water on the side where the net is being hauled. The first flounder begin to come out of the water. They wriggle to get free as they are brought in close to the net lifter and deposited on the stainless steel feed.

As each flounder appears, Kevin stops the winch and carefully disentangles the fish before dropping it into one of the bins set up by Paul and Joey. Or he feeds the net back to Paul, who gently removes the fish while feeding slack net along to Joey, who alternates between removing the fish still in the net and jumping into the stern, where he pulls out any bunched net before it tangles. These three men work efficiently and smoothly together, laughing and joking as they go about the tasks they know so well.

Noting the flow of flounder coming up in the net, Kevin explains that in Massachusetts Bay, "when the wind comes out of the east, flounder don't come out of the sand. They hibernate in December and through most of January. Then they come up in February, March, and April. When the sun's out, like today, there seem to be more moving. Their season's just starting now."

"And just ending," Joey counters, referring to the National Marine Fisheries Service closure of the fishing grounds slated to go into effect in three days.

Kevin is removing a starfish from the net before dropping it back into the sea. "The National Marine Fisheries Service should be abolished," he states while measuring a small flounder against the markings he has cut in the side of the feed to gauge whether a flounder meets the thirteen-inch minimum requirement. "They're the reason we're in this mess. They encouraged people to buy big draggers, and now we're all paying for it."

The flounder in Kevin's hand does not reach the thirteen-inch mark. Before releasing it, he stops the net lifter and turns to see if any seagulls are close enough to the boat to catch the flounder. Then he reaches over the side of *Endeavor* to let the undersize fish swim away in the safety of the boat's shadow. The flounder wriggles and picks up speed as it swims down and out of sight. Contrary to the amount of bycatch destroyed in other forms of fishing, the flatfish caught from relatively shallow depths, hauled in slowly, and released by gillnetters like Kevin, Joey, and Paul usually survive. On this trip, sea creatures ranging from starfish to a small hermit crab without a shell were in good health when placed back in the water, with one exception. One small flounder did not escape the beak of a large blackback seagull.

"Blackback seagulls are the king of the seagulls," Paul explains. "They can be vicious. A friend of mine fishes with his German shepherd on board, and I've seen the blackbacks attack that dog."

Later in the day, a small cod comes up in the net as the white body of a gannet streaks through the water. "Sometimes a gannet will be fifty feet up, then dive straight down as much as thirty feet to catch a small fish." Kevin pauses before saying, with obvious admiration, "They're so beautiful." He waits to release the cod until the gannet has moved away.

Unlike fish with swim bladders, flounders and other flatfish are not cleaned on board a fishing boat. Their yield is much lower, with a lot more waste. It is more efficient to have them filleted by machine onshore. When Joey and Paul have finished sorting the fish, the net is ready to go back into the water for tomorrow's haul. This is the most dangerous part of gillnetting for the man who feeds out the net. Joey has been feeding out nets on Kevin's boats for close to thirteen years. He is long, lean, lithe, and extremely agile. He has to be.

During hauling, the boat barely moves through the water. While the net is playing out, the boat is moving through the water at an average speed of three knots. Joey stands over the slack pile of net, which is feeding out at the same speed as the boat is moving through the water. A pole bent to curve up in the middle extends from one side of the boat's stern to the other. The net skims over the top of this pole, moving from side to side much as a thread spool on a sewing machine arbitrarily swings when the bobbin is being wound.

Joey has both sides of the net feeding through his hands—one in each hand—and he dances from side to side to try to keep the center of the net skimming out over the center of the pole. When it slides to one side or the other, Joey flings up the arm controlling that side, and tries to redirect the flow. All the while, the net keeps flowing through his hands. One slip, and it takes him into the water with it. In these waters, at this time of year, he could survive only a few minutes before hypothermia took over.

Kevin looks astern at Joey with admiration. He looks out to sea as he speaks in a somber voice, "George Kaufman, the lobsterman whose body drifted ashore a few years ago, worked with me for several seasons setting out, as Joey's doing right now." The National Research Council, which monitors statistics on job fatalities, lists the fishing industry as the most hazardous profession in the United States, with the highest rate of fatalities. Even on a good day like today, danger is always close at hand.

At 8:02 A.M., the F/V *Endeavor* approaches the marker for the second haulback. *Endeavor* is in only twenty-seven fathoms of water. As Kevin begins to winch in the net, he tells the story of two women from the Coast Guard who boarded the boat the previous week. One picked up a flounder and measured it with her own rule. "She claimed it was undersized. Now I know both Joey and Paul are very careful measuring the fish, because I've taught them how important it is. I could be fined, lose my boat, and lose the catch if we have an immature fish in the bin. It's not worth it."

Kevin echoes Jimmy Bramante's sentiments. "Most of the Coast Guard, they're all right, but this woman pulled another fish out of the bin, measured it, and said it was undersized. I was getting anxious." Kevin continues to free flounder from the net, and winch it in, as he talks. "She called headquarters on my phone, and reported that we were landing undersized fish. I asked if I could see the fish, and I put it up against my measuring notches. It was fine. I explained that it seemed to be fine, but she said no, she knew her rule was accurate, because she had used it in court with another fisherman last month, and he was fined fifty thousand dollars. Then I really got nervous." As it turned out, the Coast Guard and crew had to wait for a third party to arrive to verify that the notches used for measuring on *Endeavor* were correct, and the Coast Guard rule of measurement was flawed.

"That poor slob who was fined thousands of dollars—I'd like to know who he was," Paul says as he frees a female lobster from the net and lowers it over the side.

"I'm sure no one's chasing after him to apologize and give him back his money," Joey adds.

By 9:10, haul number two is complete, and Joey begins setting out the net. The sky is a winter gray-blue, sunny and without clouds.

As *Endeavor* reaches the marker for haul number three, two men's voices, answering each other from one boat to another, begin to come in over the VHF. "Hey, listen to them," Joey calls from the stern, where he's storing the pole before taking his position behind Paul.

The two men are heard complaining about the lack of fish where they are fishing. "I've got some cheese," Paul jokes in a shared play of words relative to the whining (or wining, as in "wine and cheese") of the two men. He carefully disentangles a flounder from the net, measures it, and drops it into a bin at his feet.

"We'll be eating the government's cheese," Kevin laughs. "Goin' to be a long year of eating cheese."

Kevin, Joey, and Paul have their backs toward the water as they focus on winching in the net, and freeing and measuring the fish. No one notices a bright orange inflatable zooming toward them through the water. Kevin turns when the sound of the inflatable's motor overcomes the sound of *Endeavor*'s engine. "Keep your hands in plain sight" are the first words they hear as four men come alongside in the rubber boat.

Three of the men board *Endeavor*; the fourth man zooms back to the mother ship, which turns out to be the CGC/*Campbell*, a 127-foot Coast Guard cutter out of Portland, Maine, with a 50-millimeter cannon on the bow.

All three men who have boarded *Endeavor* are dressed in one-piece orange flotation suits, with guns in holsters at their hips. The orange suit in charge asks, "Do you have any weapons aboard?" Kevin tells him he has a shotgun under the starboard bunk. He explains he keeps it in case a shark attacks when they are hauling in the nets.

The officer in charge tells one of the other men to go below and retrieve the gun. As he leaves, Kevin asks, "Do you mind if we continue to haul in this net so that we don't lose time?" The officer agrees, and Kevin, Paul, and Joey go back to work as the three men begin pulling the bunks apart, turning the crew's older flotation suits inside out, and rifling through any papers they find.

Above deck, the haul is complete. Joey and Paul begin to sort out the net as Kevin goes below to retrieve his documentation papers along with the various other forms requested by the officer. Quarters are cramped below, and the officer in charge moves to the pilothouse and begins to go through a checklist of items the Coast Guard provides to aid its enlisted men in conducting a search of a fishing vessel.

Orange suits number two and three attempt to relate to Joey and Paul. One states that he is the "fish expert" on board the *Campbell* because "I worked one summer in a seafood restaurant." The other man says he's probably more qualified to be in his line of work because he has "a degree in marine science." Neither voice belies any recognized irony in these statements.

The officer in charge lists his name on the checklist as Officer Timothy Brown. He volunteers, "It's the end of an industry." When asked why he thinks that, he says, "There are too many boats." Kevin, Paul, and Joey look down at the nonskid mats on the boat. A fourth man has returned from the CGC/*Campbell* and is impatiently burning gasoline at a rapid rate as he zooms in circles around *Endeavor*.

Kevin turns to the officer in charge and asks if he would please signal to the man in the inflatable to ask him to not come so close, as he is about to tear up the net and get it caught in his propeller. At first, Officer Brown does not respond. Kevin asks him again. The other two men begin to comprehend and signal to the man in the inflatable, who comes alongside simply to hear what they are saying. When he comprehends, he zooms off toward the *Campbell*. Somehow, he managed not to get caught in the net.

If the propeller to the Coast Guard inflatable had gotten caught in Kevin's gill net, the U.S. taxpayers would have bought a new motor for the boat; Kevin, a taxpayer, would probably have had to buy himself a new net. Steve Fassnacht, who makes nets in Scituate, ties each of Kevin's nets by hand. Each one costs Kevin $160, a substantial amount relative to his annual income derived from fishing. If the National Marine Fisheries Service prohibits Kevin from fishing, it will also help to put Steve Fassnacht out of business. Whoever supplies outboard engines for the Coast Guard will not be impacted by the closures.

At 2:07 in the afternoon, almost two and a half hours after boarding, the three Coast Guard officers hail their ride and leave *Endeavor* for the enclosed warmth of the *Campbell*. The episode brings to mind Phil Coates's words that the little guys' suspicions may not be "totally driven by paranoia."

At least two larger trawlers were trawling within sight. Yet someone on the CGC/*Campbell* decided to target the smallest boat on Middle Bank as the one to board. As a result, Kevin, Joey, and Paul will get back to port two hours later than expected, and after dark. For Kevin, the cost of this trip has been inflated to include the fuel burned while his boat idled during inspection. Kevin only hopes his fish buyer will still be on the dock.

He puts *Endeavor* in gear and motors toward the next marker as Joey feeds out the net. Paul calls to Joey, "Hey, did you hear that guy ask Kev if he had taken any boating courses? Jeez."

"They're just puppets," Kevin says. "You ask them anything, and they're trained to answer: 'We don't make the rules; we just enforce them.' "

"How about the guy with the seasick patch?" Paul asks. "You think he's in the right line of work?" He tips his head back and laughs. Then, more thoughtfully: "They get paid to travel around the world looking for hammerheads like us."

On the elbow of Cape Cod in Wellfleet, Truro, and Chatham, a group of fishermen is removed from the draggers and gillnetters—and not only by geography. They fish with hooks and lines the way their great-grandfathers, or men like Captain Frank Mitchell and Captain Sylvanus Smith, fished. Despite their small numbers and small boats, their landings account for 15 to 16 percent of the TAC (total allowable catch) of cod, haddock, and yellowtail flounder brought to New England ports.

Ironically, given the varying rules placed on the various types of fishing allowed, their form of fishing may be among the most profitable. They are quick to point out that it is also the purest and least damaging to the environment.

Less than twenty-five miles from Chatham, on a September day in 1999 before Hurricane Floyd is threatening to strike the East Coast, Tony Lemmi approaches the Provincetown breakwater at the helm of the *Patricia Ann II*. His wife Patty waits for him in their black pickup truck at the edge of the parking lot. Patty and Tony both fished independently before they met. At different times Patty fished for tuna, fluke, and bass. Today, she and Tony are two interdependent halves of a fishing team, connected by cell phone and a strong emotional bond.

Tony and the *Patricia Ann II* are returning from fishing in three hundred to five hundred feet of water, at the pinnacle of a geological ridge that drops off to a thousand feet on each side. The bottom is rocky. The last communication Patty had with Tony was at two o'clock. He had told her that one end of the line had caught on a rock and he had not been able to free it. When he tried to free it the other end caught, and he was trying to grapple the line.

At MacMillan Pier, Patty's anxiety level is visibly building. Tony had told her he would be in at four o'clock. At 4:05, she looks worried. By 4:20, she has checked her watch seven times, and is shifting position on the truck seat every few seconds. She looks out the truck window toward the water again and comments, "I'm surprised he's not in yet." At 4:25 she sees the bow of the *Patricia Ann II* rounding the corner, and a calm returns to her body. By the time she dons her foul-weather gear to gut the fish, her arm movements are again natural and relaxed.

The Town of Provincetown, in preparation for the impending storm, has chosen to haul the concrete float reserved for commercial fishermen. As Tony approaches, he sees the float dangling from a crane over the parking lot. He maneuvers the boat to the stationary wooden pier that usually supports the float, then hands a line to Patty along with a smile and an apology for being late. Looking up in greeting, his dark eyes register kindness, and the lack of suspicion of a man who is still able to do what he wants to do for a living.

He confirms Patty's concerns that without the float, they are going to have to find a way to gut, unload, and separate the seven hundred pounds of fish he has on board before the tide gets any lower and leaves the *Patricia Ann II* aground during the storm. Patty quickly pulls on a pair of suspendered yellow foul-weather pants and prepares to catch the ten or twelve plastic tote bins Tony sends up to hold the fish.

He tells her he lost three hundred hooks when the line caught on the bottom. "I was a little impatient today," he admits. "I was a little apprehensive. There wasn't any real danger, but you turn the radio on and everyone is yelling and screaming 'Hurricane,' and you get a little bit nervous."

Tony fishes alone in a 27-foot boat rigged for hook fishing. He is forty-seven years old. He judges that it would take him a hundred trips to cover the cost of a mate (traditionally paid one-third the catch) and a baiter and still make what he is able to make in forty trips fishing alone. "I fish single dory," he says, using the old term implying danger. "That's the only downfall. I do have a cellular phone and all my safety equipment. But I am alone."

The *Patricia Ann II* is only a year and a half old, and in excellent condition. The boat's electronics consist of a two-way radio, cell phone, radar, loran, a fish finder, and GPS (a global positioning system). H & H Marine in Steuben, Maine, built it to Tony and Patty's specifications. Hull speed is twenty knots, almost twice the average speed of *Captain Sam*, a boat nearly three times longer. Today Tony was fishing thirty-seven miles off the coast. This is the average distance he fishes from port. In the event of a storm, he can be back in Provincetown Harbor in approximately an hour and a half—assuming the seas do not build up too quickly. If he misjudges, he is a long way out to sea with not much between him and breaking waves—on occasion higher than the *Patricia Ann II* is long.

"The good side to the way I fish is I get to keep all the money I earn and I don't need to be out as many days. Someone who fishes two hundred trips in a year, what are their chances of getting hurt? It probably balances the risk of my fishing alone," Tony rationalizes. "But, the profit margin for me is much higher than the profit margin for, say, a thirty-two-foot or a thirty-four-foot boat. They may make a few dollars more than me, but they have to work out the expenses for a mate and a baiter. To me it's not worth what they're going through."

There are trade-offs. The crew member on that 34-foot boat would have been dressing or gutting the fish while Tony was hauling in the catch. Then that crew would typically place the fish in a saltwater bath and pack them in ice, ready to be unloaded at the dock. Tony states that an average hook fisherman leaving Chatham will have built-in costs of six hundred to a thousand dollars a day. "I can set the same amount of hooks in not so good a bottom and make probably a few hundred dollars less a day, but I can do it for three hundred dollars."

Tony's calculations include the cost for fuel, insurance, bait, and on down to the cost of plastic bags he brings along with him. What they do not account for is the time and labor provided by Patty and Tony.

At the dock, Tony takes each fish from the iced bin, slices down the belly of the fish, and hands it up to Patty, who then removes the entrails and places the different species in separate boxes for transport. By the time the fish are in the bins and ready to be put on the truck, Patty is covered with blood and bits of fish intestines.

Unlike most other hook fishermen, Tony baits his own hooks. For a more typical hook fisherman, the day would begin at the baiter's, where either a crewmember or the captain would have left a jumble of line and ganglions after returning from the previous trip. (Ganglions are the lines extending from the main line to the hook, usually with a snap-on connector at the top and the hook at the opposite end.) When baiting the hooks, the baiter also straightens any bent hooks, replaces worn or damaged ganglions or hooks, and untangles snarls in the line. He or she then carefully coils the line inside a fish box called the "tote" or "bundle." An experienced baiter can bait, refurbish, and coil a three-hundred-hook "bundle" of hook-fishing gear in an hour. His or her expertise determines not only the efficiency of the hook-fishing operation but also the safety of the men on board. Poorly maintained or coiled hook-fishing gear can snap up and take a man's eye out, or drag a man overboard, as the line pays out off the stern of the boat. Before arriving at the boat, a hook fisherman will stop to pick up one or more "bundles" of baited hooks, arranged in order, separated by layers of newspaper, and placed above a now-coiled line.

Herring, squid, and sea clams are the most commonly used bait in fishing. The vessel's captain makes his choice based on the price, the season, and the species targeted. Sea clams are generally used for groundfishing; herring, for dogfish. Tony uses a combination of squid and sea clams when fishing in deep water for cod and haddock. He buys clams from Royce Bassett, a clam dealer in Chatham, who buys directly from the local clam diggers. Royce shucks the clams and sells them to Tony, ready to be cut and put on the hook. Tony chooses to do his own baiting in a bait shack at his home, where he and Patty also coil the baited line and ganglions, place them in the totes, and then place the totes in the truck ready to be placed on the F/V *Patricia Ann II.*

In August, Royce charged $1.25 per pound for the shucked clams he sold Tony. He supplements the income he gets for bait by cooking up clam chowder, clam strips, and clam pie, which he sells to local restaurants. For herring and squid, Tony buys from warehouses in Sandwich, closer to the opposite end of Cape Cod, and a drive for Patty of one and one-half hours each way during the off-season, double that at peak hours during the traffic-clogged summer season.

For cod and haddock, Tony uses what is called "one-fathom gear," or $^{22}/_{32}$-inch-thick braided parachute cord. This particular line is soft and flexible enough to allow flat packing, with the line lying flat in the tote. Hooks are baited six feet apart. Tony acknowledges that for deep water, they should be eight to nine feet apart. "When you're dropping something six hundred feet deep, or even three hundred feet deep, a lot of these come really close together." He holds up one of the hooks in explanation. "They don't fall in proportion." His voice is almost drowned out by the flock of seagulls that arrives as soon as the hooks come up. Tony explains that when he is fishing in an area with a lot of kelp, especially where small invertebrates called "figs" (due to their resemblance to the fruit) congregate, "all the hooks team up, and grab into those things, and then it isn't too hard to break the line."

Hook size is constant. Because dogfish beat up the hook and line when caught, Tony uses a separate line with its own hooks for dogfish. In April of that year, dogfish were selling for twenty-six cents per pound—higher than normal. Tony paid his son to bait so he could keep fishing.

When Tony reaches the grounds where he plans to fish, he feeds out the contents of one of the totes. He then attaches a buoy, wand, weight, and radar reflector, all composing a "set." Less than two hours after setting the gear, ideally as the tide turns, he returns to haul in the catch, much the way Kevin Shea hauls his gill nets.

Tony hauls the line over the starboard rail, feeding the line back to the stern. First the wand with buoy, weight, and radar reflector comes up, then the ground line, which is fed through rollers and around a hauler, then down into the "tote" to be returned to the baiter. Holding the fish with his left hand, Tony unhooks each legal-size fish and tosses it into a bin that stretches the width of the pilothouse and is filled with ice Tony made the night before in an ice maker at home. He unhooks smaller fish, measures their length, and if they do not meet the minimum allowable size, he releases them. Untargeted species are also unhooked and then returned to sea.

Several Chatham hook-fishing boats a few feet larger than the *Patricia Ann II* developed a market for live fish. On board, the fish are kept in temporary holding tanks with piped-in salt water to meet the requirements for live produce. By being the fastest link between the fish swimming in the sea and the fish on the plate, hook fishing can provide the freshest fish caught by any of the commercial fishing gear types. The boats fish close to shore, do not stay out overnight, and often serve a market close to where they are unloaded. Bycatch is negligible to nonexistent.

Dedication and a strong economy are permitting Patty, Tony, and the few other remaining hook fishermen to stay on the water. For many years Patty owned a one-story, seven-hundred-square-foot house, together with two adjacent rental cabins, in Provincetown. Tony had previously worked as a cabinetmaker. When he saw that Patty and her two children had no room to store their clothes or belongings in the small house, he turned the interior into a boat on land. He lined the walls with cabinets and closets of all sizes. Two years ago, when the price of a home in Provincetown owned as long as Patty's had doubled and tripled in value, Tony and Patty sold the rental cabins and the house with the built-ins for enough money to buy a larger house—without a mortgage—and to purchase the *Patricia Ann II*, mortgage-free. "I just didn't want to see Tony burdened with the anxiety of feeling he had to go to sea to pay a boat mortgage," Patty says of her decision to sell the small house.

The challenge for Tony today is how to keep fishing in the face of continually changing regulations. "I'm so glad I stayed in a small boat," he says. "Six years ago, Patty and I were pretty ignorant of all the rules." Together with much of the New England fishing community, they had to learn new sets of jargon, new ways of looking at fishing and the science affecting them. And they had to do it quickly if they wanted to keep fishing. In order to understand why they were being regulated as they were, they even traveled to Seattle to sit in on a week of meetings.

"To me," Tony says, "the scariest part of this whole thing is that people making decisions about my life have never been on the water. I'll send Patricia anywhere to make sure they don't close down block one twenty-three." Tony has learned from meetings he and Patty have attended that blocks are often traded to placate a fishery in another area. "If you're not there and you don't get up and argue for your area, I guarantee you will lose your fishing." His voice rises. "It will be over that day. And you will never know what happened!"

During the Gulf of Maine closures in February, March, and April that year Patty received calls from Paul Parker and other members of the Cape Cod Commerical Hook Fishermen's Association (CCCHFA), encouraging them to move the boat to Chatham, beyond the closed area. Tony chose to stay in Provincetown, where he could remain supportive of the rest of his community. Today, another fisherman and member of that community rows over as Tony is unloading the fish. "Didn't I see you at around one in the morning on the dock, loading this boat to go out?" he calls. Tony answers the man's greeting while continuing to dress the fish. "And you're not going to be home before eight-thirty tonight by the time you take those iced fish over to the dealer in Chatham," the man says, admiration mixed with concern.

The owner of one of the other piers approaches in rubber boots, the badge of the waterfront. He notices the concrete float is missing and encourages Tony to use any of the slips at his pier if he wants. The spirit of community is apparent.

"I go to a lot of the meetings," Patty explains, "and I speak up for our size boat, I speak up for my little dragger fleet here in Provincetown. Our choice is to stick it out here and to make it right." She also drives the length of the Cape to buy bait, and all summer long she has met Tony at the dock to help unload six hundred to seven hundred pounds of dogfish per trip. Today, after picking oysters from the waters near her home, she wallpapered a room in their house and dropped the oysters at a restaurant en route to meeting Tony. She has too much energy and youth to be the grandmother of a six year old and the mother of a twenty-seven-year-old son, a graduate of Johnson & Wales, the Rhode Island culinary school, and head chef at the restaurant where she sold the oysters. The restaurant is paying forty-five cents an oyster, so Patty picks oysters for exercise instead of walking or jogging, as she used to do before the price of oysters reached today's levels.

She is disturbed by the inequity she sees in the council rulings that lump the larger boats with the smaller boats. "Whether you're a gillnetter, a dragger, or us, you can be two hundred feet in length or my husband in twenty-seven feet, and we all take the same hit. And we're limited. If it's windy, Tony can't go out; if it's too far, he can't go. If you're in a one-hundred-sixty-foot boat," she says, her voice rising, "you can go anywhere.

"Last year we went from seven hundred pounds to four hundred pounds, then the rolling closures, the permanent closures, the eighty-eight days. And yet on a small boat we could live with all of that. We don't need a large amount of fish to survive." Patty echoes Paul Vitale and other fishermen when she adds, "but they don't give anything a chance to see if it's working."

Patty allows, "I think sometimes fishermen get set in their ways. They won't accept new rules, new changes. They say, 'Well if we can't do it the way we did in 1960, I don't want to do it at all.' And maybe," her voice becomes thoughtful, "maybe that's why some fish did disappear, because the fishermen never readjusted to the amount of fish out there."

When people in the industry speak of Tony and Patty, they use terms such as "they fish responsibly" and "they've made choices to enable them to fish."

"Fishing responsibly?" Tony looks confused by the term. "I don't know of any other way to fish. You're so damned tired, and you're working so many hours, that to try to hide something when you get home would be impossible. Whether the science is right or the science is wrong, it just comes down to if it's illegal, I shouldn't be doing it. It's that simple." He describes his boat having been boarded on occasion by the Coast Guard when he had a couple of small fish in a bucket to take home to eat. "I told them what I was going to do, and they didn't like it too much, but they didn't arrest me for it because the fish weren't mixed in with the other fish like I was going to sell them."

Tony again ponders the phrase. "Fishing responsibly? I just don't see any other way to fish. Maybe they mean because we're having so much trouble with codfish. And," he admits, "there's a big decrease in codfish. Most of the fish that come up now, I'll take off the hook and get the air out of 'em, and release 'em. Years ago, we didn't think about that. Seagulls ate 'em, sharks ate 'em, or they sank to the bottom."

Tony describes how he gets the air out of fish. As he speaks, the term "fishing responsibly" takes on a larger significance. "First of all, you have to haul a lot slower so they don't get the bends. So, if it's not a stormy day, you take the fish and you gently rub them right from their throat to their—" He becomes self-conscious trying to find the proper word. "To their exit hole. And the air just comes right out. I started doing it about two years ago, and now it's just a habit. You see this little fish, and he's all bloated up, and you think he's going to die. You're pressing on his stomach, and you hear this oxygen flying out of him. Then you throw him in the water, and two wags of the tail and he's gone. So when you see that, it encourages you to do it more and more and more."

The seagulls have moved on to digest their meal, and Tony's voice softens. "When I'm fishing, I just feel like a twelve-year-old boy. I just love to fish. There's a million things I could do to make a living. I'm a cabinetmaker. I worked in boatyards. And I went to school to learn how to repair engines. But, I just love fishing. I'll just work a hundred hours and, if I make a dollar an hour, as long as at the end of the week my wife's not yelling and my kids are fed, I'll just go back. Every day to me is just. . . . I almost know what's going to be on the hooks, but it's still a mystery because you don't know how many or what size. I don't know, I just love it."

"It's a passion," Patty adds.

"It's more than a passion. It's a big passion. It's a way of life." Tony stops before expanding on this idea. "It's eccentric as hell, I think. You're definitely not in reality. At times when I'm out there, most of the time all alone out there, I see some pretty strange things. It takes a couple of years to get used to that, but once you do then you almost can't get used to reality anymore."

The seagulls are back. They are so much a part of his life that Tony is not even aware he has raised his voice to talk over their caws. "I'll fish really hard for six or seven weeks. Then the fish will disappear, and for a whole week I'll sit home and I'm all nervous. I don't know what to do. I'll get depressed. Then I'll start to come around. Then I'm O.K. I can be a human being again. I don't know what words describe it. It's—"

Patty's voice commingles with Tony's as she says, "It's not just a job. It's a way of living." She explains that if friends who fish invite them for dinner, the invitation will be: "If it blows Friday, come on over for a meal. If not, maybe Saturday or Sunday."

"It's a hell of a way to try to plan a life," Tony adds. "I can tell Patricia a year in advance what months she can have. But the nice thing is it's full months." He turns to Patty and gives a courtly gesture as if he is giving her a gift on the outstretched palm of his hand. "You can have all of October; you can have all of November; you can have all of March; and you can have all of July. But don't mess with April, May, February. Short of a family death—"

"We don't celebrate birthdays, nothing during—" Patty's voice in the background continues in counterpoint to Tony's.

"I have six-week blocks that make the whole difference in the course of a year. These past seven weeks, I've probably made about six months of salary." Tony explains that next month, in October, they will get to go to Disney World with their granddaughter, and relax. "And I don't even think about fishing during that time. When we go on vacation, very rarely do I even go near a port. I might go swimming and, if I do, it's in a pool."

Tony's outward calm belies a highly focused intensity. It is no surprise that he has to take Dramamine to go to bed on nights before he fishes, "not because I get seasick, but because I can't sleep. 'Cause I get so excited when I'm done baiting up the night before I'm going to go fishing." The excitement takes hold, and words rush out of his mouth one on top of the other. "This is twenty-one years since I began to fish commercially. Ten thousand trips later, two houses later, everything's paid for. I don't have to be excited. But yet I'll lay there all night tossing and turning, trying to decide am I going to do it this way? Am I going to do it that way? And if I don't take one Dramamine an hour before I go to bed, then I can't sleep, and I'll go out there not feeling well—too tired to fish well.

"Years and years later, every time I pull an anchor, and I've pulled a lot of anchors, I still get that same feeling of what's on there." Tony looks down at his feet, embarrassed at displaying his feelings. Then, from his eyes to his mouth, his whole face breaks out in a wide grin as he laughs at himself before asking, "Now is that ignorance? I don't know. I'm Italian, and it takes me a long time to catch on?"

The luck of location is on Tony's side, and listening to him makes you want to see it stay there. This is not a man you want to see reduced to government subsidies to keep him off the water, as are the fishermen in Newfoundland. Were Tony fishing out of Scituate, he would be having a harder struggle. But is it that simple? Is he, like Frank Mirarchi—who does fish out of Scituate—is he an unusually creative and positive person who will find a way to allow himself to do what he loves to do?

Tony puts it in terms of experience. "Every year, you get a little better, and a little better. And you make a little more money for a little less work. And even with the little money you make, you learn to take expenses out of that. And it becomes fun. Now we get paid over the Internet. And that's fun. We check the prices on the Boston Fish Exchange. And that's kind of cool." Tony's next words could easily belong to Bill Amaru or Frank Mirarchi. "And it just never ceases to amaze me that I can take all this bait out of the ocean, bring it home, cut it all up, put it on hooks, put it back in the ocean, take a whole bunch of fish back out of the ocean, sell it, and make money. And they pay me for it. It's just a good healthy way of life."

Tony is sitting on an empty plastic bin in the back of the truck. It may be the first time he has not been in motion for the past seventeen hours, and he still has to drive the dressed, packed fish to the dealer in Chatham. As he tips back on the bin, he says thoughtfully, "When you look at it all at the end of the year, I guess it's all very unpredictable. And that's what makes it great. It's very scary; it's a challenge all the time; it's an abstract way to live; there's no grid pattern; it's all egg-shaped. And that's what makes it so nice."

On September 29, 2000, Tony Lemmi made his last trip. He docked the *Patricia Ann II* at MacMillan Pier, gutted the fish, and passed them up to Patty to be packed in bins. Then he drove to Chatham, dropped off the bins at the dealer's, and returned home. Once inside the door, he told Patty he would no longer be fishing. He sold the *Patricia Ann II* and found a job as a carpenter for the Town of Provincetown. Patty took a job as coordinator for construction of the new pier being built in Provincetown.

Tony's decision was an inevitable result of the rules drawn up to regulate the fisheries, specifically dogfish. As the fishery management councils ruled to prohibit the catching of dogfish—the livelihood for fishing families in Massachusetts Bay—fishermen from Scituate and Marshfield moved to quadrant 123, where Tony fished. There, they set up gill nets to fish for flatfish. The two-to-four-month period when Tony had previously caught dogfish was now a lost fishery for him. The area where he had previously fished for groundfish was now filled with gill nets. In addition, new regulations placed on clam diggers were creating bait prices that were prohibitive and a supply that was often nonexistent. Tony, a fisherman whose passion, whose ideals, and whose ethics embodied the essence of environmentally sustainable fishing practices, was prohibited from earning a living as a fisherman. And more pressure was placed on the groundfish populations by regulations crafted to preserve a predator of groundfish.

For Patty, it is "disheartening." For the larger community, it is a sad and generally unrecognized loss.

Despite all the regulations, all the buybacks, and all the quotas imposed on the fishing industry, fish is still the number two item, by weight, shipped through Boston's Logan Airport. (It is surpassed only by the U.S. mail.) Yet the fishermen—who produce this wealth—until recently have had almost no political clout. If anything, they have had a negative political image, partly due to the popularity of endangered species causes. As people have focused on protecting the environment, many have come to see fishing as the hunter versus the hunted. This may have been one reason many politicians still feel uncomfortable arguing the fisherman's cause. Another is that a fisherman at sea hardly constitutes a lobbying force or even a constituency to be reckoned with by most politicians. Until federal regulations and a federal judge ruled to limit severely the fishermen's days at sea, he was often not even around to vote. But his wife was.

Harriet Didriksen, Judy Ramos, Ellen Skaar, and Angela Sanfilippo are four women whose names are linked with any discussion of the New England fishing industry's attempt to present its story. Harriet, Judy, and Ellen represent the New Bedford fishing community; Angela represents Gloucester. All four are married to fishermen, and all except Judy have sons who are, or have been, fishermen. Without these four women, the New England fishing industry would be in even worse shape than it is today.

Judy Ramos first began managing her family's six fishing boats at the age of seventeen when her parents went on vacation. She was the only child in a fishing family, and she was trained to take over the family business. Her mother was one of the founders of United Fishermen's Wives, the New Bedford equivalent of the Gloucester Fishermen's Wives Association.

Judy and her husband Herminio raised their two children in the same harborfront home where Judy's parents raised her. Family portraits of

Judy's parents, grandparents, and great-grandparents in Portugal line the paneled walls of the living room. She was eight years old when her mother invited her to sit in on the first meeting of the United Fishermen's Wives, held in this same room.

Judy's husband was born in Portugal. Judy's daughter Dominique (Nicky) married a man who was born in Portugal and came to this country when he was nine. Judy laughs as she describes her background. "It's just something you don't get out of. You simply have to marry Portuguese, and you've got to marry a fisherman. And if you're a boy, you have to be a fisherman. That's the mentality."

Herminio's family is from the southern part of Portugal. Judy met him when she was visiting her paternal grandmother, who lives in the north. "When my grandmother heard I was dating a man from another province, she was devastated. But the worst was that she thought he was a farmer. She felt I was a disgrace to the family to be spending time with a man who wasn't a fisherman. It's the same for the Norwegian and Italian fishing families." After relating the story, Judy shares, "I wouldn't know how to live with some man who worked nine to five, and was home every night. It took me a long time to get used to my husband being onshore after we sold our boat, the boat he skippered."

Judy and her husband presently own two boats—the 90-foot dragger F/V *Sea Siren* and the 104-foot scallop boat F/V *Elizabeth and Nicky*. They had signed up for the buyback program for one of their other boats, the 94-foot F/V *Captain Mano*, but instead sold it to Peter Bramante (Jimmy's brother) for more money than they would have received from the government. "And," Judy adds, "it would have broken my heart to have to scrap her. She's still active, still alive. We speak about these vessels as people. The dragger we have now is a beautiful boat, doing well—so far."

Sea Siren is a stern trawler Judy and Herminio own jointly with Manuel Vinegre. Manuel proposed that they apply to the last buyback program, asking a price of $200,000, which at the time Judy thought was much too high to be considered. Based on the asking price, Judy figured they would be turned down. They were accepted. Then, when Manuel thought about the realities of scrapping the boat, he decided not to accept the offer. Manuel is fifty-four years old. He owns no other boat. To buy an inferior boat would have taken most of his share of the money. He will probably not see another buyback offer again—at least not in groundfishing. "I am certain," Judy comments, "that any future buybacks will be for scallop boats, because that's where the focus is now in the council meetings."

Before the 1994 regulations took effect, before Amendment 5 mandated smaller mesh size, minimum size limits for fish species, and areas closed to fishing, 347 draggers and 187 scallop boats hailed out of New Bedford and Fairhaven, the fishing port on the other side of the channel. When asked how many draggers and scallop boats she thought there were today, Judy answers, "one hundred ninety and one hundred ten. My dragger used to go out with six, seven men. Now they're going out with three and four. My scalloper used to fish with thirteen to fourteen in crew. That's what that boat is equipped for. It's got bunks and bathrooms to accommodate that many crew members. Now it fishes with six."

Judy and other members of the fishing industry have opposed the ruling that limits the number of crew on a scallop boat because they believe it is dangerous to try to run these boats shorthanded. "It's extremely dangerous. It's a safety hazard. A scalloper that size should go out with no less than eight or nine men." In New Bedford, Amendment 5 added another danger to an already dangerous trade. Much of the waters fished by New Bedford boats are adjacent to shoals surrounding Nantucket. These geological formations left from the glaciers may shallow the water above them to a depth of twelve feet or less at low tide. A dragger has an average draft of eleven feet. In order to avoid the closed areas, the fishermen are forced to travel over shallow waters that might rip a hole in the bottom of their boats, or leave them stranded on a shoal in a storm—or both. The alternative is to add twenty miles to a fishing trip, an increase that presents its own dangers.

"I wanted to do something to try to save my industry," Judy says in explanation of why, in 1987, she chose to become the only woman member of Offshore Mariners, a previously all-male association for the owners of fishing vessels in the New Bedford area. "It's my livelihood," she continues. "More than anything, it's a lifestyle."

Judy speaks fluent Portuguese, and the Portuguese fishing community has known her since she was a child on the docks. She estimates that about 85 percent of the New Bedford fishing population are Portuguese, either by birth or by heritage. In some cases, their English is limited. Many of these fishermen would turn to Judy and ask her to explain some of the government regulations. In December of 1992, the men elected Judy president of Offshore Mariners, just when the fishermen were beginning to feel the effect of the closings of some of their most reliable fishing grounds. "I'm very proud to be from a fishing family, and I'm very proud of my heritage," she says. "So I figured someone had to speak for these guys.

"I call these men 'my guys.' They're my guys. You know, I yell at 'em, I swear at 'em, and they yell at me. They don't swear at me, though." Judy laughs and tips her head, giving an impish grin. "I'm worse than they are.

"It was hard to tell these guys down here, 'A lot is happening.' They didn't want to hear it." Judy looks out the window, across the water toward the fishing grounds. "I'd come back from the meetings, assemble notes, and tell them, 'Look, be prepared, this is what's happening. Go out and catch squid, monkfish, and other underutilized species so that you have a record, you have a history when they go to give your boat a quota for catching the species you're used to catching. And my guys didn't," she adds, "because basically New Bedford is a groundfish port. The flounder, the haddock, the cod, that's what we do.

"They didn't want to change," Judy adds. "They said, 'No, no, no, the government would never take away our right to catch groundfish.' These are immigrants," Judy adds. "They believed that this country would never do this to them. They came from a country that would. But they never believed that *this* country would limit their ability to fish. When Amendment 5 went into effect, limiting their catch, closing the fishing grounds where they had always fished, they were devastated. They couldn't believe it."

Prior to enactment of Amendment 5, the New England Fishery Management Council was advocating that the fishermen harvest the underutilized fish—the skate, the monkfish—and that they stay away from the groundfish. At a meeting of the Offshore Mariners, the men decided to adopt the council's recommendation. They thought that by doing so, they would be seen as cooperating with the government. They thought they would still be able to make a living harvesting species they had previously considered "trash fish," and that their actions would give the groundfish stocks a chance to rebuild. At the end of the meeting, the men had decided to target underutilized species, and to catch in addition only the groundfish already in the nets when they were hauling in the newly targeted fish.

Eight months later, Judy went to a meeting of the council. Allen Peterson, then director of the National Marine Fisheries Service's Northeast Fisheries Science Center in Woods Hole, announced that groundfish stocks were in worse shape than they had been before, and thus "stricter and more severe regulations had to be enacted."

Judy took the microphone and asked where he had gotten his figures.

"The landings," he replied. "Don't you check your landings in New Bedford, Judy?"

"You're getting the brunt of this information from New Bedford?" Judy was incredulous. "You're making your decisions to increase the severity of the regulations based on the landings of groundfish in New

Bedford? You're looking at the landings for cod, flounder, and haddock? Did you happen at the same time to look at the landing figures for underutilized species landed in New Bedford?" she asked. "Did you happen to notice how that's increased? And if so, did you wonder why?"

Judy was told that the purpose of the meeting was to decide what regulations needed to be enforced to reduce the fishing effort for groundfish, not underutilized species.

The result was Amendment 5, enacted in 1994. That amendment introduced minimum mesh sizes, minimum size limits for cod, haddock, and yellowtail flounder, closed areas, new fishing permits, and logbook reporting, with the stated objective of reducing the groundfishing effort by 50 percent over the next five years based on the 1989–1991 average levels of fishermen's days at sea.

"We did what they suggested we do, and then they turned it around so that the numbers were used against us," Judy later said, echoing the sentiments of the fishermen.

After returning from the council meeting, Judy called the other Offshore Mariners to a general meeting the following evening. They then spread the word to the rest of the community to meet at the Fisherman's Club in a room that holds eight hundred people. It was packed. And that was how the blockade of Boston Harbor began to take shape.

Antonio Pereira's F/V *Blue Seas* fell in behind F/V *Alentejo* owned by Luis Ribas and Jose Gonsales as they rounded the No. 2, the red, four-second flashing bell buoy marking the channel between New Bedford and Sconticut Neck to the east. Tony Santos greeted the others with several blasts on the horn of his F/V *T. Luis* as he caught up with the other vessels. More than forty fishing boats, ranging from a 27-foot gillnetter to Bobby Bruno's 95-foot scallop boat the F/V *Alpha Omega*, headed in formation to Boston Harbor. The date was February 28, 1994. Together the fishermen planned to mount a nonviolent protest against Amendment 6 and proposed Amendment 7, and what they felt were efforts to make commercial fishing a nonprofit industry.

When Tony Pereira, captain of the F/V *Blue Seas*, reached the Green Bell marking Brooklyn Rock, instead of heading straight out toward Quicks Hole, toward the fishing grounds, he turned the wheel to head toward Cleveland Ledge, the entrance to the Cape Cod Canal. The temperature was 12 degrees Fahrenheit, and the windshield was already icing up. Winds were from the northwest and gusting to twenty-five knots. At 6:15 A.M., the seas were already two to four feet in Buzzards Bay, and rising.

A group of Chatham boats, mostly gillnetters and small draggers, made it as far as the Cape Cod Canal but were too small to continue on to Boston in the stormy weather; they remained to protest in the Canal. Along the coast of Cape Cod Bay, a few men and women looked out their windows and saw the New Bedford boats bravely enduring the weather to get to Boston. And the reminder that this part of New England's maritime history had reached such a sad state brought tears to some eyes.

In Boston, the Coast Guard officer in charge was sympathetic to the fishermen's cause. He gave Judy his cellular phone to use to converse with the boats from her position on the Fish Pier. As he did, he told her, "You can't blockade the harbor, Judy. Everybody will get arrested."

"Well, we'll get arrested, then." Judy was born with pluck.

"I didn't say you couldn't protest. There's a way around it. Just keep moving in circles, and no one will be able to get through there," he advised.

Judy looks back on the blockade with nostalgia. "It was such a feeling. I was watching the boats from the pier, and I said to myself, Oh my God, this is the first time I've seen so many of my guys sticking together—wasting money on the fuel to get all the way up here in this weather." Later the cost to the New Bedford fishing community would be estimated at several million dollars in lost revenue from the boats being tied up for six weeks, unable to catch and sell fish.

Four years later, as she relates the story of the blockade, Judy is sitting in an overstuffed chair in her New Bedford living room on a gray day in February. She reminisces, "I get goose bumps just thinking about it today. When the first boats came into Boston Harbor, and hearing them on the phone, I got such a thrill. The little putt-putt *Alentejo* was sandwiched between Bobby Bruno's huge, powerful *Alpha Omega* and another big dragger, and they're yelling, 'Come on. Come on, let's go.' And Luis Ribas is calling back, 'I'm givin' the engine all she's got. She won't go no faster. Leave me alone.' " Tears welled in Judy's eyes as she watched and listened. "It was so great, and all I could think was these guys don't realize what they're doing, how important it is.

"New Bedford has always been very, very passive. It's a city of fresh immigrants who came from a country where you could not express your feelings. There was no freedom of speech. There was no assembly. They would yell and bitch amongst themselves, but—and this was great— they went to the State House! And they spoke! Guys that are just so timid, they spoke for their beliefs at the State House. They did it."

Not everyone agrees with Judy's assessment of the blockade. Jimmy Bramante thinks it showed disrespect. "You don't confront the government like that."

Rodney Avila, when asked about the effectiveness of the blockade, answers, "I don't believe that's where the fight has to be fought. Yeah, you make a statement. All the news media come out. They put a little of it on television. But after you watch the five o'clock news it's forgotten about."

"We accomplished getting the buyback program. We accomplished getting the money for the fishermen's centers, such as the one Rodney runs," Judy quickly counters. Then in a slower cadence, "We didn't accomplish all that we set out to accomplish, but we did get a few pacifiers here and there which in reality ended up helping."

By the year 2002, even Rodney appreciated the need to "make a statement," as he referred to it. The blockade of Boston Harbor was the most ambitious of the protests, but by May and June 2002, gillnetters would have held a protest in Scituate, and New England fishermen from different ports would have united in protest in Gloucester, then Portland, Point Judith, and later New Bedford, where Rodney was the master of ceremonies for what began with truckers from various ports joining together in a mock funeral procession that moved along the streets to the outer harbor. There a flotilla of fishing vessels circled just beyond New Bedford's Fort Tabor, and at least one speaker referred to the fishing community as a "discarded resource."

In the 2002 demonstration in New Bedford, Tony Pereira's F/V *Blue Seas* and Rodney's F/V *Trident* circled and honked their horns to remind the public that if it wanted to continue to enjoy fresh New England seafood, it had to support a change in the definition of "sustainable yield" and also had to appreciate that fishermen must be allowed to fish more than seventy days per year, the number stipulated in the May 23, 2002, ruling by U.S. District Judge Judith Kessler. But between the formation of Amendment 5 and June 1, 2002, as Angela Sanfilippo told the audience, more than five thousand jobs had been lost in the fishing community, and 830 fishing vessels were no longer fishing. Gloucester boats hadn't fished for more than six months. The goals of the fishing community were evident on the back of a Rhode Island fisherman in the audience whose tee shirt stated, "Respect the Ocean; harvest the bounty; feed the people."

Prior to the 1994 blockade, New Bedford had experienced a $50 million loss in fishing revenues, down to $102.6 million for the year.[4] That year, 275 fishing vessels hailed from New Bedford; over two thousand men and women listed themselves as fishermen, and over eight thousand were employed in jobs within the industry, or serving the industry. The closures scheduled to take place on March 1, the day following the blockade, were to include the South Channel, Stellwagen Bank, and Jeffries Ledge. The U.S. portion of Georges Bank had already been closed to commercial fishing as of January 1. The Canadian side was designated off-limits to U.S. commercial fishing vessels in 1985, as per the ruling at the International Court of Justice in The Hague.

After the fishing community met with Governor Weld at the State House in Boston, the National Oceanic and Atmospheric Administration (NOAA) agreed to delay a required increase in mesh size until April 1, to allow enough time for the new nets to be made in the required six-inch mesh. A provision to require gillnetters to remove their nets from certain spawning areas was delayed until April 15. And Governor Weld earmarked ten million dollars in emergency relief to be used to finance retraining centers such as those managed today by Rodney Avila in New Bedford and Angela Sanfilippo in Gloucester.

Back at the pier on the day of the blockade, the boats all started blowing their horns in unison. Because of the weather, it had taken ten hours for them to make the trip to Boston, and they were now beginning to experience the adrenaline rush that often accompanies being chilled, tired, and then reaching a safe harbor. For the first time since before dawn, they did not have to fight choppy seas and vision blurred by icy windshields.

Judy took the opportunity to tell them on the telephone in Portuguese, "You can't stop. Don't just float. You have to keep moving. So make a pattern." And that's what they did. "The boats just crisscrossed for hours, this way and that way." Judy indicates a herringbone pattern with her arms. "Little ferryboats couldn't get through, and boats trying to get into the harbor were backed up, and I heard my guys say, 'We'll show 'em what the "Portugueys" are made of.' They were hyped. They were excited themselves.

"One of the reasons my guys were so fired up is because they know there is a better way. They go to Portugal every other year, and they talk to their families about the fishing regulations there, and they hear about rules they could live with." Portugal has mesh-size regulations. It has closed areas. But it differs by alternating the closed areas every two or three years to allow the fish stocks to rebound while still permitting the fishermen to fish.

Asked why the Portuguese community has not proposed that this country adopt a program similar to Portugal's, Judy replies, "They have, time and time again, but no one listens to them." She leans back in her chair, and the passion in her voice is gone as she expresses a fear shared by many. "This country has its own agenda. It just has to follow political protocol. Just remember, it's a lot easier to take care of Tyson and Snow, and the other three major companies, than it is to manage five thousand little fishermen."

The blockade of Boston Harbor was unique in that it was one of the few times when much of the fishing community galvanized to join forces. Boat owners with differing opinions, different ethnic backgrounds, and different ways of fishing joined with owners from other ports to show solidarity. To Harriet Didriksen, a New Bedford boat owner, it showed "how bad things really were for the fishing community."

During the blockade, Harriet kept her boats tied at the dock. "I felt I was so visible because I had been on the council begging people to support our cause with money, time, their position of influence, any way they could," she explains. "But I felt that when other members of the fishing community had an idea, and were trying to make a point, I would be disrespectful if I didn't participate." Harriet's boats stayed at the dock for ten days, during which she and her crew sacrificed substantial revenues.

Judy was on the Fish Pier, where she was masterminding the blockade, at the same time she was scheduled to attend a meeting at the State House. She explained later, "I wasn't going to miss seeing my boats come in. There was no way I would miss that." Instead, Angela Sanfilippo marched to the State House in Boston to present the fishermen's case to Governor Weld. Back in New Bedford after the blockade ended, Harriet stood up at a meeting of the Fisherman's Club and said, "We've made our point. Now, it's time for the politicians to start to work for us. Our job is fishing; their job is politics."

"Since that time," Harriet now adds, "the main politician I've seen who has truly represented the fishing community is Barney Frank." The Democratic congressman from Massachusetts has stood up at meetings and told everyone present that the fishermen were hardworking people who were just trying to make a living. At the New Bedford demonstration on June 2, 2002, he spoke of "environmental extremists" who operate on the basis of "emotion and outdated science" and who are "hostile to the whole notion of fishing." And he still needs to work with the environmental community on many other issues. "That's worth something," Harriet says. "Without Barney Frank, there would be no fishing industry in the Northeast. He understands that it's better for ten families to be making forty thousand dollars each as opposed to the government's way of letting two families make two hundred thousand dollars each.

"When politicians say, 'Let's settle this,' they're concluding that an army of people are going to be without jobs as a result. We don't need to be patronized; we need to work."

Harriet's family has owned a ship's chandlery in New Bedford for over sixty years. Her father was a fisherman and her husband, Didrik, is a former fisherman. Harriet's grandfather's brother came to the United States from Norway in the early part of the twentieth century; her grandfather joined him when he was nineteen years old. By 1938, when her father and her father's brother arrived in this country, the family had a fleet of three boats fishing out of Sheepshead Bay in Brooklyn, New York. They fished in the canyons between Georges Bank and New York. In the winter months, they fished for fluke and butterfish. Then, beginning in April or May, they would shift to scallops.

Today, Harriet and Didrik fish the same way, maintaining multipurpose licenses to enable them to shift from one species to the other. Didrik is from the island of Karmøy, Norway, as are most of the Norwegian fishermen in New Bedford. His family in Norway owned the farm next to Harriet's uncle's farm, and the children of the two families grew up knowing each other and celebrating family holidays together.

When her uncle (Rasmus Tonnessen) came to the United States from Norway in 1935, he went to sea aboard a boat out of New Bedford. The sea did not agree with him, and he was sick as soon as he left the dock. Realizing he had to work on land, he started the New Bedford Ship Supply Company fashioned after ship supply stores around Sheepshead Bay.

Since its inception, the Ship Supply Company has been provisioning fishing vessels, not only in New Bedford but up the coast to Boston and south to Point Judith, Rhode Island. Charlie Butman remembers when the Ship Supply store would keep records of ten or twelve different options based on the individual tastes and preferences of each boat's captain and crew. A vessel's cook could call in an order by simply giving the number of the particular option desired. The order would be delivered to the boat prior to the specified time of departure, and at the dock where that particular boat was tied.

Those days are history. Harriet's uncle died in 1991. Since then, Harriet and her aunt have forgiven individual debts totaling as much as $125,000 to $150,000 per family when they knew it was the only way that the family could survive. After Harriet's uncle died, a park was dedicated in his memory, and many fishing families in the New Bedford area were reminded that they had been able to keep fishing in large part due to his generosity. "When a fisherman couldn't pay his bills right away, my uncle extended him credit because he knew that man was what brought him business and what kept him in business," Harriet explains. "We're boating people, and we know it takes thirty thousand to forty thousand dollars or more to outfit a boat. But, as I explained at a council meeting, we're not the Red Cross. We need help."

In celebration of fifty years of business for the New Bedford Ship Supply Company, a tall, blond fisherman in his early thirties appeared in the back room of the store. His infant son was perched on his shoulders, and in his outstretched hands he held a large haddock, which he presented to Rasmus with his congratulations. For Rasmus, no gift could have meant more.

Today, Harriet is president of the New Bedford Ship Supply Company. When her aunt died recently, the family chose to keep the store open even though a more prudent move would be to close it. Harriet manages the store and keeps her own boat on the water. "My family has always fished," she says, "so I never thought of its ups and downs. We were always able to make a good living over time. We didn't just fish and then coast until the money ran out, then go to sea again. Our boats went out every three days, unless a severe storm was predicted. Scallop boats went out every five days. We ran it as a business."

The U.S. government has never trained people to go to sea, as have many other countries. The men and women who fish in this country have, for the most part, come from fishing communities where they were trained in the ways of fishing, or their fathers or grandfathers trained them. "This is an unrecognized commodity for the United States," Harriet says. "As a product of the fishing community, I feel I have the opportunity to fish, under reasonable regulations." The emphasis is on "reasonable."

The scientific community has often exhibited a different perception of the fishermen's acceptance of regulation. In its 1998 annual review of the stock assessments for the Northeast, the National Research Council, which draws its members from the National Academy of Sciences, suggests that the logbooks fishermen are required to keep "may not contain accurate information" on the amount and location of the catch.[5] The authors of the review recommend stationing "observers" (clearly not fishermen) on fishing vessels for the purpose of collecting information.

In the cover story of the February 6, 1998, issue of *Science*, the author Paul K. Dayton, a scientist at the University of California's Scripps Institution of Oceanography, states, "Regulations often are barely tolerated by the fishing community, and poaching is rampant and minimally penalized."[6]

Harriet responds, "Would you call it 'minimal' when they take your business away from you? Would you call it 'minimal' when, because they *think* you were poaching, they take away your trip, they take all your product away from you?

"Fishermen have been fined as much as a hundred thousand dollars. They took my trip one time and fined me forty thousand dollars. The case continued two years. They lost. I beat 'em after two years, but I had two stressful years. I had to pay for all the legal fees. They told me I was fishing in Canada, and I had to prove I wasn't while my means of livelihood was threatened." How different from the conditions prevailing in May 2001, when the 78-foot F/V *General George S. Patton* belonging to New England Fishery Management Council member Barbara Stevenson was spotted by the Coast Guard in the area she had voted to close to fishing on Georges Bank. The National Marine Fisheries Service auctioned off the six thousand pounds of groundfish on board the *General George S. Patton*, and the proceeds were held in escrow pending a decision by NOAA's general counsel. But a special agent with the National Marine Fisheries Service was quoted as saying that the situation looked like "an honest mistake."[7] Maybe Harriet's net worth would be greater if she were on the council.

Harriet thinks there are still people in the business with mortgages on their boats of $500,000 to $600,000. According to Rodney Avila's calculations, the New Bedford fleet owes more than $100 million in vessel mortgages. Most of those mortgages are secured by the fishermen's homes, which also have mortgages on them. Banks are no longer lending money for vessel upgrades or refits. Many of the businesses ancillary to fishing, such as fish processors, welders, electronics repair shops, and ship chandlers, have already gone out of business or are barely subsisting.

In November of 1998, the New Bedford shipyard Norlantic Diesel closed its doors. For fifty years it had serviced the needs of the commercial fishing industry. In the 1980s, it had employed as many as sixty workers. By 1998, it employed only ten. When asked what contributed to his decision to close, Elvind H. Strand, president and general manager, answered that vessel buyback programs had shrunk the fleet and government restrictions limiting days at sea had forced vessel owners to put off maintenance in an effort to trim costs.

Mr. Strand told the press that his remaining workers would be referred to the New Bedford Fishermen's Family Assistance Center, the organization headed by Rodney Avila. More than seven hundred in the New Bedford fishing community are currently unemployed—most of them fishermen. Many of the younger fishermen and their wives have already turned to the Family Assistance Center, where they are seeking retraining for new careers. Many of those over forty cling to the idea that the regulations will let up and they should just hang on until that time or retirement age—whichever comes first.

The Magnuson-Stevens Fishery Conservation and Management Act (SFA) includes the provision that the welfare of the fishing community has to be in the equation, but many in the fishing, conservation, and scientific communities feel that provision is being overlooked for a different agenda, that of awarding fishing rights to a few large organizations. Phil Coates (former chairman of the Massachusetts Division of Marine Fisheries) and others note the obvious fact that it would be easier for the Department of Commerce and its regulatory bodies to monitor the activities of a few large fishing consortiums than the activities of a lot of boats the size of *Captain Sam* or *Endeavor*. And it would be easier to monitor the activities of one or two owners of a fleet of boats than the activities of a lot of individual small-boat owners like Mike Barry, Kevin Shea, or Harriet.

"It is so discouraging," Harriet says between coughs. "I believe we should be working to keep fishing for fishing people. What I thought fisheries management was for was to protect the species. I have never perceived my license as permitting me to own any portion of the fisheries. I see my license as a right to harvest fish, and when I get to a point in life where I can't exercise that right, I would like to be able to sell or give it to someone else who will assume that same right to fish as I have, with the same responsibilities to maintaining the stock."

Harriet is suffering from the flu, depression, and the feeling that she has to single-handedly argue the case for the whole fishing community. Harriet and Didrik have been separated for several years. Didrik is not well, and Harriet has hired a captain to skipper their remaining boat. She is fully aware that the optimum conditions are for an owner-operated boat, not for one with a paid captain.

Out of fear for her survival, she has already sold one of her boats in the buyback program, but she is quick to point out, "Buyback isn't the answer to address the community. I feel guilty as an owner taking money when the men who have been working for me get nothing and lose their jobs as a result of my being compensated. I feel they should get a year's pay also. They should be able to put fifty thousand dollars in the bank so their families have something. I want them to be included."

As she relates her frustration, Harriet is seated at Margaret's Restaurant, the only place where she will order fish, other than some of the restaurants she counts as customers. The restaurant's owner owns scallop boats and brings the fish for the restaurant directly off her boats.

If you had to define what a sense of "community" is, this restaurant could provide the definition. The only person who walks in the door and has to place an order is an outsider, but one who is treated with the same respect as the native.

A man who could be in his seventies, dressed in a pair of khakis hanging loosely on his frame, topped by a plaid shirt that has seen many washings, opens the door and walks toward the counter. "We didn't see you dancing the other evening," the owner calls to him from the kitchen.

"Well you just weren't lookin' when they played my kind of music," he counters as he takes a seat. "That was one elegant affair, Gail," he adds, referring to the marriage of the owner's daughter that took place the previous weekend at the Gothic-style church a block away from the restaurant.

The mother of the bride sets a place for him at a booth. "The regular?" she asks. He nods, and she heads back to the kitchen to prepare his preferred lunch. At another booth, a man in his forties can be overheard in conversation over coffee with a friend: ". . . it's not worth it anymore to be out for seventeen days, not allowed to catch anything, and come back to the dock only to fill out more papers."

Ellen Skaar, Harriet's friend and fellow activist for the New Bedford fishing industry, is seated at another booth. Ellen, like Harriet, is married to a Norwegian fisherman. Her father, grandfather, great-grandfather, and great-great-grandfather were all fishermen. Ellen wistfully recalls the days when women were not seen on the piers of New Bedford or any other fishing port. She raised four children while her husband was at sea, and she regularly helped him save a portion of his earnings so they could realize his dream of captaining his own boat.

"When men are at sea that long," Ellen comments, "they become more and more out of touch with what is happening onshore. My husband fished the way he had always fished, and he didn't understand when I told him that he had to take time off from fishing to go to meetings on land or he wouldn't be able to continue to fish."

Harriet and Ellen approach their work from different, often reinforcing, perspectives. They both share the same goals for the industry, but their personal goals are different. Harriet sees the fishing industry in terms of the market. Her sentences are filled with words such as "product," "market share," and "optimum yield." Once you have spoken to Harriet, you are not surprised to learn that one of her sons is a Wall Street stockbroker. She feels a personal responsibility to help save the fishing industry. It has become a crusade filling the hours that used to be devoted to family.

Ellen, in contrast, wants to get off the pier and back to her home, but only after she has done as much as she can to help the fishing community. Judy Ramos explains Ellen's ties to the pier when she says, "Ellen can't leave, because it's in her blood, and once you care about something that much, it becomes your life." All three women devote a large portion of each day to further the cause of the industry. Fishermen from

Cape May, New Jersey, to Portland, Maine, credit Harriet, Ellen, and Judy with forcing an awareness that fishermen must get involved in negotiations on land if they want to have work at sea.

"It won't make any difference" was the excuse used by many of the men who did not go to the meetings, yet who admitted to being afraid for their future. Harriet explained to them that they had to go or they would have no future. At the time, one older fisherman confided to her, "If Didrik [Harriet's husband] stood up at the meeting instead of a woman, it would mean more." Since then, Rodney Avila and others have shown that men can make a difference by going to the meetings, and by taking a position on the council.

The provisions of Amendments 4 and 5, with the exceptions granted after the blockade of Boston Harbor, were implemented in March of 1994. "Since then, they've put in frameworks to those amendments, but those two amendments were the big ones. Let me tell you a story." Harriet prefaces her tale much as Charlie Butman might. "There is an older gentleman from Connecticut who used to be on the council. At one of the council meetings, he stated, 'When you put into effect a rule which later requires twenty-five changes, that should tell us there's something wrong with that rule.' He had common sense, so they replaced him with a younger man who represents the Environmental Defense Fund."

Harriet tilts her head and looks up over her reading glasses before continuing, "Picture my going out to Bill Gates, now that he has established an industry, and I say to him, 'Your people can't work on Monday, Wednesday, and Friday. And they can't drive to work. And they can't meet on Tuesdays and Thursdays.' Then, when the company is crippled, I come in and offer him next to nothing for a company I have ruined. That's what's happening to the fishing industry with the buyback program.

"In Norway, where the concept of buyback originated, the boats are bought back at the purchase price. Here, the buyback price is negotiated based on what the fisherman will accept. If you're going to copy a plan, take it all, not just those parts that are the best for the country and the worst for the fisherman."

Rodney Avila has compiled a spreadsheet showing that 185 boats have disappeared from the New England waterfront since Amendment 4 was put in place. Of that number, 151 boats (along with six hundred crew members) have disappeared from the waterfront since 1994, when Amendment 5 was enacted: 28 of them sank; 27 were sold out of the fishery, either out of the area or out of the industry; and 16 disappeared as a result of natural attrition when their owners decided not to repair or replace them. The remaining 80 (or almost 53 percent) were sold to the government in the buyback program. "Buyback isn't the real answer to conserving the fish stocks," Harriet says. "The answer is true science, untainted by people who have to portray the fishing community as fish killers in order to protect their own jobs." Many scientists agree with Harriet in that conserving fish is more complex than just prohibiting the harvesting of fish.

Now that there are fewer fishing days permitted to a vessel, more fishermen are showing up at meetings. Harriet sees this as too little too late. "They are now getting more people than they want at these regulatory meetings. Before, when hardly any fishermen were able to be there, it was a club of regulators. They could pass anything without opposition. The government spokespeople still need to keep their jobs, and they look to the conservationists as providing an easy solution. But we are now in the eleventh hour, and I'm not sure we're going to make it."

A waitress pours more milk into Harriet's glass. The man at the booth across the aisle can be heard: ". . . so now they're talking about closing down codfishing in the Gulf of Maine." His concern is shared by the whole fishing community. Gloucester fishermen and other small-boat fishermen along the coast of Cape Cod Bay who harvest cod will be hardest hit. New Bedford fishermen, Rodney Avila included, will come out in favor of conserving the species, but regulations closing areas to the inshore fishermen abutting the Gulf of Maine do not directly affect them, since they can steam to other fishing grounds. But the larger message is that it affects them all: today it is cod; tomorrow it may be another fish species.

"There is a natural order to life under the sea," Harriet reflects. "If left alone, nature is very efficient. But when you start promoting one species over another, you tip the balance. For instance, a seal destroys many times his weight in cod because he grabs the fish, sucks out the liver, and then discards the rest of the fish. When the environmentalist is working to increase the seal population while diminishing the population of fishermen, he or she is helping to create a very inefficient system, with a lot of waste.

"Cod eat the shrimp, who transmit worms to the cod from the feces of seals. That diet produces wormy codfish. That's why you don't want to eat a cod which has been caught in an area where there might be a lot of seals."[8] "Now that the seal population is being encouraged to increase and to add to its habitat," she explains, "we're diluting the purity of the codfish farther down the coast. Pretty soon, you won't be able to find a codfish without worms, and this is because of the lack of knowledge of the people making the rules. Not the fisherman, as you are led to believe."

Charlie Butman, describing seals, says, "They dive into a school of fish, take a bite out of the liver, and discard the rest, which falls to the ocean floor." After pondering what he has just said, he adds, "I like to think that the crabs, the lobsters, the flounders, and the other fish on the bottom eat the remnants."

On the West Coast, where sea lion and seal populations have increased at an annual rate of 5 to 8 percent per year since the 1970s, they (the pinnipeds) consume an estimated three million pounds of fish per day.[9] Despite those numbers, the U.S. government is strongly committed to protecting seals and other marine mammals. Whale watching has become a significant part of the New England tourist business. Many boats previously employed in fishing now take people out to Stellwagen Bank and Jeffries Ledge to see the whales in the spring and summer months before the marine mammals head south for the winter.

"Cute" sells at the turn of the century. Seals are cute, koala bears are the cutest, and even decidedly uncute thirty-ton whales achieve cuteness through the names given them by the "save the whale" movement. Several conservation groups have raised money by promoting the idea that, for a contribution in some predetermined amount, a child can "adopt" a whale with a name assigned by humans. Fishermen, by contrast, are hardly cute. And they are the first to notice that they are portrayed as "fish killers" and "whale haters." In the present climate, it is easy to forget that seals and some whales eat fish.

"Perhaps the council should recommend assigning quotas to the seals and whales to limit the number of fish they can eat," Harriet says, with a hint of a smile on her face. "You don't hear our government talking about Canada anymore. When I first started going to meetings, all you heard was, 'Canada is doing this; Canada is doing that.' Now that Canada is easing up on the seal hunt, Canada is no longer mentioned.

"Remember, God and evolution have combined to create a world where certain fish live together in areas or habitats conducive to the needs of those fish. That is why a fishing vessel is given a multispecies license to fish. When I see a vessel come into port, and I see his hail, the required paper showing what fish are on that boat, I know where that boat has been. If I see cusk and hake and gray sole, I know that boat's been fishing east towards the Gulf of Maine; if I see just blackback, cod, and haddock, I know that vessel's been more around Georges and Nantucket Shoals.

"And that's the way it's always been. That's the way God or Nature intended it to be. These people who are regulating offshore fisheries can require a little bigger mesh; they can institute changes to the fishing gear; they can even insist on quotas; but they shouldn't try to change the balance of nature. That's what I see, is my government trying to work against nature."

3

ARE REGULATIONS DESTROYING THE FISH AND DESTROYING THE FISHERMAN?

We're not politically correct, and unless there's a new atmosphere to bring respect to fishing, there will be no fishing industry in this country in a short period of time.

—Harriet Didriksen, fishing vessel owner

Gloucester recently celebrated its 375th anniversary. Today, it is a city of stark contrasts—its future in question, its past a romantic prelude. The downtown resembles a case of urban blight. Yet Gloucester's Eastern Point and Annisquam remain the sites for some of the most desirable summer homes north of Boston, as has been the case for over a hundred years. Artists ranging from Maurice Prendergast to Winslow Homer have been inspired by Gloucester to create some of their finest work.

The Cape Ann Historical Society in Gloucester owns the largest collection of Fitz Hugh Lane paintings housed anywhere. Standing alone on a hill between the local Dunkin Donuts and the waterfront is the bleak stone structure where Lane lived while painting *Ships in Ice off Ten Pound Island*, *Fresh Water Cove from Dolliver's Neck*, and *The Western Shore with Norman's Woe*, all scenes once visible from this house. Today, that vista is interrupted not by fishing boats but by beige factory-size boxes of corrugated steel, where fish are processed as they come off the trucks from Nova Scotia, Canada, or a nomadic factory trawler that knows no country and is not bound by the regulations governing U.S. fishing boats.

Between two fish processors, the black hull of Captain Mitchell's *Adventure* is poised on a cradle—a sculpture dropped in the midst of an industrial setting. The sheer size of its mahogany wheel overpowers the landscape and challenges the viewer to reaffirm what period in time this really is. Next to *Adventure*, a cinder block one-story building, spray-painted white, proclaims in brown lettering that this is the location of the Gloucester Marine Railway. A small door located at the right side of the building, and painted bright red, identifies the occupant by a sticker stating FACTORY TRAWLERS ARE OVERKILL.

On the other side of the red door are the one-room headquarters of Greenpeace, where Niaz Dorry is fighting a battle to save fishing for the fisherman. Three-by-three-foot corrugated boxes of pamphlets and position papers are piled three high on makeshift tables and desks. Amidst the clutter, Niaz is a colorful presence in her shawl skirt of oversize birds and flowers on a black background. She is also becoming a presence up and down the coast, where she confronts fishermen to persuade them to join forces with her to prohibit factory trawlers from operating within all U.S. waters.

Her job is not an easy one. Ever since 1991, when the Conservation Law Foundation and the Massachusetts Audubon Society together sued the National Marine Fisheries Service for "failing to prevent overfishing" as defined in Amendment 4 to the Northeast Multispecies Fisheries Management Plan, fishermen have seen the environmentalist as the enemy.

The nonprofit sector in the United States accounts for 8 percent of the gross domestic product (GDP) and employs close to 10 percent of the workforce—more than all state and federal workers combined.[1] A large part of the nonprofit work is geared toward environmental concerns. Fishing has become one of the environmental community's hottest issues.

Bill Amaru, a fisherman and council member, asks where the environmental community was back in the seventies and eighties when the fish stocks were being depleted. "I'll tell you where they were," he answers. "They had other causes they were using to raise money, and now this is a cause célèbre, and that's one of the reasons that they're focusing on fisheries. The people we see at the council, like Niaz, those individuals in the trenches are working hard to do what they believe in, but the people at the top—those are businesses!"

Harriet Didriksen agrees with Bill. "The Legal Defense Fund and Conservation Law have the *premise* of preservation," she says. "A lot of the conservation people have to have adversaries so they can collect money to publish their pamphlets and pay their salaries.

"We have fished responsibly when no one noticed it, and we were left alone. Now, when fishing can be used by people to sell their pamphlets, now we're told what we can and can't do. I feel that no one has the right to replace my ability to earn a livelihood with a philosophy which creates a job for them at our expense."

When Niaz is asked to comment on the adversarial relationship between the fishing community and the environmentalists, she first points out that the rest of the conservation community does not share most of her views. Then she goes on to explain. "From my perspective, the suit brought in 1991 was probably justified. We see a lot of plans put into effect by the fisheries management services, but then when it comes to enforcement of them, sticking to the plans, there's almost no follow-up. What that suit was defending was that when you write laws, you gotta do something about them. You can't just have laws that mean nothing."

Greenpeace and Niaz have spent the last five years prodding the National Marine Fisheries Service to implement the mandates of the 1996 Sustainable Fisheries Act. "A lot of fishermen weighed in on the amendments of this act, and now they're told that those amendments work against them, which is not true. If you really tear apart the Sustainable Fisheries Act [SFA] and start to look at it, it really benefits those in the fisheries industry that should be benefiting from it.

"I approach this whole debate from the perspective that there is a line, and the line is between people who are willing to make a living and the people who want to make a killing. The ocean can't sustain people who want to make a killing. It will benefit the people who look at the ocean as a way of making a living. Unfortunately, there is this broad-brush approach to how people evaluate the fishing industry. Too many people view the fishing industry as a group of people who want to make a killing."

Niaz moved from Washington, D.C., to Gloucester because she wanted to see for herself what motivates the traditional fisherman. Before continuing, she glances toward one of the Greenpeace Action Alert pamphlets urging the ban of factory trawlers. "If there are boats which continue to ignore that the ocean is finite, those boat owners won't like the Sustainable Fisheries Act. But those who recognize it's not a bottomless pit will realize the SFA is actually beneficial to them.

"And one of our biggest concerns is that the fisheries management people—not the fisheries service as an agency, but the folks on top, those people making policies—seem to feel that the least number of people you have to deal with, the easier it is to manage fisheries. They believe the most economically efficient fleet is the most manageable fleet."

Referring to those policy makers, Niaz says, "We tend to disagree. They want laws written that will ease their management, and that will perpetuate this economic efficiency theory. The SFA doesn't do that, and so the people on the policy-making side of the fisheries, the Department of Commerce, NOAA, have been fighting the SFA. At least that's my take on the situation." Niaz shares the information that some of the people on the National Marine Fisheries Service staff worked to come up with equitable ways to implement the SFA, and then were moved out of the agency.

The New England Fishery Management Council is one of eight regional councils set up as a product of the Magnuson Fishery Conservation and Management Act. Its role is to make recommendations for fisheries management to the National Marine Fisheries Service, which is part of the National Oceanic and Atmospheric Administration (NOAA), which is in turn part of the U.S. Department of Commerce. The Magnuson Act stipulates that council members must be "knowledgeable regarding the conservation and management, or the commercial or recreational harvest, of the fishery resources of the geographical area concerned." Members include the regional commander of the U.S. Coast Guard (a non-voting member) and the regional administrator of the National Marine Fisheries Service.

Headquarters for the Northeast branch of the National Marine Fisheries Service are in an office building located in Gloucester's Blackburn Park. Howard Blackburn, for whom the office complex was named, was the legendary fisherman who, lost at sea with his dory mate in a snowstorm and presumed dead, managed to single-handedly row himself and the corpse of his mate a hundred miles to land in Newfoundland. Despite the loss of all his fingers and some toes to frostbite, he continued to sail, and later set a record for the Gloucester to Lisbon trip. Gloucester is made of stories of man against nature, but the romance is harder and harder to reconcile with a world where the human population has increased at the expense of other species whose numbers are decreasing at an alarming rate.

Blackburn's name, attached to the Northeast headquarters, should be a poignant reminder for the members of the National Marine Fisheries Service that the fisherman should not be ignored. Niaz is not sure that message is heard. "The Fisheries Service has veto power," Niaz comments, "and they provide guidance to the council. If they don't want to consider a position, they tell the council, 'Look, you don't want to waste your time doing this. This is what we want to see.' What the council wants to see doesn't always fit into the boundaries of the law. What I often see is the Fisheries Service, that is, the policy makers, trying to figure out how they can reword the law to try to satisfy the most economically powerful side of the industry at the expense of what they perceive as less efficient community-based fishing."

Many fishermen suspect that some members of the U.S. Congress want to get rid of the fishing industry as it exists today. When fishermen talk among themselves now, they say they have heard that the American people do not want to pay for any more buybacks of fishing vessels. They have heard that people do not want any more tax dollars diverted to what they see as a bailout of the fishing industry. Harriet Didriksen in New Bedford counters, "No one asked me whether or not I want my tax dollars to go towards saving the S and Ls; no one asked me whether or not I want to subsidize tobacco growers.

"As a taxpayer, I object to paying the salaries of a lot of regulators who are supposed to be helping me, but instead are putting me out of business."

When confronted with the fishermen's fears, Niaz does not entirely disagree. "I don't think Congress is trying to eliminate the fishing folks, but I can't say the same thing about the Department of Commerce. And I can't honestly say this administration is wholeheartedly behind community-based fishing. I would almost guarantee that they're not, and their behavior shows they're not," she adds. "While there is all this effort going on to try to come up with community-based management, they're pushing for privatization, for consolidation, industrialization, and for economic efficiency, which basically counteracts all that the Sustainable Fisheries Act was set up to do."

Niaz explains. "That act says move away from economic efficiency, move away from consolidation, move away from privatization, look at more benign low-impact fishing efforts as opposed to more destructive industrial-scale fishing efforts. That's what the SFA did. It said, 'determine your overfishing definitions based on the impact on fishing communities.' The National Marine Fisheries Service hasn't even come up with a definition of what a fishing community is. That's one of the things the Department of Commerce has fought.

"They have bowed to the most industrialized sector of the fishing industry, who want to keep the [1976] Magnuson Act. The factory trawlers in the North Pacific and the highly overcapitalized fleet on this coast—those two bodies combined have more influence than the environmental community." As Niaz speaks, it becomes easy to understand why she has been able to win the confidence of so many fishermen even though she initially appears to represent an alien force.

One of the concerns of environmentalists, as well as scientists, hook fishermen, and regulators of the fisheries, is that the gear used by some modern-day draggers, aptly referred to as "street sweepers" and "rock hoppers," is able to get down into the gullies where the fish breed. Photographs accompanying Paul Dayton's 1998 article in *Science* show a perfect spawning spot for groundfish both before and after a commercial scallop dredger went through. The "after" shows a sandy bottom, free of vegetation, with clearly no protection for a fish from a predator.

Up until the late 1980s, fishing boats were limited to trawling over sandy bottoms. If they fished over a rocky bottom, the rocks would catch and tear their nets. Then someone introduced a net equipped with large rollers that, coupled with higher-horsepower engines, permitted trawling without barriers. At the same time, the new gear modification invaded fish refuges or safe areas where groundfish had previously enjoyed a chance to mature and breed.

Les Watling, a professor of oceanography at the University of Maine's Darling Marine Center, began studying the rocky areas of the Gulf of Maine in 1984. Since then, he has focused much of his work on the impact of the newer fishing gear and scallop gear on fish populations. A recent issue of the *Boston Globe Magazine* quotes Watling: ". . . my feeling is that the final collapse of the fishery was the advent of gear that allowed people to go anywhere. . . . I've come to believe that those nurseries functioned for a very long time and kept the fishery going."[2]

The environmental community and many in the fishing community recommended to the council that "street sweeper" fishing gear be eliminated from the oceans. It was not until November of 1999, despite years of discussion at each council meeting, that the National Marine Fisheries Service finally prohibited this type of fishing gear. Niaz credits the long delay as yet another example of the bias toward economic efficiency. "We have gone from highly benign, low-impact gear to gear that goes places we've never been able to go before, to lines that are forty miles long [as in the case of swordfishing] to boats with enough gill nets to mark turf so that the smaller fisherman cannot enter the territory. Gear has become something other than for fishing."

Outside the Greenpeace office, seagulls call as they soar overhead. Niaz listens, and then continues. "Our intention is not to tell the fisherman he can't fish. At this point, we have a need to do an across-the-board assessment of all the gears being used, and figure out what gears have the lowest impact on the ocean, and can actually be used to catch fish.

"We're not an antifishing organization. We believe that fishing has to be limited to low-impact, community-based harvesting of fish, which allows people to be employed, and allows them to make a living off the ocean."

Conversation turns to the diversity inherent in the traditional fishing communities, and how that helps to retain a diversity of species. "I would argue that's a helpful part of the fishing community for preserving the stocks. When you have a diverse fleet, you're approaching different fisheries. You're not pulse fishing on one stock. You're fishing for different things. Different boats have different capabilities. Some boats can fish eleven months out of the year, some six, some two. That gives the ocean a break.

"That's how people used to fish here. Once you saw the industrialization of the cod fishery, you saw a twelve-month fishery. Before that people carpentered and people gardened to make ends meet between fishing. Once that lifestyle went, you started to see the fish stocks go."

Niaz could be describing Charlie Butman, who as a boy harvested sea moss in the summers. Then, as he got older, he went lobstering in the summer months, and did carpentering in the winter months when he could not fish. Or Bobby Butman and Steve Barry, who painted houses when *Captain Sam* had filled its quota for days at sea. There may be no more flexible and industrious workers than the old-time New England fishermen and their families who canned and pickled most of what was needed for the winter from their summer gardens.

"I'm not suggesting that fishermen should be living at a poverty level. But if you choose to go into a business that has limits which humans have nothing to do with, as much as we want to pretend like we do, then you have to live by the limitations of the resource, not by the limitations you set for the resource."

"As I think about it," Charlie Butman says, "the first thing you should ask these regulatory people is, 'Did you ever go fishing?' And if they say no, then they shouldn't be on that board [the New England Fishery Management Council]. That's my opinion. It's just the same as being a carpenter. If you haven't learned the trade, then you don't know a thing, and you just have to guess at everything. I don't understand how they can get all these people with all this authority about something they have never done in the first place. To me it's disgusting!"

If you are a fisherman, there are not enough fishermen on the New England Fishery Management Council. If you are not, you probably think the council is made up only of people who fish—and who have done a pretty poor job of regulating themselves. Carl Safina, a scientist who served on the Mid-Atlantic Fishery Management Council, writes, "the [Fishery and Conservation Management Act] established the regional councils and appointed those most knowledgeable about the fisheries—people who fish—to be responsible for regulating fishing activities."³

The truth is that of the New England Fishery Management Council's seventeen voting members in 1998, only three voting members are fishermen, and only two of the three earns his or her livelihood fishing. One is Eric Anderson, a gillnetter who is one of the two representatives from New Hampshire. The other is William Amaru, a forty-eight-year-old clarinet player who abandoned a career as a classical musician to fish full-time out of Chatham, Massachusetts, on the south side of Cape Cod, and who brings a musician's desire for order and clarity to his work with the council.

After graduating from college with a music performance degree in clarinet, Bill was accepted for one of the few openings available in the graduate program at the New England Conservatory of Music. Throughout his college years, he fished in the summers and left college on weekends in October, driving from upstate New York to the Cape so he could fish at night for striped bass during the open season.

Following a stint playing with the Boston Pops Esplanade Orchestra, he took a hard look at the life of a musician and decided to try fishing full-time. In 1974, he bought a converted 30-foot lobster boat and began to fish for cod with hooks and a longline. He has been fishing out of Chatham ever since.

Bill Amaru refers to himself as someone from the last generation of fishermen to enter the industry at a time of only limited controls, the last generation that had unlimited entry and opportunity to fish. He contrasts the opportunities he had to the situation in today's industry, which he describes as being totally controlled, with limited entry and limited allowable harvesting.

On a weekend in early October, Bill is briefly seated at his dining room table, where he can look out a sliding glass door over a deck to the duck pond he built in the backyard, and beyond to a wooded area that appears to stretch on forever. No other houses are visible. A visitor could be reminded of Mike Barry's home in Cohasset, which shares the same closeness to nature. Both are wood frame structures in the classic New England style.

Bill and his wife Joanne have raised a son and a daughter here. His son Jason graduated in the same class as Paul Vitale at the Massachusetts Maritime Academy and is working on an oil-drilling and exploration vessel. He has just returned home after a month at sea to spend a month with his bride of five weeks. Then back for another month's duty. The sea is a way of life for these men, and for this family.

"When I started fishing," Bill relates, "I came at the very last possible moment when you could look back in time and see the way it was once like at sea. I put a boat in the water at the end of the street where I grew up. And I could go out through the inlet and get out into the ocean, line up a particular telephone pole with the steeple of the church, be in a hundred feet of water, and pull cod all day long. I'd go home at the end of the day and make fifty dollars for a boatload of fish because the price was so low then. But I loved the fact that I could go out and, without doing anything harmful, I could bring home food.

"You created wealth. I like that idea," Bill says. "I didn't think about it much then, but I went out with a tank of gas, a hook and a line, and I came back with value." He laughs at the pleasure of his reminiscence. "That's pretty amazing to create value out of the ocean, out of nothing. It's like a carpenter taking a piece of wood and turning it on his lathe into something of value, something which people are willing to pay you for. I think that's just great. And it was sustainable. I knew that the fish I wasn't catching would be there the next day, that they would grow and have baby fish that would grow. It was a beautiful cycle of production. It looked so renewable and so good," he adds.

More people, demanding more and more fish, have tainted Bill's picture. When he realized the changes taking place, he ran for a position on the New England Fishery Management Council to help control the direction of the regulations and to help save the industry he loved. "It's hard to be a full-time fisherman and be on the council," he explains. "It's a full-time job." He does not mention that it is also a job that does not pay a salary. The fishermen who choose to do it devote a large part of their time to serving the industry in the way they feel the time spent will have the greatest results. Each council member is paid $350 per day plus expenses such as travel, meals, and hotels for each meeting. But, as one former council member stated, "To be on the council, you have to plan on spending at least two days prior to each meeting while you digest monumental piles of information. Then you have to figure a day of travel time coming and going plus the telephone conversations, faxes, and e-mail you have to stay on top of. So if you want to be of value to the council, and the American people," he adds, "there's little time to do much else."

Rodney Avila, fisherman and former council member, puts it in perspective. "When you're fishing, and that council meeting is in the middle of a trip, you either have to take the trip off or you have to bring the boat back in, and lose a day to go to the meeting." Losing a day means you are allowed to fish one day less out of your allowable days at sea. "That's why, when I got on the council, I actively walked off the boat.

And that's when I gave it to my son. I said, 'I can't do both and be fair to everyone.' If I bring the boat in to do my council duty, the crew suffer. They lose a day's pay.

"You can't have your mind on fishing, and still do a good job on the council. Even when you come home from fishing, you're thinking I have to repair this on the boat, I have to repair that on the boat. Then you go listen to the weather. When you put your council hat on, you have to forget that. You can't do both, because one of them suffers. Bill might be able to do it because he fishes alone, and he doesn't have a crew to think about."

The majority of the council members are paid by the organizations they represent while doing fisheries management work or while attending council meetings. Philip Coates (now retired) and his successor, Paul Diodati, are or have been the salaried directors of the Massachusetts Division of Marine Fisheries; John Nelson is the chief of the Marine Division of the New Hampshire Fish and Game Department; Patricia Kurkul is the division chief of NOAA, the governing body for fisheries management. Conversely, the few members working in the fisheries, like Bill Amaru, are not salaried. Former chairman, Joseph M. Brancaleone, who had been a fisherman, works for Burger King, and took time off from work when he attended council meetings or worked on fisheries management issues.

Each of these men and women has pledged to represent the industry for the most appropriate benefit to the country at large. "That's really not what's happening," Bill states. "The political situation is such that there is intended to be a balance between conservation, exploitation, and other regulatory bodies such as the individual states in order to protect their interests. So everybody's in there protecting their area.

"We've been handed a requirement to rebuild the fish stocks and try not to displace the fishermen, which is an oxymoron of sorts," he explains. "There are far too many fishermen fishing the way we fish now to effectively harvest what can be harvested without causing displacement. And we *are* causing it. We just try to balance the two together."

A fisherman serving on the council must maintain a delicate balance between carrying out the provisions of the oath he takes to rebuild the fish stocks and allowing himself the possibility to fish. Bill deftly balances the two seemingly opposite demands, sometimes tilting toward one side or the other.

Bill Amaru might be one of the few people on the council who is not representing an agenda other than his own beliefs. Fortunately, that gives him the freedom to say, "I don't have my hand in anyone's pie. And no one has his hand in mine. I'm representing the future for myself and for my industry. I want my son to be able to go fishing someday if he wants to." He gestures toward a large colored photo of his boat, the *Joanne A.*, on the wall. "I want to be able to put that boat out on the water, and catch fish like I did when I first built it in 1982. I'm doing it because I like to fish," he concludes. "I want to continue to make a good living, and not kill myself worrying about whether or not I'm going to go out and bring in nothing."

Bill is a person who needs only four hours of sleep a night—a requirement for anyone planning to enter the industry. At forty-eight, he has taut skin, dark hair and eyebrows, and seemingly unlimited energies. His ability to sit on a council and decide on the constraints that may put him out of business would qualify him to be the CEO of any large publicly held corporation. But, other than the stipend for meetings, he is not getting paid for his time.

And Bill, along with his fellow council members, is the recipient of much of the criticism of fishing regulations leveled by the fishing industry. Harriet Didriksen, for example, points out that the section on national standards at the beginning of the Magnuson-Stevens Fishery Conservation and Management Act states, in section 104–297, paragraph (8), "Conservation and management measures shall . . . take into account the importance of fishery resources to fishing communities in order to (A) provide for the sustained participation of such communities, and (B) to the extent practicable, minimize adverse economic impacts on such communities." She thinks the Department of Commerce is trying to circumvent the provisions of the Magnuson-Stevens Act by making conditions so bad that fishermen leave the industry voluntarily. "Is it minimizing the adverse economic impact on my community to put our people out of work, to take away their means of making a living?" Harriet asks.

When confronted with such criticism, Bill acknowledges the conflict between the Magnuson Act and the current regulations. "Well, when you take away the privilege of a fleet to fish, by closing off its fishing grounds like we did to New Bedford in 1994, when we closed off most of the offshore grounds, that definitely has gone against that national standard," Bill responds. "Look, if there's another way to do it, let us know what it is. But I frankly don't think there is, because you can't find anyone out there who doesn't have his or her agenda.

"Fishermen don't like quotas; they don't like mesh size restrictions; they don't like closed areas; they don't like licenses; they don't like anything. Do they like catching fish?" he asks. "That's what we're trying to do. We're trying to create an environment in which there can be fish and fishermen. That's our fundamental goal. Only they see it as, 'If you leave us alone, we can sort it out ourselves.' Well, I can tell you honestly," Bill states, "if we hadn't done what we've done in the nineties, there wouldn't be ten percent of the fishermen that are currently employed. There would be no fish left if we didn't have the controls on that we have now," he insists. "I kid you not.

"What I think has happened in the past when there's been a problem—and there has been a problem," he adds, referring to the many lawsuits brought against the council—"is that the balance has simply been out of whack. There has been way too much industry representation and not enough representation of other areas."

This suggestion that the council has given "way too much" representation to the "industry," that is, the fishermen, is of course the opposite of where Harriet and some of the other fishermen see the council's emphasis.

"Now that's been somewhat addressed, and continues to be," Bill continues, "by advancing other individuals onto the council who represent other than commercial capture industries." As an example, Bill cites the Environmental Defense Fund, which now has a seat on the council in the person of Doug Hopkins, whom Bill refers to as "a very bright, aggressive young lawyer with a good handle on the industry.

"We're starting to see a little bit more representation from other than industry, and as that swings in the direction of more conservation, I think you'll see more aggressive conservation plans put together." The ducks in the pond are quacking, attracting Bill's attention to the outside. When he returns his focus back to the room, he adds, "It's unfortunate that we had to get to the point where things got so bad before we started serious conservation plans."

Voices as diverse as those of Niaz Dorry and Gloucester fisherman Paul Vitale have been saying that the Department of Commerce and some of its governing bodies have an interest in eliminating the small fisherman in favor of a few large boats and easily controlled large fishing consortiums. Bill disagrees. "It's ironic that they would feel that way when in fact the industry is going the other way. There are fewer big boats today than there has been in the last twenty-five years."

Reminded that the big boat will catch more fish, which seems to be the antithesis of the goals of the Sustainable Fisheries Act, Bill comments, "but they're also going to go to a place where it's appropriate to fish with a bigger boat." After stopping to think about this tack in the conversation, Bill's voice gains volume. "You know, one of the things people lose sight of when they say something like that is that for years and years this industry lost thousands of participants because of the difficulties of going to sea in small boats, in boats which were not well designed for the rigors of the North Atlantic Ocean.

"Since World War Two, we've made tremendous strides in improving our efficiency, which I think is what we're supposed to be doing as a species in general, and certainly as capture-oriented harvesters or hunters. And that's what it's all about. It's not about becoming less efficient or making yourself more risk averse. It's about exactly the opposite.

"So we've made boats bigger, safer, more efficient. And we've also overfished, because we didn't put proper controls on the numbers and the ways those boats carried out their business. With virtually every other natural resource, you have a season when you can or can't hunt, you have a limitation on the number of bullets you can put in the chamber of your hunting gun, you have animals which you can or can't take. We didn't do any of that in this industry until the fish were out of the dam, were already gone. The fishing industry did what I think all industries in this country do. It strived to improve, to make the work easier, production greater.

"And now we're all charged with the responsibility for rebuilding the fish stocks and writing fisheries plans which balance the resource with the needs of the industry." As Bill speaks, his voice sinks to its previous low volume and now sounds tired. He has been driving back and forth to Mt. Desert Island, Maine, a six-hour drive from his home, to where the *Joanne A.* is in a boatyard being upgraded to increase its efficiency, as per Bill's stated philosophy. "We've got an industry which has grown dramatically," he continues, "and a lot of people who rely on us to come up with a solution. We're confronted with a real dilemma.

"So the argument that anyone is trying to put big boats in power is simply unfounded. It flies in the face of the true evidence. There are far more small-boat fishermen today, far more than at any other time in the history of the industry."

Rodney Avila, of the New Bedford Fishermen's Family Assistance Center, would dispute that statement. According to a spreadsheet he has compiled for New England, 151 fishing vessels have become inactive since 1994, either through attrition, scrapping, or buyback. At least 620 fishermen, owners plus crewmembers, are no longer fishing as a result. During the last five years, 870 fishermen, 256 fishing family members, and 104 industry-related workers have sought training to move to other industries, partly as a result of the buyback program.

"The buyback," Bill scoffs. "It took seventy-nine boats out of a fleet of several thousand!" It is clear that Bill is thinking more as a council member than as a fisherman when he adds, in a lower voice, "I mean, growing as an individual and I had aspirations, as does everyone else. So I got something bigger the next year, and in 1982 I built the boat I fish with today. And each time, I increased my catch capacity tremendously."

In some ways, times have not changed from 1946, when Charlie Butman cut in half the *Lois J.*, his first boat, to add an additional four feet in the middle. When Bill drives six hours to Maine, it is to supervise the work on his 44-foot stern trawler the F/V *Joanne A III*, presently being cut in half in order to add five extra feet in the middle. What has changed is the demand, the market, the value of the product, and most of all the technology.

"With satellites being launched to permit us to have navigation to get back to the same places, we no longer need to see the church steeple and the telephone pole to know that where we are fishing is the best possible place to target a particular species," Bill says. "The ocean is like the land. You just can't see it. There are population centers out there. You don't just throw your line anywhere or you may be throwing your line in the middle of a desert. There are places where there aren't fish for miles, and then there are individual pockets where fish are real thick. When you learn those things and you understand when they're going to be there and what to use to catch them, you can catch a lot of fish. And we've all done that."

Given his musical training, it is no surprise that listening to Bill is like listening to a Bach fugue being played. His voice rises and falls in intensity as his story defines itself. And you know that he will return, in a coda, to the theme of his conversation, to neatly wrap up a thought introduced at the beginning. "So that's why I say we're never going to go back to that point where there was a great abundance of fish. We have to learn to control our technology, not turn our backs on it. There are people who say, 'Throw away the nets, throw away the synthetics, go back to using hooks and cotton line and you'll have all the fish you want.' Well, I'm sorry, but it just doesn't work like that.

"We'll never go back to driving the kind of automobiles we drove in 1950 when we have automobiles like the ones we have in 2001. Nor will we drive around on horses the way we once did," he adds, "even though if we did, global warming might be eliminated."

To watch Bill Amaru move gracefully and knowledgeably through a myriad of subjects ranging from the fishing industry to conservation to politics and law is to marvel at the breadth of knowledge each council member must bring to the job.

Bill voices his awareness of the impression he creates when he says, "As bad as the council has been made to appear, through the press and through reports, the individuals on the New England Fishery Management Council are, in my opinion, the most expert in the industry anywhere in this country. They've got to be." He shifts pronouns. "We've got to be social scientists as well as fishing scientists because we're fishing people. The problems we've been dealing with over the years have been so difficult and we've dedicated so much of our time and effort. And," he laughs at what he perceives to be a lack of humility, "I think we as individuals have done a pretty good job too.

"When people accuse the fisherman of being the sole cause of today's problems, just remember, fishermen are a tool in the hands of society. It might sound trite, but the fisherman has supplied a demand placed upon him or her by a growing population of ever wealthier individuals equipped to buy and to want the best possible product. And," he asks, "who can say they blame them? We now know so many different benefits from eating fish which weren't known in the past."

its belly constitutes *schillerlocken* or golden curls, a popular Belgian bar food; and in Hong Kong in shark fin soup. Skates or rays, which also used to wash up on Duxbury Beach, are now harvested and flown to Europe to appear on the menu of a restaurant on Vienna's posh Weihburggasse, where they are served as *rochen* or skate's wings in a lemon butter sauce.

The diminishing numbers of both skate and dogfish have recently come to the attention of the New England Fishery Management Council, where the catches of both are being closely monitored. Richard Daley, at that time U.S. Secretary of Commerce, voted to close the harvesting of dogfish as of May 1, 2000, despite the fact that dogfish landings in the 1999 fishing year accounted for between 50 and 90 percent of the total income of fishermen in Chatham, Scituate, and Plymouth.

Similarly, the herring that provides the livelihood for the bulk of Gloucester's fishing families is shipped to Sweden, where it is marinated and served with sour cream, a boiled potato, and a glass of Mariestad beer. Herring regulations have been a topic of discussion for over a year at the council meetings.

The monkfish Jimmy Bramante's boats are bringing in to the Boston Fish Pier are flown to Japan, Korea, and France, where they may be served as *lotte* at the fashionable La Coupole on Paris's Boulevard Montparnasse. Sea robins, once considered a "trash fish," are now the preferred fish for bouillabaisse.

These are a few of the so-called underutilized species that fishermen have turned to catching at the suggestion of the New England Fishery Management Council in its well-intentioned attempts to keep a community of fishermen on the water. And these fish are part of the reason fish still constitute the second largest product (by weight) shipped through Logan Airport. Perhaps more important, that fact attests to the incredible resilience of the fishing community and the fact that the public palate has become much more sophisticated as fish stocks have decreased in numbers.

The *Boston Globe* reported in the October 21, 1998, issue that cargo flights for Chilean sea bass (not even in the bass family) had increased from one flight per day in the mid-1980s to seven per day in 1998 in order to supply the American demand for seafood. Additional sea bass was being flown in from fifteen other countries to help satisfy the ever more sophisticated American taste for fish.[3]

Susan Regis, the executive chef for Biba (now renamed) and Pignole, two Boston restaurants at the apex of the sophistication ladder, says, "The public wants to know that something is special, that it's something they can't get at Star Market. We want our fish to be as close to the ocean as possible." She tells the story of Alice Waters, the famed California chef and owner of Chez Panisse, who started putting farmers' names on her menus twenty years ago, and Susan wonders why her restaurants could not achieve the same effect with fresh New England fish. She adds, "If I could, I would like to put the name of the boat which caught the fish on our menu."[4]

These are sweet words to Harriet Didriksen and other fishermen who see a possibility of survival based on educating the public to pay more for the best fish, and less for the imports that they see as cheap imitations of the real thing. In the United States, at least 80 percent of the shellfish and 65 percent of the finfish we consume are imported.

"Much of the fish which the United States public is eating is being imported from countries where the product isn't even inspected," Harriet states. "Some of it, I am sure, is fine product; some of it is marginal product, and some of it is unacceptable product." She refers to a *Wall Street Journal* article about a husband and wife who delivered a huge truckload of "fresh" shrimp from California to a restaurant in Maine in three days. "Well, that shrimp was harvested in Thailand and flown to California before it started on the highway.

"If my boat comes in today, I have to be very alert. I'm selling a fresh product, just caught, without water, and without chemicals. If that product is going to San Francisco, I would have to have it packed, on a truck, and in Boston by 11:00 A.M. so that it could be served in a restaurant in California for dinner that next evening. I pay more and I get paid more for that quality.

"The people I see who are willing to pay for fresh—really fresh—fish, are two kinds of people. There are the highly educated, well-paid people who want to eat fish." She clarifies her last statement with the comment: "The people who have been the most elated when my husband has given them a lobster or a haddock filet are the well-off. The rest of the people, they just don't get it!

"Then there are the ethnic or immigrant people who have a fish diet as part of their culture," Harriet continues, "and thank goodness for them, because those species have become the money fish today—the squid, the monkfish, the octopus. . . ."

Harriet and her friend Ellen pack monkfish by hand, and ship small quantities to a few New York restaurants like the Oyster Bar at Grand Central. When it comes to defining freshness in seafood, Harriet does not equivocate. "You don't have to know about fish, but if you're a person who is aware of what your senses tell you, you can see it, just as you can recognize a fine suit or a piece of well-crafted jewelry. And if you look at the fish, and there's something you don't like about what you see, there probably *is* something wrong with the fish. If you look at it and the scales are shiny, the gills are red, the eyes are shiny, it's all right. If it isn't pleasing to the senses, don't eat it.

"There was a book written called *Quality*, where the author stated, 'You know it when you see it.' That's how it is with seafood. There's just something about it."

Probably no one in New England has done more to elevate fish to celebrity status than the Berkowitz family that owns Legal Sea Foods. In 1904, Harry Berkowitz, the grandfather of Roger Berkowitz, company president, opened a small grocery store called the Legal Cash Market at Inman Square in Cambridge, Massachusetts. Until the mid-to-late 1940s, the store provided a livelihood for the family. Then supermarkets like A&P, Stop and Shop, and Star Market entered the marketplace, and the situation changed. Harry decided to take his son George out of school to help him in the grocery store. One day, George was talking with his cousin who worked at Stop and Shop, and mentioned how tough it was to compete with the larger stores that had just entered the market. The cousin told him that if he wanted to compete with the supermarkets, he had to have a few niceties in the store—such as fish counters.

The Berkowitz store was packed into only 2,500 square feet. In order to incorporate fish into the product mix, George Berkowitz leased the adjacent storefront and hung a sign, Legal Sea Foods. From 1950 to 1968, they sold fresh fish along with fried fish 'n' chips to go. "It was a period when fish was not all that popular," Roger Berkowitz explains. "If you were Italian, Portuguese, or Jewish and fish was part of your background, you ate fish—especially during holidays. And we lived for those times. There wasn't a tremendous interest in seafood in general, outside of the ethnic groups. So it was a business which was constantly in and out of the red, and constantly struggling with its customer base."

Then, in the mid-1960s, an influx of Asians began to arrive in Cambridge to study at Harvard and MIT. These new arrivals would be on sabbatical in the area for six months to a year and a half. Their diet often included fresh fish, and in some cases raw fish. Legal Sea Foods suddenly became a mecca for fresh fish to satisfy the tastes and fill the dietary needs of its Asian customers.

After that, another auspicious neighbor moved to Cambridge from California via France, where she had picked up a knowledge of French cooking. Her name was Julia Child, and the rest is history. When Julia Child first started her cooking show on Boston's public television station, she wanted to cook dishes using ingredients indigenous to the area. Seafood was one of them, and Legal Sea Foods was her preferred fish market. She began to mention Legal's both on TV and in her books.

"So you had a lot of Asians eating our fish, Julia Child shopping with us. And then you had the Boston doctors and nutritionists who were studying the Asian population to see why Asians had a longer life span, fewer incidents of heart disease, and lower levels of cancer," Roger Berkowitz relates. "And after determining that it must have something to do with diet, they identified seafood as a healthy source of protein." All of this benefited the Berkowitz family and Legal Sea Foods. Roger Berkowitz describes their position at that time as "being in a renaissance. And, we were so close to the Boston Fish Pier that we were able to have access to the product all the time."

Roger's grandfather had previously closed the grocery store. A cousin who had been operating a meat market in the old grocery store space decided to retire in 1968. The Berkowitz family chose to turn the space into a seafood restaurant. On picnic tables with paper plates, the family served the old staple fish 'n' chips, along with fried clams, fried shrimp, and fried scallops. As seafood became more popular, so did Legal's. Today, Roger Berkowitz is a familiar face on TV commercials for his restaurants and also for Blue Cross Blue Shield of Massachusetts and the regional telephone company. And Legal Sea Foods has twenty-six upscale fish restaurants where cherry paneling and halogen lights on paintings have replaced the picnic tables and paper plates.

"Seafood is no longer a commodity," Roger Berkowitz states. "It's no longer an inexpensive product. As it gets scarcer, people are going to take better care of it in order to get the highest prices they can for it. When I was a kid and fish was selling for three to four cents a pound, no one cared whether it was gutted; they didn't care whether it was iced; they didn't care whether it was washed. And now they're really paying attention to those things because they understand that quality does make a difference."

Roger Berkowitz is seated in a high-backed swivel chair behind a desk in his office in an industrial area on the outskirts of Boston. What appears to be a large, curved desk is covered with piles of papers, letters, and trade journals, as is the matching credenza behind him. Despite the clutter, he is totally focused and all business, but with a kindness that prompted him to agree to discuss the fish business today without constraints.

Legal Sea Foods is a significant player in the fisheries equation. In an average week, Legal's processes close to one hundred tons of groundfish. Fifty to 75 percent of the groundfish served at Legal's comes off American fishing vessels. Jimmy Bramante points out that Legal Sea Foods has always stayed in touch with the family-owned boats. "They advertise that, and they actually do stay in touch with us. They always buy for quality. Sometimes the price is low, sometimes the price is high, but they absorb that. It's a quality restaurant."

Jimmy's words would be reassuring to Roger Berkowitz. "We've been marketing quality assurance by virtue of the fact that it's a Legal Sea Foods–quality fish. That's our branding," he says. "It has to hit a certain standard when Arthur and his crew [the buyers for Legal Sea Foods] go down to the Fish Pier. That fish has to meet a certain standard similar to a fine-quality beef. By virtue of the fact that it even gets back here, that makes it Legal Sea Foods quality."

As more people become aware of quality in the seafood they purchase, fishermen are looking to nontraditional ways of marketing their product. In New York City, Stephanie Villani used to operate a stall for selling fresh apples from her family's farm. She and her husband, Alex, a fisherman, now drive two hours each way on weekends to the same farmers' market, where they sell the fish he catches during the week. Stephanie estimates that this method of selling fish is 20 to 50 percent more profitable than selling wholesale. It also gives Alex the flexibility to catch whatever species meets the quota requirement and is available. The negatives are that they must be outside selling fish in all kinds of weather, they are dealing with some of the world's most demanding consumers, and they cannot leave the selling to someone else.

Jim Ostergard is a fisherman who introduced this country to the concept of boxing fish at sea. As he points out, "It's not easy to peddle good fish." In an effort to expand the time a fish will remain at top quality, Jim has experimented with using boxes from Norway that drain from both sides and have teeth to hold the box off the surface below. This permits fishermen at sea to remove fish from the hold of a boat and pack them to show at the display auction. The advantage is that there is less chance of fish stacked on top of one another contaminating the fish lower down in the hold or vice versa. Fish at the bottom of a fish pen on a vessel customarily lose 17 percent of their weight. Boxing can bring that weight loss down to as little as 3 percent, thus preserving the fish and retaining a high moisture content when it is brought to the table.

The first vessel to try Jim's boxing method was the New Bedford F/V *Odin* captained by Ellen Skaar's husband Gabriel. When the boxed fish were brought to auction, the dealers offered fifteen cents less. The message was interpreted to mean that the fishing community did not want to have to deal with anything new or different. Then Gabriel and Jim went to the end user and received fifteen cents more than the highest price on the auction board for that species. Jim concludes, "Quality is about people, not about the product."

In 1986, fishing vessel owners in Portland, Maine, teamed up with the city and some of its fish processors to create the only nonprofit display auction in the United States. Their model was the display auctions in Reykjavik, Iceland, which have been operating successfully for about twenty years. At the display auction, boxes of iced fish are unloaded before the auction begins and are placed in a temperature-controlled room. Buyers then have a chance to see and handle the fish prior to placing a bid in the auction room. Prompted by the success of Portland's display auction and having learned from several earlier attempts, New Bedford established the first electronic fish display auction in the United States. In New Bedford, as in Gloucester, the fishermen unload their catches when they return to port. A buyer then has the option of looking at the fish and handling them before placing a bid. Next, the buyer either e-mails or telephones an order to a broker at the auction building, where the scene resembles a commodity broker's office except that the commodity is fish. The success of the New Bedford electronic display auction is partly the result of two factors. First, the buyers know the quality that typically comes off certain boats and may elect to buy on the Internet, sight unseen, from the holds of those boats. Second, more fish are unloaded in New Bedford than in any other East Coast port. In 1998, the New Bedford auction traded 15,869,564 pounds of groundfish, at a dollar value of $21,153,709. A year later, due to the regulations in place, 14,047,655 pounds of groundfish were traded in New Bedford, for $18,493,786.

Larry Ciulla and his sister Rosemary are third generation in a Gloucester fishing family. Years ago, their father and mother had the foresight to acquire two and a half acres of Gloucester waterfront property. In 1998, with software provided by the owners of the New Bedford auction, Larry and Rosemary converted that property into Gloucester's first display auction. They noticed a need to highlight quality fish, and they built a forty-thousand-square-foot facility for unloading, displaying, and selling fresh fish. Jim Ostergard says, "the display auctions upgrade an appreciation for the quality of fish, because people can see exactly what they are getting."

A visit to the Gloucester display auction underscores the frustration voiced by Gerry Frattollilo when she laments the lack of space available for a display auction in Boston as a result of Massport's displacing the Boston Fish Exchange. At the Gloucester display auction, a large warehouse next to the dock provides for the display of boxed fish. Adjacent to that space, a room at least twice the size of the existing room in

Boston is fitted out with modern recessed acoustical ceiling tiles and glare-free lighting. A screen mounted at the front of the room displays trades as they are made. Each two-person writing surface available to the bidders is equipped with a keypad and microphone, and each is labeled with the company name of the particular dealer who sits there. North Coast, Legal Sea Foods, and Atlantic Coast (all Boston dealers) are a few of the regular dealers whose names appear at the bidders' desks.

Bidding is done on a wholly different basis in Gloucester than in Boston. The morning auction is held at 6:00 A.M. Fish are unloaded and tagged with their date of arrival the night before, and buyers arrive at 4:30 A.M. to look them over. Bidding is in blocks of ten lots, or pallets. After the bid for ten lots is accepted, bidding begins again for the next block of ten. The opportunity to "scratch" or turn down a bid is still available to the vessel owner, as it is in Boston. A vessel owner pays seven cents per pound to unload fish at the Gloucester auction; the buyer pays four cents per pound.

Sal and Frank Patania buy from both the Boston auction and the display auction in Gloucester. When asked if he thinks there is an advantage to purchasing from a display auction, Frank answers, "Not really. In Boston, you pay a little more, but you get to handle every fish. And what better display can you have than when you have to handle the fish one by one? In Gloucester, you can tell them to throw the fish out of a box, and then throw them back in. But you still can't handle every fish. They're all in hundred-pound boxes. You'd have to start the night before. And someone else loads up the boxes. If they feel they want to dress up the top, they can do that. Whether they do or they don't, I couldn't tell you, but it's possible. You can get top quality in Gloucester, but you're going to pay for it."

At the display auction, a box of haddock unloaded that morning from a boat that goes out for only two days at a time is going to command a higher price than a box unloaded from a boat where it might have been in the hold for a week. A fish caught by hook will bring the vessel owner twenty to thirty cents more than a fish caught by a dragger. Frank maintains that in Boston, "it may be more of a shot in the dark, but you can get top quality every day. At the boat, you unload the fish one at a time, and if my brother or I find a fish or two we don't like, if it's soft, if it's broken, if it's got a tumor, or if it's just old, we throw it aside. And we know the boats," Frank adds. "That's always been a factor, whether there are ten or one hundred boats. Certain boats do a better job of taking care of the product."

The display auctions provide a calmer environment, Frank admits.

"The idea is you saw it; you bought it; you've got nothing to be upset over. In Boston, you're face to face with the producer. The fisherman thinks it's good. The guy who's buying it who's going to process it knows what he's buying, knows what he's going to get. Instead of getting a forty percent yield, he knows he's only going to get a thirty-five percent yield, so he's not going to be able to compete on the market, and he starts yelling." Frank is referring to the fact that the fisherman and the buyer don't necessarily come in contact at the display auctions because the boats are unloaded prior to the bidding. When Frank speaks of the "yield," he is referring to the amount of fish that will be lost in processing. A fresh fish that has been well cared for will lose little to the filleting process and vice versa.

Barry Sullivan, chief operating officer for the Gloucester auction, points out that the prices received for fish have gone up substantially since the display auction opened. He credits this in part to a heightened awareness of the correlation between quality and price brought to the fisherman by the display auction. Of course, supply and demand have had a lot to do with price increases. Barry voices the example, "Today each tote holding fish shows the fish displayed neatly head to tail, head to tail. You never saw this two to three years ago." He adds that today the fishermen will remove the gills from all the fish prior to their being shown at the auction. "Any fish not gilled will bring twenty-five cents less than a dressed fish. The fisherman now knows that. And the consumer benefits from the higher quality."

Today, the Gloucester fishing community cannot imagine not having the display auction. It is the one positive they have seen in the past few years. And they are grateful for it. When the New England Fishery Management Council voted to virtually eliminate codfishing by reducing the trip limit to thirty pounds per vessel, Gloucester fishermen went to Barry and told him he had to charge them more to unload in order for the auction to stay in business. This despite the lack of income imposed on them by the ruling.

The auctions are running simultaneously, which creates a complication for Frank Patania. "You can't even keep up. Over here it's eighty cents; over there it's ninety cents; over here it's a dollar fifty. Now try to explain to your customers that there's a guy [dealer] in Gloucester who paid a dollar fifty a pound for his fish, and he's quoting prices off a dollar fifty a pound, while the guy [another dealer] in New Bedford bought the same species at fifty cents a pound. The customer is going to think he's getting robbed. You just have no idea what the other port is bidding."

In addition to having a seat on the Boston Fish Exchange, Legal Sea

Foods buys from both the display auctions in Gloucester and the display auctions in Portland. Arthur Kloack, Legal's chief buyer in 1998, was at the Boston auction every morning, and he bought regularly from the catch of *Captain Sam* when Mike Barry was still fishing with his brothers and Bobby Butman. "The display auction benefits the people who don't handpick the product off the boat," Roger Berkowitz says. "We're down at the docks every day handpicking, so we know what we're getting. If we were farther removed, and in the grocery store business or the supermarket business where we might not have the knowledge and the relationships, then the display auction alone would suit us well."

"You have to look at the fish," Arthur interjects. "They're all caught differently. You have to look at the way they're caught, how much was caught at one time, how they were put away, and how they were washed. Washing fish is probably the most important thing you can do," he emphasizes. "It's the key to everything." By this, Arthur refers to thoroughness, to making certain that the fish is thoroughly cleaned, without any detritus left on the fish to cause premature spoilage.

One way to accentuate the importance of quality is labeling. Larry Ciulla says, "labeling is the greatest thing you can do for the industry." Jim Ostergard agrees. His boxed fish are packed head to tail with the belly down and the dates they were caught listed on the outside of the box. "Of course," Jim cautions, "it's important to monitor that people are in fact working under the criteria rules in order for labeling to succeed."

It is also important that they speak the same language. One of the differences between Boston and the other ports is that when a fisherman who fishes out of Boston says he has been fishing for five days, he figures it from the time he leaves the dock to the time he returns to the dock. That number is calculated on the basis of the number of days the crew members are unable to sleep at home. To a Boston fisherman, a five-day trip is a trip where three days were spent steaming to and from the fishing grounds, and two days were spent fishing. Thus, a fish labeled with a five-day label in Boston may be two days closer to the sea than one from another port with the same label.

"Don't even come to Boston if you don't have quality, because you won't be able to sell it," Jimmy Bramante advises fishing captains from other ports.

When discussing quality, Bill Amaru thinks labeling might give a false impression. "We're pretty much on a par with the offshore vessels," he says. "There may be a time, especially in the midsummer, when the fish by nature is just more perishable because of what they're eating, the temperature of the water, the difficulty of getting them to market." Niaz

Dorry would be horrified to hear Bill say, "If you're out on a factory ship where there's a climate-controlled environment, you're going to get a much better quality than you probably could get in the States. Those fish are alive when they go into the processing portion of the ship, where it's chilled to forty degrees, and they're bled and immediately placed in ice water and instantly frozen. When you take the average quality of fish handled in the United States and compare it with that processed fish, there isn't a hell of a lot of difference. The main difference is price. Those so-called factory-processed fish are cheaper. And they're cheaper," Bill adds, "because those factory boats operate much more efficiently than a bunch of little boats."

After stressing that Legal Sea Foods uses no previously frozen fish, Roger Berkowitz comments, "Arguably, if a fish is caught and then held seven or eight days, a case could be made that the previously frozen fish would be better. But for us, one or two days fresh is always going to be better." His next words would elicit a cheer from Niaz. "The problem with factory trawlers is they are much *too* efficient in what they pick up. That's always a danger, and that's why we need legislation written to get those trawlers off the water."

Jim O'Brien, one of the owners of Jake's Seafood Restaurant in Hull, Massachusetts, would qualify Bill Amaru's comments on the quality of fresh versus frozen fish by saying it depends on how you define quality, and how you prepare the fish. "Ninety-nine percent of the people couldn't tell the difference between a PF (previously frozen) fish and fresh fish if I fried it for them," Jim states. "Baked, you could because you don't have that encasement to keep the moisture in. The difference is texture. Remember, when you freeze anything, it blows the capillaries out. It alters the chemistry of the fish. It alters the structure of the cells, just as it does with meat or anything else."

Jim is seated in the dining room at Jake's on the edge of Hull Bay, where the fall colors on trees at Worlds End, the Trustees of Reservations property, are visible, reflected on the water. He slowly returns his gaze from the window before adding, "Freshness-wise, that frozen fish is fresher than what ninety percent of the restaurants in America are serving today. You could do a roasted cod filet in a lobster broth, or something like that, and it would be absolutely elegant. I mean," he laughs at the thought, "it would taste just wonderful. The flaking might be a little bit dryer, but like I said, most people wouldn't understand that."

Jake's started as a wholesale lobster pound, founded by the Jacobsen family in 1949. Today's restaurant is built over and around the original structure, a shed that previously covered the saltwater lobster tanks and a large scale for weighing the lobsters. Today's parking lot for diners used to hold delivery trucks that transported fresh lobsters to restaurants up and down the coast.

Eventually, the owners of the Nantasket Lobster Pound, as it was originally named, decided to offer some prepared lobster. "I'm sure it was to cook some of the weaks and almost deads, and then turn them into some type of money," Jim explains, "which unfortunately still goes on in this business. It's not a health issue, but it's not a very palatable issue either."

In addition to boiled lobsters, the Jacobsen family offered cod and haddock, then expanded the menu to include a variety of seafoods. The first fish 'n' chips were offered in 1966. A complete meal, including french fries and coleslaw, cost $1.95. At that time, cod was sometimes given away as part of the catch. Haddock sold for around sixty cents per pound at auction. If you bought one hundred pounds of wholesale haddock off the boat, the captain would often throw in twenty or so pounds of cod. It was that plentiful. Today, a moratorium exists on catching cod, and the dogfish caught in Scituate and destined for fish 'n' chips is selling at auction for twenty-four cents a pound.

Jim grew up catching dogfish the same way the boy walking on the beach did—as something that was just there for the catching. He was first introduced to it as a culinary option in the late 1980s in the test kitchen of Legal Sea Foods, where he was invited to sample different species. "The drawback to dogfish," he explains, "is that its shelf life is terrible. The minute it's off the bone, it deteriorates or ammoniates overnight, whereas cod or haddock, if it's iced properly and cut in a fresh state, you get two to three days out of it if you know how to handle it properly."

Until 1971, Jake's was all take-out. That year, the Jacobsens opened a dining room, and began to keep records. Jim O'Brien started working at Jake's when he was thirteen years old. He dreamed of someday owning it. In 1984, Mrs. Jacobsen, then a widow, called and offered to sell. Jim was twenty-three. Jim and his father and mother bought the restaurant and transformed it from a paper plate operation with a limited menu to a full-service dining room, and the new owners quadrupled the variety of ways of preparing fish. Cod and haddock are no longer served just as fish 'n' chips. Now they are baked, fricasseed, sautéed in wine, or served over pasta with a marinara sauce. Today, on a Friday or Saturday evening in the summer, a line of people waiting for tables stretches out the door and around one corner of the building.

Shortly after the O'Brien family bought Jake's, Billy Conti, then the buyer for Legal Sea Foods, showed up in his pickup truck. Billy and Jim had known each other growing up in Hull, the town next to Cohasset, where each had fished as a boy. Billy said, "I want to sell you cod and haddock."

Looking back, Jim relates, "I didn't know what I was doing." He answered, "Sure, Bill, no problem." Billy told Jim he wanted to take him to Legal's commissary for a tour and to see how they did things. After that, Jim bought all his fish through Legal Sea Foods. Thirteen years later, Jim still speaks with amazement when he says, "They portioned fish for me. They sent the stuff down as if they were sending it out to their own restaurants. For four years, I was basically a Legal Sea Foods restaurant with a different name. I did more volume than two of their own units." When Jim realized he could buy the same quality for 30 percent less money by buying directly, he broke away from the relationship, but even now says, "The only place I'll eat swordfish other than at Jake's is Legal Sea Foods. I know how they handle their products. I mean, Legal processes their fish like they're in a laboratory."

The laboratory simile is not far from reality at Legal Sea Foods headquarters. Men and women dressed in garb similar to that worn in a hospital are carefully inspecting and logging in the catch of the day. Each fish is certified, probed, and recorded. Even though the fish have already been separated into different species at the Fish Pier, each is again checked for blemishes or other unacceptable qualities. From the time it leaves the boat to the time a fish is on the plate, it may have gone through seven different inspections.

Today, Jim buys groundfish from two sources. One is Ideal Seafood, which supplies fish to about fifty restaurants, most of them family-owned. Frank Patania allows that Jim is "very particular about the fish he buys. He can't afford not to be," he adds. "Quality costs. It's like anything else. If you're going to buy a cheap car, you get a cheap car, and vice versa."

Frank is not convinced that the public is more aware of quality in fish than it used to be. "I wish the consumer was more aware of quality, but they're not, they're really not. Price is everything. It's sad but true. There are very few people who care about quality first. Everybody's got their price."

The other source for Jake's fish is a fish processor that buys from Canada and is located by the railroad tracks in Boston's wholesale market district. "The difference is staggering," Jim says. "I can call them on Monday, and they may not be able to tell me the price, but they can tell me what they will and what they won't have for the week. Conversely, I call Sal at Ideal at eight in the morning, one half hour *after* the auction, and he can only then tell me what he has available. And now it's getting to the point where they're taking free orders from us, it's so bad. And that's not good," Jim laments. "That's not a buyer's market. He can't give me a price on that fish. He has to go out and somehow 'find' large cod for me."

Frank would answer that he supplies only top-quality fish. "My customers protect themselves by sometimes writing 'Market Price' on their menus," Frank says. "Not too many can commit to a price and then play the stock market. Sadly, there are not too many of those people."

Wholesale prices of seafood have increased at a much more dramatic rate than the wholesale prices of most other perishable foods. Jim estimates the price of cod filets over the last ten years has increased by an average of five to eight cents per year, which is about double what the annual price increase has been on similar commodity items such as chicken breasts. "When seafood prices go up, it doesn't necessarily mean the quality goes up accordingly," Jim says. "Often it just means there's a tight market or a lack of supply. You have to get what you can get and pay the price. And that's it.

"I don't go through the headache of creating the specials we bring to the tables on blackboards because I like to do it. I do it because it puts people closer to the chef. It makes people think, 'That's great. We got a good buy today; this is special for me.' We do that sort of thing in very subtle ways." He explains that when Jake's runs out of some fish, it is part of a larger plan. "Halibut is a good example. I may bring in enough halibut with the knowledge that I will probably run out Saturday night. But I do that on purpose so that people will understand they have to buy it while they can get it. Then on Sunday morning I can special some items that may not have moved on Saturday." He admits, "It's all showbiz.

"I grew up in a very business-oriented family. We're very analytical about the way we do things." He chuckles as he adds, "I also married a CPA for a wife. But over the last few years, due to the shortage of fish, we've been forced to be magicians with every aspect of the business. We've had to offer cod, for instance, cooked in so many different ways that it permits us to manipulate the portion cost of cod by averaging it with the cost of the supplemental items we add to it."

Jim's voice is incredulous as he laughingly says, "If you had told me a few years ago that the stuffing on the cod—a crabmeat stuffing—was going to be used to offset the cost of the cod, I would have said, 'You're nuts; I'll never be in the business.' But that's exactly what's happened. And I'm still in the business!"

Jake's closes around Thanksgiving for the winter months. Jim's parents head to Florida, and Jim goes backstage to prepare the restaurant for another season. In February, when he began to put his final menu together for the 1998 season, he did not even put haddock on the menu. He made a conscious decision to make cod the main whitefish on the menu. "I told my wife that I had to do it. I had no choice because haddock was at such a premium. She suggested that maybe I could bring it in and offer it as a blackboard special if it sold at a good price at some point in the summer. And look what happened." Jim throws his arms towards the ceiling. "It [Jim's advance planning] just blew up!"

In 1993, the National Marine Fisheries Service, prompted by legal action initiated by the Conservation Law Foundation and the Massachusetts Audubon Society, instituted emergency measures to close down areas to haddock fishing and to limit the harvesting of haddock. The result was that haddock became scarce at the dock, but subsequently became more abundant in the sea.

By the summer of 1998, scientists were reporting low biomass in cod. As a result, the National Marine Fisheries Service closed two additional quadrants on the fishing grounds to the harvesting of cod.

A week and a half after Jake's opened for the season, Jim stayed up for two nights in a row to reprint his whole menu. He admits to having been caught off guard. "I think it caught a lot of people in the business off guard. For the past four or five years, we've been dealing with a severe lack of haddock. We've come to expect that, because of the regulations and closures which have been in effect. Then, this year, haddock became very available," he adds, "and cod for the first time since I've been in this business was not available. And I still haven't gotten a firm answer as to why that happened this year."

On the waterfront, the effects of El Niño were being discussed as possible causes for the disappearance of cod. Jim does not rule out the fishermen's explanation. "I'm still a firm believer in weather being a huge factor in all of this. When you have the kind of strange weather phenomenon we had last year, it has to have an impact on other animals other than us. We all heard of bigeye tuna in the San Francisco Bay area, but this year it was just as bizarre here. There were weird sightings at sea of things that never come this far north." Warm water masses or eddies spun off from the Gulf Stream brought a Caribbean triggerfish to a lobsterman's trap in Rye, New Hampshire; a red bigeye was caught by a fisherman in Jamestown, Rhode Island in December; and the New England Aquarium sent divers to Newport, Rhode Island, to collect pipefish, trunkfish, and other tropical fish for an exhibit titled "Southern Visitors."

"The Canadians have done a great job, not only with closing the spawning grounds for haddock, but also with enforcing the closures," Jim says. "They can estimate pretty closely what next year's harvest will be. And they've been doing this for fifteen or twenty years." When asked why the United States has not been able to do the same, Jim answers, "When the Canadians set their rules and regulations, they set them. They haven't held hearing after hearing after hearing, after hearing." He qualifies his remarks by saying, "I'm not against hearings, but I'm against giving everyone too much time to talk about it. In contrast, my Canadian supplier knows within a week when he is going to have product, which is pretty amazing given what is going on in this industry."

Jim likens his experience over the last few years to that of constantly creating new recipes. "It's not a matter of going in like a Ninety Nine Restaurant does, where they're buying frozen cod out of Iceland"—then he qualifies his remark—"a good-quality product as long as the people know up front what they're getting. The unit cost is set; it's all ready to go; and you just put it on the menu and you know what you're going to make on it." Jim echoes Harriet's views on the cadre of people who recognize quality fish. "My customers are educated. They're not just educated about fish, but the people who come through the door here are educated people. It's not an inexpensive place to shop, and we understand that."

"What we're dealing with here, and what Legal Sea Foods is dealing with [or trying to deal with], is taking raw product in a very volatile market, and delivering it to a customer on a daily basis, in a consistent portion, with consistent quality, and at a consistent price."

After commenting that until someone learns how to manage the fisheries, he does not see having much direct competition, Jim adds, "Fifteen years from now, if they've brought back the stocks of groundfish like they have the stocks of striped bass, then all bets are off. I'm not afraid of that, because then I get a chance to breathe a little easier."

American consumers at the beginning of the twenty-first century are used to having ready access to fresh fish, filleted and ready to cook. Or they expect to see it on a restaurant menu and then have it served—without bones, head, or tail, thank you—after they place an order. As fish stocks have dwindled and as the human population has increased, consumer demand has also increased. But what you think you are being served may not always be what you ordered—or thought you ordered.

The "fresh" salmon appearing on your plate may now come trucked from a pen in Campobello's Head Harbor, where its growth has been monitored and nurtured by former deck hands. The fluke or summer flounder served to you on Martha's Vineyard may have been flown in from a fish farm in Argentina.

Niaz Dorry tells a story of driving to Alaska in 1995. For two days, she drove on a road through the Arctic National Wildlife Refuge to Prudhoe Bay. When she arrived, she found she could not stick her toe into the waters of the Arctic Ocean because, from the shoreline out, the offshore "land" is leased to oil companies who make it off-limits for any purpose other than drilling.

"We're sort of reaching that point around here where we may not have access to some of the traditional species, because somebody wants to line up the coastline with aquaculture so they can do their thing. And aquaculture would probably occupy the waters close to shore.

"And we may not have access to fresh fish," she continues, "because the only kind of fishing effort some scientists and regulators are suggesting we should have is the factory-style, processed type, which is going to be happening out on the high seas where fishing will have been consolidated to larger and larger boats fishing out past the aquaculture pens. And this probably will not have reduced our fishing effort. Rather it will have consolidated it into the hands of significant lobbying powers.

"We will no longer be able to see either the diversity of species in the ocean, nor the diversity of traditional fishing methods," Niaz predicts. "Is that the way we want the ocean to look—like Prudhoe Bay when you get up there?"

As the world demand for fresh seafood is increasing, the wild supply is decreasing. Legal Sea Foods now owns and operates twenty-six restaurants, and by the time you read this book, the company will have opened an additional three restaurants. The demand for groundfish is estimated to be five billion to seven billion dollars greater than the supply. Aquaculture production will have to increase 500 percent to supply world seafood needs expected for the year 2025.[5] For the consumer, this already means that the fish on the plate may have been flown in from a fish farm where it has been coddled and raised within a man-made environment, or at least an environment controlled by humans. For the entrepreneur, it is a dream come true.

Aquaculture, unlike commercial fishing, is virtually unregulated; the public cannot tell the difference between the genuine article and the copy, and the U.S. government is providing large sums of money to keep it that way. In one year alone (1994), the federal government allocated more than sixty million dollars to advance the cause of aquaculture.[6] Commercial fisheries have been awarded only a fraction of that amount. In most cases, the fisherman never sees the money allocated, and yet local newspapers, at least on the East Coast, are quick to pick up on monies promised the fisheries. Who has ever read an article about federal assistance to aquaculture? And what level of accountability is expected, if any?

In 1999, aquaculture generated an estimated $42 billion in revenues worldwide. By the year 2025, it is expected to generate $60 billion and produce over 160 million metric tons of seafood. Presently, one out of every five fish consumed is raised instead of being caught in the wild. Scott Soares, a marine biologist and aquaculture coordinator for the Massachusetts Department of Food and Agriculture, believes aquaculture has increased between 10 and 15 percent each year in the five-year period from 1995 to 2000. In 1993, fish and seafood imports "represented the third leading contributor to the trade deficit, behind petroleum and illegal drugs," with a value of $5.8 billion.[7] The Food and Agriculture Organization (FAO) reports that Asia presently accounts for over 90 percent of the world production. Sixty-three percent of that is produced in China, where shrimp is often grown in converted rice paddies and "Chinese bay scallops" have been cultured from an original brood stock of twenty-six Nantucket bay scallops.[8] No wonder the U.S. Department of Commerce is allocating monies to aquaculture in hopes of reducing the seafood trade deficit.

The term "aquaculture" encompasses a vast array of species and methods, basically reduced to the following three:

1. Land-based, involving recirculating water and producing hybrid striped bass, various species of trout, salmon, carp, tilapia, American eels, and summer flounder.
2. Coastal, dependent on tidal waters, allowing for the production of the various bivalves such as quahogs, surf clams, various types of oysters, sea scallops, bay scallops, soft-shell clams, and mussels.
3. Offshore, utilizing nets or pens as in the salmon farms in the waters east of Schoodic Point, and so-called sea ranching, the introduction of cultured species into the ocean for later harvesting by traditional fishing methods. This last form of aquaculture is of the most interest to commercial fishermen, as it provides a means of eventual livelihood for them, but with the drawback that it removes yet another portion of the seabed where they have traditionally fished.

According to Joshua Goldman, president of Fins Technology, "Aquaculture now supplies about fifteen percent of the world demand for fish." The bass that is served to you at Legal Sea Foods, for example, may have come from a fifty-thousand-square-foot building in an industrial park in Turners Falls, Massachusetts, where Fins breeds close to one million pounds per year of a hybrid saltwater striped bass and freshwater white bass. Mr. Goldman's bass know no season and are available to restaurants and fish markets on a daily basis.

Fins is a greenhouse for raising fish. The medium is water. Water bubbles in purification systems; water is transported overhead as it moves flapping fish on a slow-moving conveyor belt from one tank to another; water fills vast plastic vats where fish circle round and round as they would in schools in the sea. Male saltwater striped bass, each valued at more than a luxury car, are the thoroughbreds in this environment. The females are the freshwater white bass. Combining the characteristics of both creates a product that will not breed in the wild and thus cannot contaminate the wild population.

Jim O'Brien, at Jake's Restaurant, believes that when aquaculture products came on the market around 1996 or 1997, "they started taking the pressure off for the restaurants. At that time, a lot of people were just crazy about aquaculture. They predicted that in ten years the wild market was going to have the pressure off it completely, and people wouldn't be demanding wild fish. And that just didn't happen. And it's not going to happen," he insists.

Jim continues, "Aquaculture probably helps [profits] one-half of a percent to one percent a year, depending on how aggressive I am with putting it on the menu and with pricing it. In the short term, it does affect our profit margins, but we try to do a menu mix offsetting that possibility, so . . . ," Jim opens his hands, palms up, and laughs as he explains, "there are layers of variables we try to manipulate. He qualifies his previous remarks by saying, "The aquaculture route is the way to go, offering our customers the incentives to try it on a short-term basis to build business on a long-term basis." Jim has no intention of dropping cod and haddock from Jake's menu as long as the conservation measures work and cod and haddock continue to be available to him. "I think the measures will work," he states, "if they stick to them, and don't allow new amendments and changes to them year after year."

But will the public agree to pay more for fish harvested in the wild than for the fish raised in captivity? "From a marketing standpoint, I kind of have to separate the issue into two categories," Jim responds: "traditional aquaculture products and traditionally wild products someone is trying to grow in a laboratory condition. They're separate industries and they're going to have two separate success rates." As for dealing with the shortage of commercially caught fish, what Jake's is going to try to do is change consumption habits from those wholly based on cod and haddock consumption to consumption of tilapia, rainbow trout, and Chilean sea bass. If someone finds a way to grow haddock down the road, then we'll have to deal with that on a separate basis," Jim adds.

Legal Sea Foods has a two-prong approach to the supply versus demand issue. In explanation, Roger Berkowitz refers to his philosophy that seafood is no longer a commodity. "As it gets more and more expensive, fewer and fewer people are going to be competing for the product," he says. "It will be looked upon more as the Europeans treat fish. It will be as prized as beef, if not more so. That's the mentality change that has to take place. The result is going to be that those who are selling fish inexpensively are not going to be able to continue to do so." He adds, "We're in the business of conservation as well. It's not just consume as much as you can without caring about the future. So I think, strategically, we have to look at a few different things. We have to take what's available to us as more quotas are put in place. Secondly, what's going to become increasingly more important is the aquaculture prospect."

Aquaculture is clearly the area of his business that most excites Roger Berkowitz. Legal Sea Foods proposed a joint venture with the New England Aquarium and two aquaculture firms to build a fish hatchery in excess of forty thousand square feet, with the capability to raise summer flounder and tautog fingerlings (immature fish). The proposed location was in front of the Boston Design Center, beside a dock for luxury cruise ships at the edge of Boston Harbor. The incongruity of this site did not seem to faze anyone. The pedigreed fish this location is being programmed to spawn seem to fit well into the Boston Harbor Seaport Plan calling for luxury condominiums, hotels, and an upscale neighborhood.

Roger Berkowitz sits up in his chair, and his voice is livelier as he says, "The Department of Commerce is very anxious to get this underway." Again it becomes apparent why the fishing community is fearful of the Commerce Department. "It will happen," Roger Berkowitz assures us. "There are some brilliant people involved in this project. Science has progressed to such a degree that we can really develop and monitor the project to develop the stock where size and meatiness of the fish are at optimum levels for consumption.

"The science has improved so radically in the last two or three years that in addition to the rainbow trout, salmons, and Arctic char, you now have shrimp, shellfish, turbot, and summer flounder being farmed. A few weeks ago," he relates, "I had some summer flounder which was absolutely magnificent."

That summer flounder was the product of a 1995 grant for $654,000 awarded by the National Marine Fisheries Service. The project title was "From Fishing to Farming, a Demonstration of Commercial Summer Flounder Aquaculture in New England."[9] Fins Technology, then called AquaFuture, was a recipient of a portion of that grant. The money came from the disaster relief fund earmarked to help the fisheries. And it demonstrated a pattern that would emerge again and again, where individual U.S. senators and the Department of Commerce would herald sums of money supposedly appropriated to shore up the fisheries. Yet none of that money would go directly to the men and women trying to fish commercially despite an ever tighter noose of regulations. If anything, grants for research coming on the tail of closures have permitted tighter and tighter regulations to be mandated for the fishermen because the money is often presented by the media as being awarded directly to the men and women who still fish for a living.

"At the time the grant was awarded, some very promising technology was in an infant stage at the University of Rhode Island, where a wonderful guy named Dave Bengston had succeeded in figuring out how to do the early life stages of the flounder," Joshua Goldman explains. "As we move to striped bass, which, unlike salmon, trout, and catfish, have small eggs, and marine fish where the eggs are often smaller, the tricks of the trade get even harder because meeting the nutritional needs of this animal that you are measuring in microns is pretty tricky." The University of Rhode Island was successful in figuring out how to reproduce the summer flounder on a modest scale in a laboratory. "We wanted to fast-track this commercialization," Joshua relates. "We said, 'Let's get this out of the lab. And let's see if we can't make the beneficiaries of this effort the commercial fishing sector.' " Thus, Joshua Goldman's company, whose role was to provide water recirculation technology for aquaculture, qualified for part of the disaster relief funds. Two commercial fishermen were paid to build facilities and operate hatcheries utilizing the recirculation technology provided by Fins Technology. But then the economics of summer flounder (whether the fish was hatched on land or caught off Menemsha's Lucas Shoal in Vineyard Sound) were severely impacted by a drop in the Japanese yen. *Harami*, the sushi made from summer flounder, is highly valued in Japan. That fact was surely a motivation for funding the summer flounder project. Today, the value of summer flounder is half what it was when the grant was awarded in 1995, and, as a result, only one of the two participating fishermen, New Bedford's Cathy Downing, still finds it commercially viable to operate a hatchery for summer flounder.

Why raise summer flounder, a species whose marketability is so dependent on foreign currency? Joshua Goldman explains. "Flounder are unique in that it's a marine fish grown on land. Flounder need bottom area. So, raising them is more of a two-dimensional effort than a three-dimensional effort." Because summer flounder could be raised inland, the grant recipients could bypass the extensive permitting process required for marine aquaculture in the United States. "But," Joshua points out, "it still took an enormous effort to get the facilities permitted." When asked if he sees other marine species being successfully raised in conditions similar to those envisioned for the summer flounder, he answers with a qualified "yes, but I think the time frame is longer rather than shorter." He estimates that thirty million dollars has been spent to try to grow hybrid striped bass on land, and "there's just beginning to be controlled reproduction of this animal. And now there are a whole series of new problems entering the picture." He expands on this thought. "It's fairly easy to get fish that were conditioned in the wild, that eat all the things they eat in the wild. You bring that fish in and they spawn. You grow that fish in captivity, and the product is delicate, not robust."

Judy Ramos still has a hard time accepting a fish grown on land as a quality fish. "They just eat and . . ." she hesitates while choosing her words, "they expel. And they eat and they expel. There's no motion there. There's no movement there. There are no currents to clean it out. People are going to get sick. It is not going to be a healthy food source. Healthy is out there." Judy points with her eyes toward the water side of her home.

The Food and Agriculture Organization shares Judy's concerns. The FAO estimates that the untreated discharges from Salmon farms in British Columbia are the equivalent of the raw human sewage produced by a city with a population of 500,000 people.[10] Salmon farming has also had to contend with water pollution due in large part to excess nutrients fed to the fish. A less-understood threat to the fish is *Pfiesteria*, a single-celled organism that lives in brackish water and, during one stage of its development, produces toxins lethal to fish and possibly to humans. *Pfiesteria* is claimed to be responsible for a $20 million fish kill in the lower Chesapeake Bay area.

Monitoring the health of the fish is the full-time job for a Fin Technology employee, who checks the gills for forms of disease when a fish dies and then advises adding more salt or other treatments to the water to protect the other fish sharing the same tank. According to Joshua Goldman, "There are some advantages to this system from a health standpoint in that some of the parasites (like grubs), that live in connection with fish in the wild, can't go through a life cycle here. We can't have them. But," he allows, "we have other issues that we have to manage." One issue could be that some of the antibiotics used to keep fish healthy might contribute to the evolving inability of antibiotics to fight off diseases in humans.

Another concern is that cultured fish could escape and breed with fish in the wild, and possibly change the genetic pool by their cohabitation. By combining a freshwater fish with a saltwater fish, Fins has virtually eliminated the concern about changes to the genetic pool, but within the Fins Technology tanks no two fish are identical. And Joshua would like to see fewer differences. He speaks of Fins as the "pioneer of large-scale recirculation." In explanation, he points out that striped bass are a warm-water fish. In the ocean they migrate thousands of miles to follow the warm currents. At Fins Technology, the temperature of the water can be controlled to create a more desirable climate for the fish. The goal is to produce a fish that grows faster than the fish in the wild. That goal is still elusive.

In the early days of Fins, when it was AquaFuture, Joshua Goldman and his partners went to hatcheries to purchase striped bass fingerlings and white bass fingerlings. From a production point of view, this method created a problem. After each generation of fish was raised, the company was forced to go again to the wild source via the hatcheries in order to recruit new fish. Joshua Goldman likens it to "standing there at the craps table throwing your dice genetically." Despite the control of the environment, each fish was, and continues to be, unique. This bothers a geneticist, who envisions a "perfect" specimen. And it bothers a business mentality that likes to deal with predictability. The answer is to control the genetics, a decision that has resulted in grants from the Department of Agriculture and Sea Grant, a program initiated by NOAA in connection with various universities and institutions.

Today, Fins Technology produces its own breeding stock in captivity. On a day averaging 20 degrees Fahrenheit, with winds outside gusting to twenty knots, three Fins employees are in a plastic-covered greenhouse shelter, where they stand over a small tank gently massaging the bodies of seven anesthetized egg-producing female bass. They are hoping they have plucked the fish from a larger tank at the optimum time for each to throw its eggs. Too soon, and the eggs will not be ripe enough for fertilization; too late, and the ripe eggs will already have been thrown before they can be captured and placed in a smaller vessel filled with milt, the fertilizing agent produced by the male striped bass.

Not surprisingly, Joshua Goldman holds a degree in bioengineering with a focus on water filtration. In this laboratory for creating bass, genetic engineering coexists with, and depends on, the engineering of the basic hardware required for experimentation. Water filtration plays a major role in eliminating bacteria and the other forms of contamination that concern Judy Ramos. River water flowing over the namesake falls of Turners Falls is filtered through the ground to wells accessed by Fins. One-half million gallons per day of water are pumped through the "A" building, where the spawning stock is housed; forty million gallons per day are pumped through the "B" building, housing the hybrid stock.

The two other founding partners at Fins Technology are Scott Lindell, a geneticist, and Tim Joukowsky, who handles the financial side of the business. When the issue of profitability is raised, the ethics of the West prevail: asking a rancher how many head of cattle he has is akin to asking him how much money he has in the bank—poor form! Joshua does allow that the cost to raise one Fins bass is based on what he originally spent to purchase a fingerling from a hatchery (approximately twenty-five cents per fingerling), fish food (the largest expense), and labor to raise the fish. Obviously, profits are higher if the fish can be engineered to grow faster and spend less time being fed and tended at Fins Technology.

The bass you eat at Legal Sea Foods will have left Turners Falls weighing between one and a half and two pounds (the smaller size becomes one portion; the larger is filleted). It will be approximately twelve months old. The product may be on your plate tonight, where it could be the focal point of a culinary creation by a name chef who chose to pair it with Dijon mustard, fresh herbs, tomatoes, capers, and maybe a touch of dry vermouth. It will be delicious, but the texture of the meat will not be the same as the texture of meat from the game fish that likes to fight the surf on the back side of Nantucket at the edge of Muskeget Channel.

Asked if he still sees a market for fish caught in the wild, Roger Berkowitz replies with a resounding "Absolutely!" He then proceeds to describe the process of releasing harvested fingerlings back into the ocean, as is being done in Japan. "As the science gets better and better, and we learn to grow disease-free fish, the same will happen here."

"And," he stresses, "we *would* like to give something back to the industry."

Joshua Goldman's goals parallel those of Roger Berkowitz. He expresses a desire to someday see the results of the work being done at Fins configured into smaller production units with fishermen as owner-operators. "Aquaculture is farming," he points out, "and it takes a lot of commitment and experience on the part of the people involved. We've worked to come up with the technology to grow fish in captivity, and we continue to learn, but ultimately we'd like to share some of what we've learned with the fishing community."

Herminio Ramos, Judy's husband, likens the fish grown in man-made conditions to the hothouse tomato versus a tomato grown outside and in season: "There's no comparison in the taste." Judy concurs, then draws a parallel to scallops. "I don't even bother ordering scallops from a restaurant anymore. They're not our scallops. They might be from Peru, or China, or they might be Mexican calicoes. There is nothing you can compare to deep-sea New England scallops. Those farm scallops are rubbery, and they have a . . ." she crinkles her nose and twists her mouth, "a sweet, nauseating taste. The menu may say they're New England scallops, but that doesn't mean they've ever been in the sea."

"Well, I'll admit that a striped bass caught by a rod and reel off the beach at Tuckernuck on the south side of Nantucket is a sweeter, oilier fish than the one grown in captivity," Roger Berkowitz agrees. "That's why I'm so excited about raising summer flounder. Because it tastes so much more like the natural fish—with a really clean taste. It's sort of a cross between flounder, gray sole, and turbot."

As Roger Berkowitz describes the fish he plans to raise, it is difficult not to share his enthusiasm. Here is a man capable of selling a lot of fish. And he is talking about a way to protect the stocks and still provide a means of livelihood for a community of fishermen.

"Hatch and release" is not a new phenomenon in the United States. Jimmy Bramante tells the story of finding a lot of old books and records at the Boston Fish Exchange when he was helping clean out the building prior to its conversion to Massport's conference center and offices. He and his sister tried to salvage what books they could to donate them to a college or library. "The contractors were tearing that building apart without even wrapping it for asbestos," Jimmy recounts. "Asbestos was in the air all around us, so we didn't want to risk staying around to save too many books."

Jimmy noticed a book appearing to be a ledger of some sort, listing different fish, how many eggs were hatched, how many survived, and how many were released. "It suddenly dawned on us that they had fish hatcheries years ago," Jimmy says. "I mean, we're talking turn of the century, and they had fish hatcheries!"

Prompted by his discovery, Jimmy stood up at one of the New England Fishery Management Council meetings and asked why they did not have a hatch and release program today. Phil Coates, then chairman of the groundfish committee, replied that the National Marine Fisheries Service had sponsored hatch and release programs up until 1960. They had one on Gloucester's Ten Pound Island, in the middle of Gloucester Harbor, but they stopped because they "had no proof it was helping."

"Well," Jimmy countered, "I know one thing for sure: it wasn't hurting."

Jimmy and other fishermen have a hard time understanding why money is not put into something positive, such as hatch and release programs, as opposed to putting so much money into hiring so many regulatory and enforcement personnel whose only job is to watch the fisherman.

In 1994, when Ronald Brown was secretary of commerce, he ear-marked thirty million dollars in aid to the fishing communities in the Northeast. Contrary to a commonly held belief that fishermen are the beneficiaries of large federal subsidies, no direct financial assistance to a fishing family resulted from the appropriation. Instead, many in the scientific and business communities who understood how to apply for grant money were able to fund fisheries-related projects. A significant portion of the monies went to support the desk personnel in the offices of the National Marine Fisheries Service who would review proposals, award funds, and evaluate the outcome of the various projects funded.

Nine million dollars of the total was assigned to what was labeled the "Fishing Industry Grant" (FIG) Program. At that time, Dana Morse was Northeast regional operations officer for the National Marine Fisheries Service. He describes the program as "a means to stimulate ideas for new business opportunities, new processing technology, and fishery development."[11] Nine aquaculture projects were funded, and received a total of slightly over two million dollars. One of the projects funded was the joint Fins Technology–Legal Sea Foods project.

Each striped bass raised by Fins requires 150 gallons of recycled, purified water, piped into its habitat. After the expenses of piping, personnel, purification systems, and housing, that fish has to command a high price in order to cover the costs of raising it.

Bill Amaru, fisherman and former member of the New England Fishery Management Council, does not think the market can bear the cost to raise too many species. "Remember, this is profit-driven. If it costs you more to raise a fish than you can charge for it, that's not a business that will be around long. I think aquaculture will have a growing but still relatively small part as compared to what the wild fisheries can handle."

Asked if he thinks aquaculture will be a significant entity on the East Coast, Bill replies, "Significant? Personally, I don't think so. Because of the economics, you can only do aquaculture in a relatively small area." Bill points out that the dollar value of coastline real estate is too high to permit large-scale farming where people are willing to pay a premium to live in condominiums with a view. Also, the volume of the sea far surpasses the linear feet of the coastline. "If you give the natural system the opportunity to do its production, it far exceeds anything aquaculture in the coastal zone can do."

Jim Stavis is one of the largest fish processors in New England. His company, North Coast Seafood, recently completed construction of a fish-processing center near the Boston Fish Pier and adjacent to parcel C1, the site envisioned by Roger Berkowitz for his proposed hatchery. Jim points out that aquaculture is "a very capital-intensive operation." In addition, it is difficult to secure funding, because it takes five years for a successful aquaculture operation to show a profit. And there have been few successes. North Coast Seafood is betting on the natural resource. "In three to five years, because of the efficacy of the regulations, we're going to see a very viable resource," he states. "If I didn't believe that, I wouldn't have put my money into bricks and mortar to build this new building."

Rodney Avila punches keys on his computer as he speaks. "There'll always be some need for fishermen. Look at swordfish. New York chefs have a ban on serving swordfish, but our local restaurants on the Cape, on Martha's Vineyard, Nantucket, Block Island, they buy harpooned swordfish. They buy fish from the harpoon boats because it's better."

Asked why harpooned swordfish is better than swordfish caught with a longline, Rodney explains that longlines are typically set at night and not hauled back until the following morning. The hooked fish may lie in what may be warm water for twelve to fourteen hours before being brought aboard, dressed, and iced. In addition, a long-liner swordfish trip (as described by Linda Greenlaw in *Hungry Ocean* or Sebastian Junger in *The Perfect Storm*) might run twenty-five to fifty days. During that period, the fish are in the hold. A harpooned swordfish is harpooned and removed from the water within one to two hours, then dressed and put in the fish hold, where it is immediately iced down. A harpoon boat will stay out for only ten to fourteen days. Thus the harpooned swordfish is brought to market about two weeks after being caught; the long-lined swordfish could possibly be brought to market six to seven weeks after being caught.

Rodney flips to another set of figures on his screen. "Let's take a look. See, in 1966, over a million pounds of fish was caught locally for a total of one hundred seventy-nine thousand dollars. I just want to compare this. Just before the restrictions started in 1994, we caught two hundred twenty-three thousand pounds for about three hundred fifty thousand dollars. A lot more money." Rodney continues to pull up data on the screen. "This year, our stocks have increased, and I know we haven't landed the fish as we generally do. But the prices have gone up as a result." He searches the screen for clarification. "So I agree with Harriet Didriksen when she says that people will always pay more for quality— for fresh fish."

If fish stocks rebound as expected, and the gap narrows between fish caught in the wild and the demand for seafood, the market for aquaculture will disappear—but only if a community of fishermen is allowed to fish. At the moment, the Department of Commerce is supporting aquaculture projects, not fishermen.

Aquaculture has its environmental costs. Importation of exotic species threatens the wild supply through the possibility of escape and eventual interbreeding. Coastal birds are slaughtered to protect the farm-raised fish from predation. And native fish that might have become food for larger wild fish are instead killed to provide food for fish raised through aquaculture. Global landings of fish caught in the wild (less bycatch) are approximately 96 million tons. Almost one-third of that amount is used for fish meal to feed animals and farmed fish—one-third of it to aquaculture. An article in *Nature* estimates that a fish raised by humans in a controlled environment devours two to five times more fish protein (derived from wild fish) than that same fish provides for human consumption.[12]

By encouraging and financing aquaculture, we promote killing the species we should be protecting. And we are doing this in part to feed the farmed fish. If we instead allowed the big fish in the sea to eat the small fish, and if we allowed the fish caught by fisherman to go directly toward feeding humans, we would be going a long way toward protecting the fish. Instead, we prohibit the small fisherman from fishing, and we are considering wiping out the food supply for the wild fish in order to feed a farmed fish that does not taste as good as the native fish.

Many people in the United States might turn their nose up at the thought of eating herring and some of the other small pelagic fishes. But the larger fish, whose taste we relish, rely on these small fish for food. If we are catching herring and turning them into fish meal for farmed fish, we are limiting our opportunity to continue to enjoy the delectable taste of our native fish. From an ethical point of view, we are robbing the inhabitants of poorer countries of much-needed protein in order to provide a preferred fish to richer countries.

Despite the romantic image of the lone fisherman pitting himself against the forces of nature as portrayed by Ernest Hemingway and Winslow Homer, today's commercial fisherman is often perceived by some as a barbarian who is single-handedly destroying the environment and wiping out endangered fish populations. But who is protesting the legally permitted slaughter of some of our coastal birds at or near aquaculture facilities?

Between 1989 and 1993, the U.S. Fish and Wildlife Service collected data indicating that 51,373 birds had been killed legally in order to protect farm-raised fish, which naturally are an attraction for the birds. In that four-year period, 9,443 great blue herons, 1,197 kingfishers, 48 white-winged scoters, and 19 green-backed herons were among those killed legally. No numbers exist for those birds killed illegally. Since then the numbers have risen, and in June of 1997 the Fish and Wildlife Service altered its regulations to allow aquaculturists to kill double-crested cormorants without a permit. Prior to the 1997 ruling, 25,930 double-crested cormorants were legally killed during the four-year period monitored.[13]

If the rationale for the 1991 lawsuit filed by the Massachusetts Audubon Society against the National Marine Fisheries Service was to protect food fish for seabirds, coastal birds, and other swimming birds, why is the Audubon Society not motivated to protect these same birds from being legally killed? Is it easier to quietly eliminate the small fisherman and his community than to protest government support for a substitute to wild fish as long as we have some kind of fish on the table when we want it?

5

ARE WE LOSING OUR NEW ENGLAND FISHING COMMUNITIES?

> As fishermen we feel as though without the fishing industry, Washington would have one less headache.
>
> —the late Joseph Novello, captain of the F/V *Vincie N.*, quoted in Peter Prybot, *White-Tipped Orange Masts*

Fishermen are independent by nature. That independence, together with a love of the water, may be their primary motivating force. The challenge, the excitement, and mainly the desire for independence drive fishermen to sea in relatively small boats, which they have to provision for any eventuality. Even in terrible storms, the fisherman has to be prepared to fix anything with only his ingenuity and what he has on board.

Those same qualities explain why the fisherman is such a poor representative for the fishing community. At meetings of the New England Fishery Management Council, a Gloucester fisherman might give an impassioned, well-documented plea *against* closing Stellwagen Bank or Jeffries Ledge, only to be followed by a fisherman from New Bedford who gives an equally well-reasoned argument *for* closing Stellwagen Bank or Jeffries Ledge. Yet both men agree privately that the council is trying to close their business down and never listens to what the fisherman or woman has to say.

A small group of fishermen in Chatham, Massachusetts, is trying to change those conditions and trying to exemplify how fishing communities can work together to keep fish in the water while keeping fishermen on the water.

Chatham, Massachusetts, is what the island of Nantucket was before families with vast sums of money propelled themselves to the island in search of coastal simplicity with a high price tag. Weathered clapboard homes, their doors and windows outlined in white, face sweeping views of marshes, estuaries, and the white tops of waves rolling across sandbars between the shore and Pollock Rip.

Down the hill from the lighthouse, a road leads through salt marshes to a wooded peninsula where in 1999 Paul Parker managed the activities of the Cape Cod Commercial Hook Fishermen's Association from the basement of his grandmother's house. Today is the first warm spring day. The sun catches rows of white waves undulating toward the shore from Monomoy Point, a sandbar that has claimed many a sailing vessel over the centuries but today looks blameless. Paul tips back in a deck chair on the second-floor balcony of his grandmother's house facing the sea. He has the lean body, large hands, and grace of a basketball player, or of the hook fisherman and scientist he is.

Paul is twenty-nine years old. As he looks out over the water, he speaks of why he is here in Chatham, living the life he is living, making the choices he is making. "I just think it's very important for my generation to take a strong role in conserving the environment, because I think we're at a real crossroads. We can go with capitalism and pure economic theory and say, 'O.K., strip malls and fish farms, that's the way to go. That's the most efficient.' Or we can take a step back and ask ourselves, 'You know what? In the fifties and the forties, were we any happier?' I mean did we have something in our society that was worth something . . . something that's been lost?" Paul transfers his focus back from the water to the land. "I think there's something unique worth fighting for right here in Chatham. Likewise there's something unique in some small farm town in Iowa, as there's something unique in a small ranching town in Montana. There are still communities where folks go out and interact with nature. And they need to be represented."

Paul has options, and he makes choices. He holds a bachelor's degree in biology from Cornell and a master's degree in marine environmental management from Duke University. And he has the courage to believe he can reconcile the often-competing positions of the scientist, the environmentalist, and the fisherman. "I became interested in the fact that there are these resources and everything comes from them. Some people have to go harvest them, and, generally speaking, those aren't people driving around in nice cars and making the rules. Those are people who work hard and never get appreciated."

After college, Paul did not have a job. He asked himself what he loved doing best. The answer was fishing. He weighed the possibility of working as a scientist in an office somewhere and fishing on weekends. "It occurred to me that I should just do what it was I wanted to do, where I wanted to do it, and just eke out a living at it. I've always loved Chatham. I just love being on the water. Ever since I was a kid, summering here as a boy, my happiest moments have been fishing and interacting with my environment in that way. I guess everybody finds their niche. Mine is on the water."

Paul's father and mother fished commercially for striped bass in the summers to supplement his father's winter income. "I think they purchased a lot of their appliances and first cars on striped bass," Paul reminisces. Today, Paul fishes out of Saquatucket Harbor in nearby Harwich, Massachusetts, on board the 35-foot F/V *Peggy B II* captained by Ronald Braun, Jr. Besides long-lining (using multiple hooks attached at intervals to a three-hundred-foot line), they "jig" for fish; that is, they drop a line with four hooks spaced about eighteen inches apart over the side of the boat, and pull it up when they get a bite. On an index measuring the most sustainable methods of fishing, Paul would put jigging at the top, with coastal long-lining next (as opposed to offshore long-lining described earlier).

Jigging today differs from jigging in the days of Captain Sylvanus Smith, when hemp lines were lowered over the side of wooden fishing schooners. Just ten years ago, jiggers were all handliners using thick, three-hundred-pound-test monofilament. Today, they use rods and reels and something called "spider wire," a thin, extremely strong synthetic thread. The advantage of the new line is that it goes straighter down in the current and fish do not see it. "Jiggers today may use funky rubber lures; they use electric reels [allowing the fisherman to hit a button to reel in the fish while he tends a second reel]; a lot of boats will fish two rods per person. I mean it's a lot different."

Paul tells the following story: "One day last month we were all fishing close together on one area of bottom. We were fishing with two poles apiece—one electric, one nonelectric. A boat next to us was fishing with two poles, both electric. There was another boat there with old-fashioned handlines. Now I know the guy who fishes with the old-fashioned handlines well, and I know the guy who fishes with the electric reels well. And I can tell you that on that particular day on the *Peggy B II* we caught about twelve hundred pounds; the guy with the two electric reels caught closer to two thousand pounds; and the guy with two handlines caught about two hundred pounds. And we were using bait. They weren't. So it just shows you there can be a wide degree of difference in technology even with something as simple as jigging."

Paul manages to fish approximately 140 days per year. In addition, he spends more hours than seem humanly possible as the executive director of the Cape Cod Commercial Hook Fishermen's Association, a trade organization proving itself to be a major player in environmental management of the ocean's resources.

"I think we have a really important message and an important perspective to bring to fisheries management," Paul says. "We've started to amplify a national voice on issues like habitat protection, bycatch reduction, and overfishing, all issues which are plaguing us all around the country." To bring their message to a larger audience, hook fishermen are aligning themselves with some powerful environmental groups and celebrities in a position to lend cachet to their cause. Paul recently returned from Los Angeles, where he showed a video the American Oceans Campaign helped create. The video furthers the work of scientists Page Valentine and Les Watling in their efforts to protect fish habitat. It shows areas of the ocean before and after a scallop dragger towed its gear over a sandy bottom. "Before" pictures an underwater garden with sea ferns, rocks, and sea urchins. To Paul and the other scientists, this is what a breeding ground for groundfish looks like. "After" shows a sandy desert stripped of all life.

The video's purpose is twofold: to educate while helping to raise money to support a 1996 lawsuit brought by the Cape Cod Commercial Hook Fishermen's Association against the Department of Commerce, NOAA, and the National Marine Fisheries Service (NMFS). The lawsuit claims the defendants have failed to manage the fisheries in a way that would protect essential fish habitat, reduce bycatch, and prevent overfishing. Paul voices a theme dear to environmentalist Niaz Dorry as well as fisherman Paul Vitale. "The council just continues to rely on single-species management without considering the ecosystem, without considering the unquantifiable things such as habitat impacts of fishing."

Many in the industry thought the original Magnuson Act was pretty clear on those issues. When it was revised as the Sustainable Fisheries Act in 1996, protection of fish habitat was a provision many environmentalists lobbied hard to see included. Those same environmentalists and Paul feel habitat degradation has contributed to diminishing both the fish stocks and the fishing communities. "These things were recognized in all the best available science; these things were pointed out in habitat committees, groundfish committee meetings, and full council meetings," Paul states.

In June of 1999, in connection with the American Oceans Campaign, the Cape Cod Commercial Hook Fishermen's Association filed a second suit. By this time, the group had come to the attention of the Pew Charitable Trust, which today provides financial support.

Four years after the original suit was filed, and to the amazement of just about everyone involved, Judge Gladys Kessler, a U.S. district court judge, ruled in favor of the Cape Cod Commercial Hook Fishermen. "This victory should go a long way to get NMFS to protect undersea habitat," Paul stated after receiving notice of the victory. "We are not looking to put mobile-gear fishermen out of business. In fact we are working alongside dragger interests in the fisheries management process to develop fair means to protect the rocky bottom that cod and other groundfish species need for food and shelter."

Paul Vitale in Gloucester doesn't see the CCCHFA lawsuit as helping the industry overall. "Every gear has its problems. There's no one-hundred-percent environmentally safe gear. You've got animals getting caught in the buoy lines of lobster traps and gill nets. There's no sure way or the right way to do it. Every fisherman has his way to fish."

The Sustainable Fisheries Act mandates that groundfish stocks have to be rebuilt to a level that will allow for what the scientific community refers to as a "spawning stock biomass." This means a large enough number of sexually mature fish to raise the stocks of that species to a predetermined level, one that will still allow for a maximum sustainable yield. The act further stipulates a ten-year period for the rebuilding plan.

Phil Coates, past chairman of the council's groundfish committee, essentially agrees with Paul Vitale. Phil rates the Sustainable Fisheries Act as "a very, very aggressive rebuilding regime." He credits "a coalition of environmental groups, recreational groups, and a few commercial fishing organizations with stepping up the timetable for rebuilding the stocks. They said, 'Well, here's a law we can fix and make more accountable.' They basically got their oar in before the rest of the fishing community had the time to react and see that there were things here that might not be acceptable to them."

Many of the environmental groups involved in crafting the 1996 Sustainable Fisheries Act are based in Washington, D.C., and can easily lobby congressmen and staffers while fishermen are at sea. Phil says, "There was such impressive lobbying that the Senate passed the new [1996] act with a one hundred to nothing vote—a unanimous vote. And the House only had a couple of dissenters."

"I'm a member of that lobbying group, and I think it's great," Paul Parker says. "If we don't have any fish, you can see what happens to the fisherman. So I think it's important for fishermen to choose their allies well and to work with people they trust. I think there are conservation and recreational organizations that are not particularly interested in the long-term welfare of the commercial fisherman."

Paul speaks in laudatory terms about the work Niaz Dorry has done and continues to do. "In terms of conservation, she's right on, but let's be honest: I'm a trained conservationist. That's what I was raised to do. My professors would never have imagined that I would be working for a commercial fishermen's organization. But fishermen are working on the water every day. I trust their views on how to conserve these fish, and I trust their views on the necessity for conserving fish habitat more than I trust the views of other people who are more disconnected from the fish." Paul could be Charlie Butman when he says, "I mean I don't know how often some of these conservationists, scientists, or managers actually get out on the water.

"But, if there are fisheries managers who never get out on the water, it's our responsibility to take them out on the water. If there's a council meeting where they're talking about stuff that's all a bunch of BS because they don't know or understand, well, it's our responsibility to be there and to provide comment." Paul mainly represents the communities of Chatham, Provincetown, and Harwich, which he acknowledges did not participate in management until recently—"because they didn't organize, they didn't mobilize, they thought there was this big conspiracy against them. Whereas it was their failure to be part of the system that left them out of the regulations."

Contrary to the picture portrayed by the press, a lot of the younger men and women fishing today have college degrees, business degrees, and various other advanced degrees. They are educated people, people who are managing businesses, people who are thinking in terms of their children and in terms of long-term sustainability of the resource. "Of course, when you get in situations of crisis management," Paul says, referring to the National Marine Fisheries Service, "in that arena everyone gets messed up." He admits to the difficulty of having to weigh the hook fishermen's ideals against what he sees as impossible options. "I mean right now we're looking at a two-thousand-pound trip limit or taking four months off during the year. I know a two-thousand trip limit isn't going to work. We've already tried it. It isn't going to work. It's only going to get us to where the Gulf of Maine is—down to four hundred pounds. And possibly down to thirty pounds. You want to be helpful and supportive of something, but there is just nothing on the agenda that's going to work."

Paul echoes the feeling of every other fisherman when he says, "I dread going to the council meetings. It's a nightmare. I dread every single meeting I've had to go to, and I try to minimize it. I've never come out of one of those meetings with any confidence that what we've accomplished at the meeting is going to do anything to improve the situation."

Chris Glass, a marine biologist at the Manomet Center for Conservation Sciences, maintains that the problem arises because the whole Gulf of Maine is treated as one block. "Management can only do it that way. They can't really submanage. It's difficult enough for them to manage all the different stocks of fish, and submanagement just isn't possible with the system we have."

Chris cites the Japanese system as a better model. In Japan, a series of local cooperatives of fishermen and scientists manage the fisheries of each area. Here, that would mean that Cape Cod Bay would be managed by a local prefecture composed of people whose livelihood is based on the group of fish in Cape Cod Bay. "Under that system, the people involved know they are protecting their own livelihood, so they have a much more open and active system of management because they're managing themselves."

Paul Parker has some doubts. "Well, the bottom line when you are involved in that type of grassroots management is that you really need investment from all your stakeholders. We're still at a point in our management where we don't even agree on the problem. So as long as we're in a mode where we are reacting to what the federal government defines as the problem, we're always going to be in a tough position."

Japan's system is unique.[1] Most countries manage their fisheries much the same way the United States does or, in the case of Iceland, with the use of ITQs (Individual Transferable Quotas). None seem to be doing a particularly good job of it, or the fish stocks would not have diminished to today's levels, and fishing communities would not be in such an impoverished state.

Despite his abhorrence for attending meetings of the New England Fishery Management Council, Paul serves on the advisory board for both the habitat committee and the groundfish committee. Both committees meet regularly, and both take up at least a day a month of Paul's time plus transportation. Preparation for the meetings takes additional time.

Paul attempts to identify what he hopes to accomplish from participation in the regulatory management of the fisheries: "We've put a lot of effort into the existing infrastructure. As frustrating as it may be, that's what we're stuck with right now." He adds that one of the real goals of the Cape Cod Commercial Hook Fishermen's Association (CCCHFA) is to get more people involved in the system. Each newsletter from the association gives the reader an update on the latest regulations to be discussed at that month's council meeting, and it offers rides for anyone who wishes to attend the meetings.

"We're trying to take some foreign concept, like going to some meeting in Gloucester to talk about some ill-defined problem that you don't even believe in, and to reduce it to something manageable where fishermen in town [Chatham] can stop into our action center on the street and make a phone call or write a letter to voice their concerns without having to sit through hours of statistics. That's not their bag." Paul stresses that they also have no choice. "There's a resource out there that needs to be managed. If we want to harvest that resource, catch it, kill it," his voice rises as he brings home his point, "we have a responsibility, as businessmen, to participate in the management of that resource. If we're not going to do that we have no right to benefit from the use of a public resource. And if we don't do the job, somebody else is going to take it away from us." Paul's eyes narrow and he purses his lips before saying, "And I can tell you, we're not going to like the results!"

As the Cape Cod fishermen have begun working together as a community, they have also become aware of a power they have not had as individuals. When a boat captain purchases fuel from either Monomoy Fuel or Whitely Fuel, two small locally owned fuel companies, the captain or boat owner chooses to pay a local industry tax of five or ten cents extra per gallon. That money then goes to help support the work of the CCCHFA. Paul sees it as "fishermen investing in their own futures." The quiet clout of the fishermen became apparent to Oil Express, a fuel company from outside the community that claimed it was too large to pass the fuel tax along to the CCCHFA. Oil Express is no longer in Chatham—a direct result of a boycott by the community of fishermen.

Chatham hook fishermen are protesting the lifting of an existing moratorium on ITQs, or individual transferable quotas. They fear the ITQ would privatize that portion of the ocean that is harvestable—where the fish are. Shares or quotas would be allocated by the government and could then be sold or traded. Allocation would be decided on the basis of the number of fish landed over a set period of time. To the small community-based fisherman, this translates as a license for the least environmentally sensitive forms of fishing to destroy the resource for everyone. In Iceland, where the fisheries have been managed by use of ITQs since 1984, most of the fifteen million dollars worth of ITQs are now owned by a few large corporations and politicians, with an overall loss of many of the traditional fishing communities that existed prior to 1984.[2]

Paul unequivocally states that the concept behind ITQs is "totally unethical. You're taking something that belongs to the public and giving it to a few select individuals." To Paul and most of the men and women who fish for groundfish in New England, prohibiting the use of ITQs is critical to the survival of fishing as a way of life. To them, ITQ stands for "all that is bad—corporate domination of the public resources." The ITQ issue, more than anything else, may have tipped the scale in the balance Paul tries to maintain between his environmental allegiances and his identification with the rest of the fishing community. His voice is a combination of sadness and anger when he speaks of some of the environmental organizations who are choosing to embrace the concept of ITQs. "They have no right to fight towards lifting the moratorium on ITQs. They don't have the investment in the communities; they don't have the investment in what's at stake. What's at stake is a way of life, a tradition, a culture."

Paul believes the fish are in jeopardy with or without ITQs. "That isn't going to change, whether a corporation owns the fish or whether the public continues to own the fish. But what will change is us, the real people, the cultural assets we have and the history. Those are the things that are going to be lost. And you can't put a price tag on that—the fishing Provincetown, the Gloucester port . . . Chatham. Those are priceless commodities.

". . . So this is just where I started. I started here in Chatham. And we work on fisheries issues here, but I could just as well be someone who grew up in a small timber town in the Pacific Northwest, and I would be living the same life, dealing with the same issues."

More and more fishermen are seeing themselves as part of a larger community of men and women who work outdoors, polarized against what they see as corporate America and the intrusion of government in their lives. It is no longer a stretch for the fisherman to identify with loggers or, vice versa, for New England's cranberry bog owners to identify with the fishermen and keep a low profile to avoid the sorts of government regulations they see the fishermen facing.

Paul admits to having been lucky enough to make some money fishing, and, he adds, "I've really grown attached to it. And it's pretty addictive." The lot of Paul Parker and other men and women fishing out of Chatham is markedly better than that of Kevin Shea, Paul Vitale, and others fishing in the Gulf of Maine, separated from the waters off Chatham by only a four-mile strip of land. Paul Parker is still permitted to catch two thousand pounds of cod per trip, and he does not have to contend with additional closures—at least not today.

The resilience that permits fishermen to adjust to extreme weather changes while their small boats are battered by winds and waves on the

Atlantic Ocean may be one reason they have allowed their livelihood to be threatened by bureaucrats, politicians, and scientists, who often collect data without consulting the fishermen, and who for the most part have never fished in the waters they help regulate.

On Thursday, January 28, 1999, the National Marine Fisheries Service and the New England Fishery Management Council agreed to close off portions of the Gulf of Maine and all of Cape Cod Bay to codfishing through a series of rolling closures scheduled to begin in Maine in May and June 1999 and to continue down the coast through April 2000. By that act, they put many of the inshore fishermen, including those who did not fish for cod, out of business.

Phil Coates later defended the reasoning for the council's actions. "Unfortunately, because of advice we got from the Fisheries Service stating that cod stocks in the Gulf of Maine were precipitously low, we embarked on this closure, which caught a lot of people by surprise." He added, "We couldn't let everyone go out there and bang cod for another year, because we had gone so far over our targets, like two-and-a-half-fold." Phil admitted that the closures scheduled to take place in February, March, and April are a "draconian" action. "We only hope it will pay off."

At the groundfish committee meeting on February 11, 1999, a few days after the decision to close portions of the Gulf of Maine, Joseph Brancaleone, then council chairman, with a calm and patience usually reserved for priests, replies to a Rhode Island fisherman who is calling him a fascist. "Mike, I got on this council as a fisherman trying to help fishermen. I'm off in five months, thank God. You know why I'm going to get off the council? Because of the law [the Sustainable Fisheries Act]. That's why we're doing what we do. We can't lobby Washington. We're not the ones who made the law. Change the law, but don't call me a fascist," he gently urges. "I don't need to be treated like that."

In advance of this meeting, the New England Fishery Management Council sent out an agenda listing a 2:00 P.M. discussion to "Develop proposals for exemption and/or experimental fishery certification for closed areas for groundfish vessels targeting specific species." The council was indicating that it would consider making exceptions to the rolling closures for inshore fishermen who target groundfish other than cod. In hopes of receiving exempt status for the gillnetters, Kevin Shea, Bob MacKinnon (president of the Massachusetts Gillnetters Association), Jan Anderson (secretary and treasurer of the association), Bob's son (a fisherman), and several other gillnetters fishing out of Scituate sit patiently on folding chairs in the audience. They have driven down to a Holiday Inn in Warwick, Rhode Island, from their homes that morning. It is

5:15 P.M., and the committee members are still discussing Georges Bank cod instead of the exempt issue dealing with Gulf of Maine Cod, even though they have already voted on the motion made by Bill Amaru relative to the previous item on the agenda.

The Scituate gillnetters are prohibited from fishing, because the grounds where they have always fished are closed to protect the cod. They do not fish for cod. They fish for flounder. The U.S. Department of Commerce, in the new regulations that took effect February 1, 1999, has exempted the following vessels from the rules prohibiting Bob, Kevin, Joey, and Paul from fishing in the area off the shores closest to their homes:

1. charter, party, or recreational vessels
2. vessels fishing with pelagic hook and line, pelagic longline, spears, rakes, diving gear, cast nets, tongs, harpoons, weirs, dip nets, stop nets, pound nets, pelagic gill nets, pots and traps, purse seines, shrimp trawls, and surf clam and ocean quahog dredges
3. midwater trawls

All the above are permitted to fish in the area off Scituate. And they are permitted to catch cod on the basis of their cod bycatch being less than 5 percent. Yet the gillnetters, who live in the area and also fish with a cod bycatch level of less than 5 percent, are not allowed to fish. If, in fact, the closures were designed to protect the cod stocks, the committee should grant the Scituate gillnetters an exemption, without further discussion.

While philosophizing about issues unrelated to the gillnetters' predicament, one council member reminds everyone they must wrap up the meeting and be out of the room by 6:00 P.M. It is now 5:20. Still no discussion on an exemption for the gillnetters. Barbara Stevenson, who owns three trawlers in Maine, recommends the committee jump to the item scheduled for 3:30. Up to now the gillnetters have shown unbelievable restraint. With only forty minutes left to the meeting, Bob MacKinnon jumps up and says, "No! You are not jumping over the two o'clock item."

Barbara Stevenson says, with a calm provided by authority, "We'll get to that."

Two men representing the National Marine Fisheries Service rise in turn and walk to the microphone. Neither has spoken in any of the previous discussions. Something about their dark suits and sudden appearance is reminiscent of the council meeting two months earlier in

New Hampshire where the decision to close the fishing grounds was announced as police filed into the room. Each of the two men expresses a desire "to regulate the [closed areas] on the basis of other species." A new ramification to the ruling has been introduced, that is, the possibility that the closures were for reasons other than to protect cod stocks. This does not look good for Kevin and Bob.

Eric Anderson, fisherman and council member, responds, "If that's the position of the National Marine Fisheries Service, then we closed the wrong areas."

Phil Coates asks that the industry be considered.

Jim Kendall, a council member, reminds the committee, "We did design this framework to exempt certain fisheries. If fishermen meet exemptions, they should be able to fish."

Phil Coates suggests a "blanket experimental exempted program" with observers in order to "keep as many people on the water as possible." He raises the possibility of requiring vessel-tracking devices (VTS) on the exempted boats, with the provision that the government pay for them. VTS devices of the type being discussed list for five thousand dollars. Up to now, a vessel owner required by the government to use one has had to pay for it. Jimmy Bramante had to buy and pay for a VTS for one of his boats—not because he wanted it on board.

Maggie Raymond, another owner of Maine trawlers, rises and takes the microphone. As she speaks, it is clear she is protecting her own interests. "I oppose exempted fisheries targeting a species other than cod if it closes other stocks in my area."

An exasperated Jan Anderson takes the microphone, and requests that the committee grant an exemption to the Scituate gillnetters. She points out that they do not fish for cod and they do not catch cod, two points documented at the meeting both by an independent observer and by records kept by the Manomet observers.

The matter is "out of our hands" is the final word issued from the chairman. The groundfish committee recommends that the Scituate gillnetters "write to the director of the Department of Commerce to request an exemption." Things are looking decidedly bleak for Kevin, Bob, and all the other small inshore fishermen. If the intent in closing the fishing grounds where they fish was, as stated, to protect the cod stocks, there is no reason they should not be allowed to fish. By the time they write letters, wait for replies, and hope for someone to address their plight, February, March, and April, the season when Kevin and Bob earn the bulk of their year's earnings, will have passed. At the speed this issue is being addressed, so will the same months have passed in the years 2000 and 2001.

The Department of Commerce has left only one avenue open to Kevin and the Scituate gillnetters who fish from even smaller boats than Kevin's 42-foot *Endeavor*. It is an option that exposes the fishermen to some of the most dangerous winter conditions, in an area where there are no safe harbors for them in the event of a storm. And it is an option that does just the opposite of protecting the cod.

The gillnetters have been left the option to hang cod gear off the stern of their boats, steam for four-and-a-half hours to the outside of Cape Cod, an area with more shipwrecks than any other area save Cape Sable Island off Newfoundland, and fish for cod instead of flounder. *Endeavor* is not designed for these waters. Unlike *Captain Sam*, it has neither the space nor the hull design to permit its crew to fish round-the-clock for several days during the winter weather in this part of the Atlantic, and still get safely back to their home port.

Months after the closures went into effect, Tony Lemmi would describe the men he encountered on the offshore fishing grounds who had traveled seventy-five miles from port in 30- to 36-foot boats to fish in February, March, and April. "I couldn't believe the distance some of the men in those small boats were forced to travel to earn a living."

Patty Lemmi calls it "criminal." She echoes the words of the Gloucester fishing families in the second half of the nineteenth century, the days of the sailing schooners, when she adds, "Only after someone goes down will something be done about it. As long as fishermen are willing to take the risk, they're going to be pushed to the limit."

If, as many in the industry are coming to believe, the Department of Commerce is operating with a plan to eliminate the small fisherman in favor of a few large trawling operations, this is a ghoulish way to carry out the plan. Paul Vitale sums it up. "You have the choice of going bankrupt or getting into serious trouble."

A monthly council meeting is scheduled for February 24 and 25, 1999, in New London, Connecticut, where Phil Coates, chairman of the groundfish committee, will present the recommendations from this groundfish committee meeting. The day before the council meeting, a newspaper serving communities south of Boston, including Scituate, prints a seemingly unrelated article titled "Whale Protection Rules Are Finalized." There is no byline to the article, but it seems to have originated from a press release sent to the Associated Press.

In the fourth paragraph, the article states, "The rules requiring gillnetters and lobster boats to avoid certain types of gear and fishing areas in order to protect the endangered right whale were finalized by the National Marine Fisheries Service earlier this month." It then goes on to say, "The rules are to protect the delicate population of about 300 right whales estimated to remain in the North Atlantic. . . . In Cape Cod Bay, a critical habitat for the right whale, gill net fishing is barred from Jan. 1 through May 15. In the Great South Channel—a large swath of sea located 20 miles off the coast of Hyannis— . . . gillnetters, who hunt for fish such as cod and flounder, also will be forbidden in that area, except for one sliver of sea in the southwest area of the channel."[3]

Bob MacKinnon's response to the article is to point out, "A right whale has *never* been caught in a gill net." Right whales have been hit by whale-watching boats in the same area. It is significant that, other than mandating how close whale-watching boats can come to the whales, no legislation exists to restrict whale watching, a popular $24 million industry expected to grow larger as Massachusetts attracts more tourists.

Dan McKiernan, who chaired a team to reduce the entanglement of right whales, replies, "There have been a lot of cases of right whales entangled in unidentified line. There haven't been many cases of right whales being hung up in gill nets. Our point is that we don't want the next one to happen. It's not worth it."

Dan and his team were under a court order to come up with a plan to comply with the mandates of a lawsuit brought by one individual who aligned himself with the Conservation Law Foundation. The case revolved around the role of the Massachusetts Division of Marine Fisheries as the agency issuing permits to fish. A permit to fish was defined by the plaintiff as an opportunity to alter the habitat. Federal law prohibits altering the habitat of an endangered species in any way that endangers the animal. The judge ruled in favor of the individual bringing suit. In an effort to negotiate a resolution, Massachusetts prohibited fixed gear use in what is deemed the critical habitat for marine mammals. Thus, fishing is essentially not allowed in Massachusetts Bay from January through mid-May.

Anyone who has ever seen a whale surface or read Victor Scheffer's *The Year of the Whale* knows the reverence and awe inspired by these magnificent cetaceans. Each man or woman with the good fortune to see a whale and to realize how few still exist is naturally committed to their protection. The fisherman more than others must feel an affinity for a fellow creature living on and from the sea. Whales have been transformed into different types of metaphors by mankind, as has the fisherman. The days of whaling, when the whale was the hunted and the fisherman the hunter, still remain a poignant and embarrassing tableau to those living in the developed world of the New England states. No fisherman wants to see any fish species decimated to the levels of the whales, and no fisherman wants to see whales exterminated.

At neither the council meetings nor the groundfish committee meetings leading up to the decision to close the area fished by the Scituate gillnetters was there any mention of the protection of right whales as the driving force behind prohibiting these fishermen from earning a living. Protecting the cod biomass was always the stated aim of closing quadrants or blocks 124 and 125 in February and March, and quadrants 124, 125, 130, 131, 132, and 133 in April. So what is the underlying goal? Or are decisions to close down portions of the fishing grounds based simply on who is willing and able to spend the most time and money promoting a cause? And, if so, do those people understand or want to understand the ramifications of their actions?

NOAA issued a fisheries strategic plan in 1997 stating, "Many human activities such as fishing . . . lead to conflicts between humans and protected marine species. If these species are to be protected, the effects of these conflicts on the species must be minimized or eliminated."[4] In the hierarchy that controls how, when, and where commercial fishermen fish, the regional councils report to the National Marine Fisheries Service, which reports to NOAA, which reports to the Department of Commerce, which reports to Congress. The 1998 budget for the National Marine Fisheries Service was $344 million. Of that amount, $20.2 million went to the endangered species effort. An additional $9.5 million was allocated to conserving marine mammals.[5] In addition, drivers in Massachusetts who choose to do so may pay a premium of twenty dollars per year for an RW or RT (signifying "right whale") license plate. This money goes to a quasi-public department working with an environmental group to protect the three hundred or so remaining right whales. To date, the Commonwealth of Massachusetts has issued 43,236 RW plates and 12,905 RT plates.[6] The annual revenue from these environmental plates amounts to about $1,122,820 of additional funds. Over $250,000 was spent in the summer of 2001 in an attempt to save one right whale who is believed to have died by September of the same year.

Most right whale deaths have been attributed to encounters with large offshore ships. The National Marine Fisheries Service report for the period of January through September 2000 for the Northeast region lists five right whales who showed signs of having been entangled and one entangled right whale who died.[7] Yet until the fishermen can prove that each yellow polypropylene line found wrapped around a right whale is not from fishing gear, newspaper articles will continue to connect the fishing industry with the death of these endangered mammals.

Right Whale 1102, named Churchill, was spotted June 8, 2001, entangled in what the *Boston Globe* described as "fishing line" and later in the same article as "fishing gear."[8] A member of the disentanglement crew, one of the few people who has actually gotten close enough to see what type of line was wrapped around the animal's jaw, determined the line to be "either a mooring line or part of a lobsterman's offshore lobster gear." Yet the bias connecting the line to the fishing community is stronger than fact, and just about everyone except those in the fishing community speaks about the "fishing line" entanglement when discussing Right Whale 1102.

Buoyed by the success of its case against the Commonwealth, the Conservation Law Foundation issued a press release in March of 2000 indicating its plans to sue the National Marine Fisheries Service for its perceived failure to protect the largest marine mammal on earth. The National Marine Fisheries Service already faces ninety-six lawsuits previously brought against it, so it is difficult to see this action in terms other than grandstanding.

At least one scientist is working with the fishing community and the Center for Coastal Studies in Provincetown to try to understand how to conserve the few remaining members of the right whale population while preserving a way of life for small fishermen like Bob MacKinnon and Kevin Shea. David Wiley is a conservation biologist and scientific adviser for right whale recovery efforts. At a lecture at the Whaling Museum in Nantucket on a rainy July evening, Mr. Wiley, surrounded by the instruments used to hunt whales and one of the remaining whaling longboats, discussed his efforts to bring the fisherman and the conservationist together. After describing why the present efforts of the National Marine Fisheries Service and the efforts to regulate fisheries are not working, he added that the judgment ruling in favor of the Conservation Law Foundation and the individual who brought suit "has not been efficient in conserving whales."

Wiley's research is focused on studying how fishing gear might be modified to reduce the possibility of right whale entanglement. Bob MacKinnon is one of the fishermen who has worked with David Wiley and has helped set up experiments on land to duplicate conditions underwater. Unfortunately, regulations prohibiting the fishermen from fishing have preceded the results of the collaborative research effort.

The February 24–25, 1999, meeting of the New England Fishery Management Council adjourned at 7:30 P.M. in the midst of a nor'easter. It adjourned without any discussion of an exemption for the Scituate gillnetters. The result is that relatively small boats not fishing for cod, and using larger mesh than required in order not to catch cod, are being penalized on the basis of "saving the cod."

It is Friday night at Tosca's restaurant, located in Hingham, Massachusetts, a town adjacent to Scituate. Chef de Cuisine John Hanley picks up three of the order slips lined up by the waiters and turns to the five cooks between him and the stoves. "Salmon at tables forty-three, sixty-nine, and thirty-four; tuna at forty-three; cod, sixty-nine and thirty-four."

Several food aficionados rate Tosca's as one of the five or six best restaurants in New England. At one side of the dining room, flames from a wood-burning fire stretch up to a height of eighteen, twenty, twenty-two inches to consume the oxygen above. The cook grilling meat and fish gently places two salmon steaks on the grill's red metal strips. In the red flame, the salmon become translucent. The cook moves to the spigot behind him to run cold water over his hands—a regular part of the ritual. In early March 1999 the first entrée featured on Tosca's menu was "Local Cod Roast with Clams and Mussels, Lobster brodo and Chorizo mashed potatoes for $19." John Hanley created this recipe, and plans to keep it on the new menu.

Each morning, in preparation, the sous-chefs at Tosca create a lobster stock using the lobster bodies left from the preparation of a lobster ravioli first course. To the bodies in the pan, they add onions, celery, leeks, fennel, bay leaf, thyme, parsley, tomatoes, garlic, white wine, and brandy, which is then flamed. When the flavors have cooked long enough to mingle and create a full-bodied stock, the juice is strained through cheesecloth into a saucepan. Lightly sautéed onions and fennel are added, and the brodo, or broth, simmers until ready for use.

When John joined the staff at Tosca, he found that only thin filets of cod, close to the tail, were being supplied to the restaurant. John wanted a dish that would allow him to pan-sear a thicker piece of cod. He asked Mullaney's market in Scituate to supply him with center-cut cod loin, with the skin on, so that when it was seared over a high flame, the skin would be crispy and the meat of the cod would remain moist. He wanted to use local cod.

Asked where he gets his cod, Mullaney's counterman indicates the chart on the wall of his retail store, showing the areas closed to fishing. He then points to a section northeast of Gloucester and between the shore and Middle Bank. "I believe the boats are catching the cod in here and in the Great South Channel. To me, that's local."

Come April 1, the area off Gloucester will also be closed to commercial fishing boats, except for those qualifying for the exemptions, and not allowed to land cod.

On one of the four industrial stoves at Tosca, a black sauté pan, rounded at the sides from the heat of the stove, holds four mussels and five cher-rystone clams, open and simmering in their own juices, together with the white wine used to cook them. John Hanley is quickly and profes-sionally assembling the pieces of the roasted cod for table 34. He holds out a white rounded dinner plate to one of the cooks, who proceeds to mound the chorizo mashed potatoes in the center of the plate. Then John turns to the next cook, who places mussels and clams around the edge of the mashed potatoes before pouring a stream of lobster brodo around the sides. John decorates the potatoes and shellfish with wilted greens before topping the dish with the loin of cooked cod. "I use farm-bred clams and mussels in this dish because of their availability. I wanted them in the recipe because their salt brine would lend itself to the taste of the cod, and also complement the rich flavor of the sausage in the mashed potatoes."

John hands the plates for table 34 to Joe Simone, Tosca's head chef, who gives them a final inspection before releasing them to the waiter. As he does so, four more orders come in for the roasted cod.

Clearly, Frank Patania was right. Where there is a demand, the in-dustry will find a way to fill it. A careful look at the charts showing the areas closed to fishing indicates that all of the Gulf of Maine is wide open to fishing for Gulf of Maine cod except that area comprising quad-rants 124 to 133, or the western end off Gloucester and including Cape Cod Bay. In February, while Kevin, Paul, and Joey were prohibited from fishing for flounder, for fear they might catch a cod, the cod consigned to the Portland Fish Exchange totaled 90,031 pounds. The dollar value was $157,585. Council member Barbara Stevenson's boats are reported to have landed cod on a regular basis in February. So why are Bob MacKinnon, Kevin, Joey, Paul, and most of the small community-based fishermen prohibited from fishing?

In the year 1999, the Saltonstall Building in Boston's Government Center would hardly inspire idealism in even the most dedicated government employee. All bags are x-rayed, and visitors are screened in the lobby. Paint peels from most walls, and the elevator doors open onto floors with unlit corridors. The building meets few code requirements of the City of Boston, the Commonwealth of Massachusetts, or the U.S. gov-ernment. Several floors have been shut down for asbestos removal, while people continue to work in the rest of the building.

Philip G. Coates, then chairman of the groundfish committee for the New England Fishery Management Council and director of the Division of Marine Fisheries for the Commonwealth of Massachusetts, is working out of an office on the nineteenth floor. Bar graphs, flow charts, reports of stock assessments and biomass are stacked several feet high on every available horizontal surface. The only amenity is a commanding view over the city to the north. At chair level, the view is lost behind the stacks of paper.

Most weekday mornings Phil leaves his home at 4:00 A.M. to catch a 4:35 bus from the Cape Cod Canal in order to be here by 6:00. Increased participation of the fishing community in council meetings, together with the complexity of the frameworks and amendments, often combine to extend the length of the meetings to long after midnight. In ten months, Phil will retire, after nineteen years as the senior fisheries manager for the Commonwealth of Massachusetts. His work with the council will end at the same time.

Many council members, Phil included, admit to having been frustrated with the inability to get things moving in the days before the Sustainable Fisheries Act was put into effect. Phil hoped the act would give them more tools to work with. Today, he says, "I think what we got is a little more than what we had bargained for. The absolute inflexibility of the act is of real concern to some of us."

One of the problems fishermen see with the way they are regulated is that rules for large boats and small boats are all lumped together. "To categorize a thirty-five-foot boat with a ninety-foot-boat is ridiculous," Patty Lemmi states. If the owners of the F/V *Captain Sam* had decided to keep fishing out of Boston rather than accept the government buyout, they would have been held to the same Gulf of Maine closures as Kevin, Paul, and Joey on the F/V *Endeavor*. But *Captain Sam* would have been able to cross the Gulf of Maine, and safely stay out on the fishing grounds to fish beyond the closed areas for five days or more. Tony, Kevin, Paul, and Joey are not fishing on boats designed for onboard living or designed to withstand waves of fifteen feet or higher washing over them. As a result, they are infinitely more exposed.

"Personally," Phil responds, "I'm absolutely in support of maintaining a labor-intensive, small-scale fishery, together with the existing and necessary larger draggers that can fish on Georges Bank and stay out for five or ten days at a time, in marginal weather, to provide fresh fish for the consumer." As Phil speaks, his white beard, round cheeks, and eyes peering over reading glasses create the image of a trim St. Nicholas, trying to deliver the gift of fish to future generations while still providing employment for his elves. "The small boats and draggers provide employment; they provide character to the New England coastline; and they're one of the major reasons hundreds of millions of tourist dollars are spent by people who want to see the coast and say, 'Oh, isn't that quaint, the fleets and all. . . . ' Plus, they provide a hell of a lot of income to a lot of people."

Phil thinks most, if not all, members of the council share his views. But, he says, "It's very difficult right now because many of the fish the fishermen have targeted are the ones in the worst shape. And we're trying to figure out how we can keep them [the fishermen] going.

"We gave liberal access to the fishermen with multispecies licenses, and as a result, we now have a lot of permits being held by people. A person only had to land a couple of codfish during the season to get a full-scale limited access permit. Whether it was a full-time fisherman like Bob MacKinnon or a guy who went out once and sold a couple of fish, he has the same permit as Bob does." Phil allows that the council probably should have been stricter in the number of multispecies permits it allowed to be issued. Some permits are held by speculative investors, similar to the people who speculate in the price of pork bellies on the Chicago commodities market or buy up taxicab medallions to hold them until the price increases. Chances are good that the loyalties of those investors lie neither with the fish nor with the fishing communities.

How to deal with the "latent fishing effort," where the permit has been issued but has not been used, is one of the dilemmas Phil is pondering. "When the stocks start coming back, are we going to let all these doctors, dentists, and others who have dreamed of going to sea at some point—are we going to let them go in and garner the results of other people's broken backs?"

The natural answer would be to invalidate permits to all except those who can demonstrate they have been regularly fishing for a living. Phil counters: "But remember, within that category, you have full-time commercial fishermen who have permits to catch groundfish, but have said, 'Well, I don't want to catch groundfish if they're in trouble, so I'll target underutilized species, or whatever, until the groundfish stocks rebound.' Do you penalize them? The government says, 'Catch dogfish. There's a big imbalance in dogfish. They're eating up everything. So, let's go catch 'em.' So we went out and caught 'em, and now the fisherman says, 'We can't get back into what we want to catch now that you are shutting off the dogfish fishery. Is that fair?' And that's a legitimate issue."

In all aspects of the fishing industry, the government is usually perceived as the bad guy. But who constitutes the government varies widely, depending on who is doing the talking. To most in the fishing community, Phil would be considered a part of the government. He is supported by tax dollars, and he does govern in the sense of making decisions to establish rules and regulations that others must abide by. But when he speaks, he allies himself with the fishing community and speaks of the government in the third person.

Phil points out that one difference between the New England council and other regional fishery management councils is the degree of openness and public access to the meetings. "We've been extremely liberal, far more liberal than any other council. I think it's reflective of the social and attitudinal approach we have in New England. When you have public forums, town meetings, why shouldn't people be able to speak? But," he adds, "I think it's now becoming an impediment to the way we conduct business."

Many of the regional councils limit public comment. In some cases, anyone wishing to speak must submit a statement prior to the meeting. "And that's not fair to the fisherman who finds out for the first time that there's a real threat to his way of life. Then he shows up at a council meeting, and is horrified at what's going on because he hasn't been exposed to the system." Phil laughs to himself as he looks up from under bushy brows. "Yet, I must admit, some of them are far more eloquent than some of us sitting around the table."

Does Phil see a way to preserve the fish stocks and still preserve a community of fishermen? In answering, he cites the pyramiding of regulations, or what Frank Mirarchi calls "layers of regulations," as an effort on the council's part to circumvent the creativity of the fishing industry in order to rebuild the stocks. "One example is the running clock closures," Phil says. The reference is to the regulation permitting a fisherman who catches more than the allowable catch, and wants to avoid throwing fish back, to stay at the dock for a number of days while using up some days at sea. The fisherman still subtracts those days from his yearly allowance, today eighty-eight days, but he can sell the fish he caught.

"The intent was very noble. It lets a guy go out fishing." Phil creates a hypothetical scenario whose main character appears to be not unlike Kevin, Paul, and Joey. "He's a conscientious fisherman. He doesn't like throwing away dead fish. He sets his nets in a very conscientious way, and he thinks he's avoiding codfish. Lo and behold, he comes up with a thousand pounds. At the four-hundred-pound level, he's two and a half times over what he should catch. So what does he do? He figures, well, I'll sit at the dock for two and a half days. I will have burned up some groundfish time for that extra amount of fish. That's great."

What Phil neglects to take into consideration is that for the fisherman, the economics do not translate to "That's great." At the Boston auction on the day Phil related his story, cod sold for $1.82 per pound. And that is higher than average. Even at a seasonably high price, four hundred pounds translates to only $728. That does not pay a crew, and pay for gas and maintenance, and still leave anything for a boat mortgage, food, clothing, or rent.

Phil continues to build his case. "In the same category, are guys who have these same eighty-eight-day permits, and they're lobstering. So Joe, who's a lobster guy, sees Bill, a full-time groundfish fisherman, coming in, and Bill drops the comment, 'There's a lot of cod out there.' Joe says to himself, 'Gee, I've got a groundfish permit. I've been hauling my traps six days a week. Maybe I better set some longline gear on Sunday, instead of resting." Phil pauses to enjoy his humor before continuing. "So out he goes with his longline gear, and he estimates if he gets four hundred pounds a day, he can use this running clock ruling and catch a whole week's worth of fish. So he comes in with two thousand eight hundred pounds of codfish, and he doesn't go groundfishing for six days. But he continues to lobster.

"So, now," Phil's voice rises, "he's parlayed his six days of lobstering and one big day of groundfishing because he's taken advantage of this running clock allowance. Now that was never intended. But that's what's happened.

"Our noble efforts have created a whole new opportunity for a whole group of people who say, 'Well, you know all these protective measures are showing some signs of working, the fish are spawning, so let's go out and see what we can do to take advantage of it."

The picture painted by Phil still leaves the hypothetical fisherman Bill, and the real Kevin, Paul, and Joey, with only four hundred pounds per day of codfish, and three less days to fish.

Phil refers to the gillnetters when he says, "We're trying to deal with the days at sea for Bob MacKinnon and other gillnetters. They've got eighty-eight days. However, the gillnetter goes out and sets his gear. Then he comes in, and goes out the next day to pull his gear. And it only takes twelve hours."

When Kevin Shea calls in before leaving the mooring and after picking up the mooring, that time is calculated in hours, not as a day of fishing. "So Bob gets two days effort, and he is really only charged for one day. So, he's got twice as many days," Phil exclaims. "Plus, unlike the dragger or handliner who brings his gear back, he leaves his nets in the water. His gear is fishing, even though his boat may be tied at the pier. So he's not really being restricted to eighty-eight days."

Asked why fishermen with various gear are allowed to fish in the closed areas when the Scituate gillnetters are not exempted, Phil replies simply, "Because the other gears don't catch groundfish." The issue appears to be larger than cod. Phil elaborates. "The exemptions apply to gears that don't take groundfish, like lobster gear, although we know there's some bycatch of groundfish there, but hopefully when they pull the traps, they dump the cod, if they don't stick 'em in the bait bag."

In five hauls, Kevin, Paul, and Joey caught only three legal codfish and one juvenile they released, so there is more at stake here. "What we were trying to create was for people like Bob MacKinnon, who's got his data showing he didn't catch cod, to go out and set his flounder nets and still catch his flounder. Now that raised a whole host of issues, mainly the fact that right behind the cod problem came flounder problems." Phil is referring to the stock assessment levels for flounder that the National Marine Fisheries Service presented to the council just before the February council meeting.

"The feds said, 'There's no way we're going to grant an exemption to someone to go out and fish for a species that's now in the same mess.' So that kind of wiped that opportunity out. We're still going to pursue it, but on a different basis." Phil explains, "We're going to promote experiments which will allow a guy to go out with an observer on board to verify what the fisherman says he can do."

The National Marine Fisheries Service reports that the stocks of both yellowtail flounder and winter flounder in the Gulf of Maine are below the levels needed to meet the biomass numbers required by the Sustainable Fisheries Act. Phil maintains there may still be an opportunity for Kevin, Bob, Paul, and Joey to fish, but "it's not going to happen in this period of closure. These guys will still be able to catch some flounder, just the way they can catch two hundred pounds of cod after May first. We're not shutting 'em off."

Charlie Butman's only comment: "That man's never been fishing, or he would know that it takes a lot more than two hundred pounds of cod to buy fuel and run a fishing boat." Charlie shakes his head in disgust. "They think they can squeeze a nickel so hard that the buffalo will jump off it."

"Oh, no, they'll catch flounder," Phil continues in a placid tone. "They're worried, I know, that they'll also catch a lot of cod, and the minuscule cod quota is going to be caught so fast. The big fear now of the fishermen is that they won't be able to avoid cod, and they're now saying that once the quota's caught, we're going to say we need more area closures.

"So, I'm hoping we can work with these guys to avoid the cod while they're doing their other things. I don't know whether we are going to be successful or not, because there are some mind-sets on the council that keep repeating, 'We've got to close those areas down.'"

Phil's shoulders relax, and his body conforms to the shape of his chair as he reminisces about the days thirty years ago when thirty-to forty-pound cod were living in the Cape Cod Canal. "When people used to go down to the Herring Run in Bournedale to fish for bass in the spring, the smart guys were there even earlier catching big cod. They'd say, 'Who the hell wants to eat a striped bass? I'd rather get a cod.' " He walks toward a wall chart showing the southern end of Cape Cod Bay, and he points to Scusset Beach, an area between the Canal and Manomet. "I used to take my son to fish for cod right off the beach here, and I remember a lobsterman in the spring going up right off the rocks at Manomet and coming back with fifty-, sixty-pound cod.

"And look where we are now." He shakes his head, and presses his lips together. In a second, the jubilant voice returns. "But we'll get 'em back. We'll get 'em back. And I hope in my lifetime. In our lifetime," he adds.

Menemsha Basin, inside the western tip of Martha's Vineyard, is the quintessential picture-book fishing village. A traditional white building with gray roof at the head of the harbor houses the only functioning Coast Guard station between Woods Hole, Massachusetts, and Newport, Rhode Island.

Only two moorings in this harbor are set aside for cruising sailboats, and only three boats are permitted to raft together at each mooring. Spaces between pilings mark off just enough area for a total of fifty-two pleasure boats to back into slips. The dockage area paralleling the one road from the main part of the island to the beach is marked Commercial Fishing Boats Only. This is in sharp contrast to Vineyard Haven, where fishing schooners by the hundreds used to lie at anchor while waiting for the shifting tides and winds before setting sail, and where today only pleasure boats and cruise boats lie at moorings, while the passenger ferries occupy the dock space.

A wooden walkway (called the "bulkhead") is all that separates Larsen's and Poole's, the area's two wholesale/retail fish markets, from the fishing boats tied at the dock. Both markets buy fresh fish off the boats tied up at the back of the store. The fish is then filleted inside the store before it is sold at the front or street side of the store. This fish is about as fresh as you can get short of being on the boat when it is caught. And veteran fisherman Charlie Butman claims that the flesh of the fish is better the next day than it is on the day it is caught.

The F/V *Mary Verna*, a 47-foot wooden-hulled side trawler with the documentation no. 519489, is tied alongside the dock, to the south of Larsen's. Hanging from the vessel's backstay is a hand-printed sign written in black paint on plywood:

THIS BOAT TIED TO DOCK BY STUPID FOOLISH REGULATORS, WHO WOULD
STARVE TO DEATH IF THEY HAD TO WORK FOR A LIVING!!

A second sign warns:

EXPECT TO SEE NO FISHING BOATS IN THIS HARBOR IN NEXT 10 YEARS!!!

Jim Morgan, the owner of the *Mary Verna*, is seventy-five years old
and has been fishing since he was ten. He is the owner of the last remaining true "fishing shack" on the spit of land leading to Poole's and
Larsen's. The others belong to the owners of the five houses on the hill
to the southeast. The largest of these shingled houses sits on less than
one-quarter acre of land. None has more than two floors. Each has
existed in essentially the same footprint of land since 1901. The major
visible difference between a 1953 photograph of the houses and a view
of the houses today is the addition of some trees and a porch or two.
Yet the desirability of these houses and their location overlooking Menemsha Harbor and Vineyard Sound motivated Carly Simon to purchase
one for $500,000 and sell it three years later for $1,200,000, and it is
the reason Billy Joel is rumored to have paid $1,800,000 for another
one. Both houses have since been sold for even higher amounts. Local
lore relates that one of the houses and its fishing shack dependency were
purchased for the sheer purpose of providing a dock for the owner's
Boston Whaler. The vessels tied up alongside those curtained "fishing
shacks" range from a Hinckley "picnic boat" (popularized by Martha
Stewart) to a seagoing replica of the open-cockpit vessels that fished out
of Menemsha at the beginning of the twentieth century.

Inside Jim's shed, a workbench runs along the south side, underneath
the one window. On the opposite wall, paintings created by Jim hang
alongside yellowed photographs showing the harbor when fishing boats
the size of *Mary Verna* were rafted side to side to fill Menemsha Basin.
Today, four boats, including the *Mary Verna*, are tied up at the dock.
The F/V *Quitsa Strider II* and the F/V *Unicorn* are two offshore stern
trawlers with detachable bows designed to keep them within a 72-foot
state limit. They are owned by Greg and Jonathan Mayhew, brothers
whose ancestors are reported to have once traded all of Nantucket Island
for "two barrels of salt cod and a beaver hat." Jonathan has been involved in just about every aspect of commercial fishing, including flying
a spotter plane for the few remaining fishermen who harpoon tuna. He
has just returned to port after complying with a requirement to throw
overboard a thousand pounds of fluke or summer flounder worth
$2,500. He is disgusted with the whole system regulating the fisheries.

"We need to start all over again, and throw out the present system," he says, his eyes flashing. "What we need is an Alan Greenspan to regulate the fisheries the way he regulates the dollar. A sign reading 'Fish Need To Spawn At Least Once Before Being Harvested' should hang over his desk so he can't avoid seeing it."

Jim, in his shed, is putting the finishing touches on one of the weather vanes he designs and makes to sell in his wife's craft shop just down the road. The scene on the weather vane is that of a fisherman and one of the fishing vessels similar to the 1917 design presently docked in a slip on the other side of the Basin, the type of wooden-hulled boat that used to fish out of Menemsha Basin before the days of steel-hulled trawlers and before the days of quotas, catch limits, and closed areas. The boat and the weather vane represent a time when fishing was perceived as a romantic, simple way of life. It is difficult to equate the gentleman and craftsman who creates these weather vanes with the person who wrote the signs hanging on the *Mary Verna*'s backstays.

"When I was a kid, there would be fifty or sixty fishing boats in this harbor on a stormy day," Jim says with his soft-spoken manner. "I used to fish off No Mans [an island used today as a government bombing range] in the shoals because the *Mary Verna* only draws six to seven feet, and we would fish for two or three days." Now Jim fishes in Vineyard Sound, where he can return home each evening. "It's not so bad for me," he says. "I'm more or less retired. But the guys that are hurting are the guys like Tommy here. He opens his hand toward Tom Phaneuf, whose six-foot two-inch frame is presently filling the doorway to Jim's shed.

Tom is the owner of the F/V *Mattia-C*, presently docked just ahead of the Mayhews' *Quitsa Strider II*. He has been fishing commercially since the age of seventeen, when he first went to sea with his older brothers. Jim and Tom both harvest fluke or summer flounder, which they catch just outside Menemsha in Vineyard Sound. Tom and Jim are the type of fisherman Niaz has in mind when she expresses a hope that the small fisherman can continue to earn a livelihood from the ocean. Tom has a seventeen-year-old son who is learning disabled. He would like his son to have the option to fish but doubts it will be possible for the small fisherman to fish out of Massachusetts unless a drastic change takes place at the state level.

Tom fondly speaks of Jim as "an artist." Then he looks out the door at the *Mattia-C* and adds, "but this is what I do. I don't want to do anything else. I can go get a job as a carpenter or roofer or whatever, but fishing is what I do best.

"Six years ago, when the feds gave us a quota, they put a moratorium on commercial fishing permits for fluke. There's no more. You can't get 'em." As Tom speaks, the villain in Jim Morgan's sign emerges. "Didn't happen in state waters, because these numskulls kept issuing permits, and permits, and permits. Now, there are so many permits out there, you've got this huge handline fishery that went from between five and ten percent on any given year to what is probably approaching between forty to fifty percent of the catch.

"And this has exploded!" Tom refers to the effect of the Magnuson-Stevens Act and its amendments as he explains, "The first year of the plan, we fished one hundred ten days." Normally Menemsha fishermen fished for about five months of the year or 150 days. "The second year was one hundred days. The third year was one hundred one days. The fourth year was fifty-six days. The fifth year was fifty-two, and this year, when they were supposed to go up on our quota, it was reduced to thirty days." Tom's voice lowers as he says, "When my wife heard this year's quota limit, she cried."

Tom thinks the reason for the low quota imposed on commercial boats is the result of the state issuing so many permits to hook-fishing vessels. "We've been complaining to the state for four years. They've gotta stop selling permits to fish. There's only this much, and the pie keeps getting smaller and smaller. Yet they just keep expanding the number of participants."

Dan McKiernan, at the Massachusetts Division of Marine Fisheries, points out that, contrary to Tom's estimates, the percentage of handliners fishing for fluke was 26 percent in 1998, and dropped in 1999. [Both men may be correct, but it may not be a valid comparison because Tom Phaneuf was referring to a percentage of the catch, not of fishermen.] In February of the year 2000, Dan counted 274 licensed Massachusetts draggers. Forty to fifty of them fish for fluke. He calculates that the draggers would use up the present quota of 500,000 pounds in five weeks—without the help of the hook fishermen.

Dan issued Tom his permit to fish in 1985, two years after a 1983 moratorium went into effect prohibiting the draggers from fishing in state waters from May through October. In Dan's view, Tom made a conscious decision to enter the industry as a boat owner knowing the imposed limitations. "It's an issue of competition between the day boat like Tom Phaneuf's and the vessel with a crew of three. And we've made a lot of decisions that favor Tom Phaneuf." Dan points out that "draggers have more versatility and range than hook fishermen, who need access to grounds fairly close to shore." And that is where Jim and Tom fall through the cracks, because draggers are lumped together whether they are the size of the F/V *Captain Sam* or smaller ones not designed to be offshore that fish by day close to shore and then return to port in the evening, as do Tom's *Mattia-C* and Jim's *Mary Verna*.

Present law states that if there is a federal plan requiring permits, anyone with a permit is bound by that plan, regardless of where he fishes. If a fisherman fishes in state waters, he must still comply with the federal regulations. So Tom and Jim are bound to comply with both state and federal requirements where they fish.

The boundaries of the so-called territorial sea were originally based on the maximum distance from shore a cannonball could travel. In 1977, when Congress declared a two-hundred-mile limit for U.S. waters, the area comprising the "territorial sea" was set aside as state waters, with its own regulatory bodies. In Massachusetts, these state waters expanded beyond the earlier limits to include some of the bays and sounds, such as Vineyard Sound. This sound is also the habitat of the fluke or summer flounder Tom and Jim Morgan harvest. Nantucket Sound is closed to draggers—but not to hook fishermen—from May 1 to October 31, as is Buzzards Bay.

To complicate the issue, fluke is managed by the Atlantic States Marine Fisheries Commission, and is not under the auspices of the New England Fishery Management Council but rather under the authority of the Mid-Atlantic Fishery Management Council because it is perceived as a "southern" fish. The Mid-Atlantic Fishery Management Council has jurisdiction from New York State down to North Carolina, and it operates under different principles from those of the New England council. It is known to favor quotas, and has set a TAC (total allowable catch) that is then subdivided into portions for each state that historically harvested fluke. The state quotas are based on the dragger landings prior to the enactment of the Northeast Multispecies Fisheries Management Plan.

Phil Coates, director of the Massachusetts Division of Marine Fisheries, perceives the Mid-Atlantic council as "not terribly receptive to the needs of small-scale fishermen, such as the small draggers out of Menemsha. They've kind of discarded them, in a sense, by saying, 'Well, they're not really commercial fishermen.' We argue that they have been, and that they are a traditional part of our fisheries. The problem is that there aren't good records to back us up. It gets very frustrating."

Jimmy Bramante in Boston points out, "Massachusetts takes ninety percent of the brunt of the regulations, yet the bulk of the prime fishing grounds are off our shores." In addition, Massachusetts fishermen were more environmentally conscious than fishermen of some of the surrounding states; that is, they were using larger mesh and had a higher minimum size for the fish allowed to be kept (fourteen inches long versus nine to eleven inches). Yet they were, and continue to be, penalized by the Mid-Atlantic council's quota system. They were throwing back the small fluke when fishermen in other states were keeping them. This meant that Massachusetts was registering smaller landings. And that was the basis for their smaller allotment.

Frank Mirarchi, who served on the Massachusetts State Council for fifteen years, describes the situation in Menemsha as being ruled by "a patchwork of different rules by different regulatory entities, just laminated one on the other. When you stop to look at the composite, it doesn't make any sense at all. And to add to the insult, the hook and line people are allowed to expand and siphon off some of the catch from the historically enfranchised draggers."

In August of 1998, after an emergency meeting of the New England Fishery Management Council to determine whether or not to close the Gulf of Maine to cod fishermen, the *Boston Globe* in a front-page story stated, "There are too many fishing boats." Later in the same article, the writer referred to the "oversized fishing fleet." Sportfishing was never mentioned.[9]

Almost nothing angers a commercial fisherman more than the idea that an area closed to him for fishing is open to a charter boat with a hundred recreational fishermen and no limits on their catch. Paul Vitale speaks for the fishermen when he refers to the fluke or summer flounder in southern New England as "a disaster. Commercial guys are only allowed to land fifty pounds a day, and some guy only doing it for fun is allowed a greater catch. That's bogus!"

Paul, Tom, and most other fishermen credit the lax regulations for sportfishing as due to a well-funded recreational fishing lobby. As a possible outcome of successful lobbying, NOAA (the governing body overseeing the National Marine Fisheries Service) stated in its May 1997 strategic plan, ". . . we will focus on . . . increasing recreational fishing opportunities."[10]

In Scituate, when Frank Mirarchi speaks of sportfishing, he points to the economic realities driving the tolerance for the recreational catch. "A dead fish caught by a sportfisherman means a lot more to the economy than a dead fish caught by a commercial fisherman. More money accrues to the national economy from people chasing fish for recreational than for commercial purposes." Frank estimates, "They may spend ten dollars a pound to kill a fish, and we spend a dollar a pound to kill the same fish.

"To me, the loss of community spirit is more important than the value of the fish, though the value of the fish is important to the taxpayers. But to throw all this away in favor of a bunch of millionaire playboys that go out and catch fish at ten dollars a pound. There's something wrong there."

Phil Coates takes the position that a recreational fisherman should also have access to the resources. "If there's bycatch being caught by commercial fishermen, why can't there be a recreational harvest? We are after all the public." The argument is that a charter boat should not be penalized just because it happens to make money. Of course, this argument conveniently clouds the issue of how much of the natural resource is being diminished by an operation with relatively few restrictions placed on it.

An article in the *Boston Globe* states, "Nearly one-third of all the cod caught in the Gulf of Maine . . . was taken by both charter boat customers and other sportfishermen in 2001." And that number promises to increase as more charter boats are launched. The same article indicates that the Massachusetts Department of Marine Fisheries (Phil's department) issued 48 percent more permits to charter boats in the year 2000 than in 1996. During that same period, Phil's vote helped decrease the number of codfish a commercial fisherman is allowed to land from one thousand pounds to four hundred pounds (up from thirty pounds) per day for the allowed days at sea. Ed Barrett, a Green Harbor fisherman prohibited from fishing for cod for all but four months of the year, is keeping tabs on the charter catch. His records show that the amount of cod being landed by the charter boats is larger even than that indicated by the *Globe* article.[11]

Phil ponders the question, "If the grounds are closed because the stock is in bad shape, should they [sportfishermen] have that access, and particularly fairly liberal access?" He then divulges, "Look at what happened when we put Amendment 7 together [the Georges Bank closures]. The recreational folks said, 'Let us develop our own plan. If you accept it, then we can continue to fish, and have access to these grounds.' "

The plan proposed that in return for permission to fish in the closed areas, recreational fishermen would catch fish larger than twenty-one inches, release the small fish, and prohibit use of the vessels to anyone who sold fish. "You have to understand," Phil says, "that when someone pays anywhere from sixty dollars to two hundred dollars per trip, they're hoping to get some remuneration in the form of fish flesh. These people generally aren't going out for the aesthetic aspect of fishing. They're not like a fly fisherman who wants to go out, catch fish, and then release them because it's enjoyable. They're out there to get some meat. Flesh. So you've got to make it worth their while."

On the basis of the argument made by the recreational fishermen, the council agreed to their plan, with the proposed restrictions. Thus, a man or woman who chooses, and can afford it, is permitted to be transported to an area closed to commercial fishing, catch an unlimited number of fish, have them filleted on board, and pack them in iced coolers for consumption onshore at a later date. "So if you're a good fisherman, it's a good return," Phil acknowledges. "I mean, it's a nice little way for the public to have access to the resource. At the time, it seemed a reasonable compromise. Now, there's some feeling some of this should be re-thought." Phil is referring to the fact that there were fewer fish larger than twenty-one inches at the time the deal was cut. Today, due in part to a severe reduction in commercial fishing, there are more groundfish larger than twenty-one inches than had been anticipated. For the recreational fisherman to be allowed to catch those fish while the commercial fisherman who made their growth possible is not allowed to fish sends a message that conservation is not rewarded. And it accounts for the fury engendered in the eyes of a commercial fisherman regarding the recreational sector.[12]

In Jim's Menemsha fishing shack, Tom says, "One of the things happening now, and this is proof of the recovery of fluke, is that these guys are catching their limit with handlines on a Saturday or Sunday when they're off from their regular jobs. This is great, but there are too many of 'em." His voice softens as he laments, "and the fish are so easy to catch."

Tom, Jim, and other fishermen who fish in and around Vineyard Sound went to the Division of Marine Fisheries five years ago and asked for trip limits. They saw the fish recovering and did not want to see the stocks taken too quickly. Based on the strong market for sushi at that time, the fishermen recommended three-hundred-pound trip limits for each boat. At that time, they were able to get four to five dollars per pound for summer flounder.

Dan McKiernan comments, "It was a good day's pay, and continued for four or five years. Now that the Japanese economy has plummeted, that fish is only one-half to one-third of its value on the export market." Meanwhile, the fish are prevalent, so it takes a dragger only a couple of hours to fill a three-hundred-pound trip limit, and the fishermen receive a fraction of the value on which they had based their proposal. "The dragger men are now campaigning for limiting the hook fisheries to a fixed quota, while the draggers would get the majority of the quota. Now the draggers' gear has been around for a long time, and they don't want to see competition coming from this less efficient gear type, because with increased abundance of fish, the less efficient gear types suddenly are profitable."

When Dan next speaks, he echoes the amazement voiced by just about everyone involved in every aspect of the fishing industry at one more change that has recently taken place. "If you had told me ten years ago that you could go out with a hook and line and catch the daily dragger limit of fish, I would say, 'No way!' But, my God, now they're doing that! And," Dan predicts, "the same thing's going to happen with codfish in ten years. Codfish are going to start to come back. The catch is going to be kept constant. And until that stock is brought back to some high level as mandated by the federal government under the Sustainable Fisheries Act, you're going to have fixed quotas.

"So you're going to have a guy go out with a rather efficient gear type—whether it be a gill net or a dragger—and load up, and probably exceed what he was allowed to catch. And you're going to have hook fishermen showing up at hearings and saying, 'Hey, wait a minute. This is a wasteful gear type, because I never would catch that much. I can catch just what I need; I'm going to use less fuel; and I'll have less impact on the bottom.' "

The economics of the scenario predicted above would dictate that the commercial fisherman with higher overhead would be put out of business by the hook and line fisheries unless, as Dan points out, "management doesn't make a decision to give him the larger share of the fish. If the managers continue to allow more participants, and if things like trip limits are kept constant, the consumer loses access to fish. So," Dan concludes, "this is a lot about economic manipulation and social engineering. It's just not about fish behavior anymore."

Both Dan's wiry eyebrows and his voice rise in unison as he prefaces his next remarks. "Take stock of this! Summer flounder is symptomatic of the future. Ten years ago, the stocks were absolutely collapsed. There was practically nothing. The dealers came to the hearings saying, 'Do something about summer flounder because it's just awful.' " The result: the Mid-Atlantic council, which regulates fluke, instituted strict state-by-state quotas for fluke or summer flounder. "Why is this symptomatic of the future?" Dan asks rhetorically. ". . . because the quotas are not going up as the fish recover. And I'd say the stock has probably tripled in size in the last five years or six years. We see that in the daily catch rates of the draggers."

Three months later, on May 26, 1999, the prescience of Dan's comments rings true at a meeting of the New England Fishery Management Council, held in Plymouth, Massachusetts, where the number of fishermen's trucks in the parking lot at the Sheraton Plymouth Inn together with the policemen stationed at the door to the Mayflower Meeting Room signals conflict. And conflict threatens to become anarchy unless something changes.

Bob MacKinnon and Kevin Shea sit in folding chairs beside other gillnetters from Scituate and nearby Green Harbor. For three months, they were prohibited from fishing. The fishing grounds have just been opened as of May 1. Scheduled to take effect on May 28 (two days from now), the catch of adult cod is to be limited to thirty pounds per boat, per day. This is less than one-quarter the weight of one cod caught by Charlie Butman in the 1970s and approximately two and a half times the average weight of fish caught in the 1990s. Gallows humor being spread around the room asks for a clarification on how the fishermen should deal with the half.

Standing at the back of the room, Rodney Avila, in a pink polo shirt, folds his arms and leans back in order to best absorb the goings-on. At the front of the room, Dr. John Witzig, director of fisheries statistics for the Northeast Fisheries Science Center (NEFSC) in Woods Hole, is presenting stock assessment figures for what is now labeled "Gulf of Maine cod." Dr. Witzig points to various graphs and charts indicating that the biomass for juvenile cod has reached a level that can no longer support harvesting. He speaks of spawning biomass, of yield-per-recruit models. He uses symbols such as F_{max} and $F_{o.1}$ to refer to what amount of fishing the species can sustain and still increase to a preordained number set by the Sustainable Fisheries Act.

As Dr. Witzig speaks numbers, the audience hears consequences. To them, the numbers translate as loss of income, inability to pay mortgages, trouble brewing on a personal level when the fishermen are prohibited from providing for their families. At the conclusion of Dr. Witzig's talk, the thirty-pound limit still hangs in the air.

Paul Cohan, fisherman and president of the Gulf of Maine Fishermen's Alliance and an eloquent and clear-headed speaker, rises and walks to the microphone. His full head of curly hair is only partly reined in by a visored cap, the only attempt to contain the appearance of directed energy he projects. First he details the many incidents of fishermen having to discard thousands of pounds of cod as dead bycatch because the species is so prevalent and has made such a dramatic comeback, thanks to the efforts of the fishermen and the efficacy of the regulations. He contrasts what the fishermen see with what Dr. Witzig is indicating on paper. He reminds the council members that if they persist in voting in favor of an emergency measure to limit the catch of cod to thirty pounds, they will completely lose the respect of the fishing community. "We can rip up citations as quick as anyone. If you vote this measure through, it will set the course for anarchy." The room explodes in cheering.

If you had to pick one word to best describe how the regulations are

destroying both the fish and the fisheries, that word would be "bycatch."
On several occasions, Paul Cohan and other fishermen have practically
begged council members, men and women in state regulatory positions,
and even the director of the National Marine Fisheries Service to at least
allow them to use the dead bycatch—specifically cod—to feed people in
soup kitchens and shelters. The mind-set prevails. Men and women paid
to produce numbers still maintain that the bycatch problem cannot exist,
that there are no cod, or no dogfish, or no flounder despite the numbers
indicating that in 1999 twice the amount of cod was discarded as landed.

Vito Calomo, executive director of the Massachusetts Fisheries Recovery Commission (later to become a council member), stands up to
speak. He deliberately is dressed in a dark suit in order to project the
same sense of authority as the statistics experts. "We are seeing more
codfish on Middle Bank than we have ever seen." He points out to the
council members that the fishermen in the room are not protesting the
measure to limit cod to thirty pounds. Instead they are protesting all the
cod that will be needlessly killed should the thirty-pound limit be implemented.

A spokesman for Bruce Tarr, the state senator from Gloucester, echoes Mr. Calomo's concerns and warns the council, "The thirty-pound
trip limit will not manage the fishery; it will terminate it."

Carl Bouchard, a fisherman from New Hampshire, moves calmly to
the microphone. He places a letter on the table before taking the seat
placed in front of the microphone. Mr. Bouchard begins to read from
the letter addressed to Joe Brancaleone from David T. Goethel, a fisherman and member of the board of directors of the New Hampshire
Commercial Fishermen's Association. The letter details Mr. Goethel's
attempts to fish in the nearest area open to New Hampshire fishermen
since May 1. It chronicles four-and-one-half-hour trips each way and
twenty-one-hour days due to the limitations posed by the short melting
time of the ice used to preserve fish and the closed areas that are mandated by the regulations. The letter relates the writer's efforts to avoid
known cod areas despite the prevalence of this species in all sizes.

> ... it became apparent that towing on top of Stellwagen Bank would gen-
> erate enormous catches of cod. However, towing in the deeper water along
> the edge of the Bank yielded a catch rate of 200 to 400 pounds of cod
> per day. Towing in this area also yielded increasing amounts of legal size
> cod with ratios approaching 30 to 40 dead fish for every live one.

Mr. Goethel then goes on to relate the story of one tow he made on
May 17 at a depth of forty fathoms. This day, while towing for dogfish,

he brought up the cod end from a vessel's fishing gear. It was filled with ten- to fifteen-pound codfish that were too numerous to be landed. Mr. Goethel slit the net and emptied the fish back into the sea. In his letter, he estimates that five to ten thousand pounds of fish swam away while five thousand sank to the bottom dead. David Goethel's steersman later confirmed that he also had seen an estimated seventeen thousand pounds of cod released to the sea when David Goethel cut the cod end of the net.

The chasm between what the fishermen are witnessing on a daily basis versus what the scientific community is presenting on paper, and the surrealistic choice of a thirty-pound trip limit for cod in the face of the numbers stated in Mr. Goethel's letter, beg for a new approach to fisheries management.

Mr. Bouchard recommends either closing the entire Gulf of Maine to the catching of cod-for *both* recreational and commercial fishermen, while subsidizing the fleet until the cod reach a level acceptable to the council—or relaxing the regulations and increasing the cod limit to five hundred pounds per trip.

Paul Vitale walks to the microphone. Justine Vitale is seven and a half months pregnant, and Paul is about to become a new father, with new responsibilities. He laments the "wasting of a beautiful resource, a resource which could be used to feed my wife and child." To audience applause he adds, "Let the previous frameworks and amendments work. If you limit the cod catch to thirty pounds, you will destroy all the benefits of Amendments 5 and 7."

Paul relinquishes the microphone to Bill Crossen, another member of the Gulf of Maine Fishermen's Alliance. Crossen questions the abilities of the crew aboard the *Albatross*,[13] the National Marine Fisheries Service vessel that provided the samples referred to by Dr. Witzig: "I have been taking codfish samples on my vessel since the early 1990s. I use a four-inch liner, and I have found an ever increasing amount of one- to two-year-old codfish each year since 1992." It is important to note that he is referring to spawning-age cod, whose numbers are shown by the scientific community to be at dangerously low levels to sustain recovery for the species. Bill Crossen culminates his comments by inviting the council to "put people on our boat to see what I am seeing. Give yourselves some credibility."

Kevin Scola, a gillnetter who fishes out of Green Harbor, just south of Scituate, jumps to his feet to speak. He does not use the microphone. He does not need to. He raises the issue of the inequities posed by permitting the charter boats to continue to land cod while the gillnetters were prohibited from fishing for three months and now are going to be limited to thirty pounds. He tells the story of being forced to keep his boat tied at the dock through February, March, and April as he watched men and women return from charter trips where they had paid $850 per day to fish. "They were unloading seventeen to twenty coolers filled with iced, filleted codfish. And those fish were coming right off the areas where I'm not allowed to fish. Aren't those dead fish just as dead as the ones I would catch?" His voice rises in frustration. ". . . and they aren't even being counted in your statistics!"

After applause from other fishermen, Kevin lowers his voice. As he addresses the council members, his voice telegraphs disgust. "I am insulted that you would even propose a thirty-pound limit for cod after what I've seen. Each Saturday and Sunday during the closures, I watched forty recreational boats whose combined catch exceeded the whole TAC target you established to enable the stocks to recover. My neighbor in a Grady-White can catch ten times what I, as a commercial fisherman, am allowed to catch. After today," he concludes, "I have lost all respect for the data of the National Marine Fisheries Service."

The tone of disdain in Kevin's voice cuts through the word "thirty" and penetrates to the front table, where council members sit silently in front of their individual microphones. At the recommendation of Chairman Brancaleone, the council agrees to break for lunch, but not before being advised to "think seriously about what we have heard here today from the fishing community."

When the council members return from lunch, Bill Amaru and Eric Anderson, the two fishermen on the council, look revitalized. For the last few weeks, they have been back on the water, doing what they love to do. And it shows. Each is tanned and vigorous. In contrast to the emotional exhaustion they exhibited at meetings in the winter and spring months, they appear focused and energized.

Eric Anderson proposes an emergency action. He asks for clarification on what action would be permitted that would take effect in the shortest period of time.

Bill Amaru adds, "We must try to give the industry what little they've asked for." He positions himself with the other fishermen in the room when he declares, "I don't agree with the science they are giving us. I have personally seen more cod in the last few years, and I have to conclude that the best available science is what I see with my own eyes." He suggests readdressing Framework 27, and allowing boats that encounter codfish in their nets to take them home, not throw them back into the sea as food for the dogfish population. He points out that the concept of a thirty-pound trip limit for cod will cause catastrophic levels of discards. The audience cheers. Bill turns to the other council members.

"The fishermen want to work with us. They are not asking for a lot." He then proposes a seven-hundred-pound trip limit for cod, with no running clock.

James O'Malley is executive director of the East Coast Fisheries Federation, a commercial fisheries organization based in Rhode Island. At the time of the Plymouth meeting, he was also a council member. He asks, "How do you deal with a recovering resource?" He likens the situation with cod to that of fluke in Vineyard Sound, and his words echo those of Dan McKiernan. "We must find a balance between accommodating the problems presented by bycatch when the regulations don't allow for the increase in numbers of fish versus the need to nurture and protect the stocks."

Patricia Kurkul, the division chief of both NOAA and the National Marine Fisheries Service for the region, by dint of her position, has the most clout in the room—and what appears to be the least empathy with the fishing community. She states, "We talked about all of this in January. There are no surprises." She asks how the council can justify allowing for additional fishing mortality when the members had agreed in January to lower the trip limit for cod to thirty pounds as part of Framework 27.

Bill Amaru responds, "I don't know who said the world is a dangerous place to observe from a desk. If it can be proven that a boat leaving a fishing dock will kill fewer fish by being allowed to land a reasonable amount of fish, then what is best for the resource is not to place unreasonable limits on the industry." He addresses his next remarks to Chairman Brancaleone. "We must get away from the level of animosity we are creating, and which is going to get worse for the Coast Guard and worse for the National Marine Fisheries Service unless we address the needs of the fishing community."

Eric Anderson turns to Patricia Kurkul as he asks, "Do we have the tools to get something done within thirty days?"

In response, she gives a synopsis of the legal requirements for crafting a framework, amendment, or emergency action, then ends with the words ". . . too complicated to give a definitive answer."

Undeterred, Eric Anderson proposes a motion to increase the daily trip limit for cod to seven hundred pounds, with no running clock.

Eric Smith, the assistant director of the Marine Fisheries Division for Connecticut, says he cannot support the proposed seven-hundred-pound catch limit. He points out that Framework 27 already allows for a two-hundred-pound catch limit.

Jim Kendall, a council member and lobbyist representing the New Bedford Seafood Coalition, an association of wholesalers, rolls up his shirtsleeves as he begins to speak. He likens the council process to a "runaway train with no brakes. We don't even have the ability to protect the resource," he responds to Patricia Kurkul's additional comments on the legal requirements of responding to the fishermen's requests. "We've got problems beyond codfish. I honestly don't see how we can vote to support killing the fish [through bycatch discards]. If fishermen get used to killing fish just to meet a thirty-pound limit, we are heading in a dangerous direction," he warns. He voices his support for the seven-hundred-pound limit and the existing allowance of eighty-eight days at sea.

Bill Amaru assures the council members, "If allowed, the industry will come in with only seven hundred pounds of cod. That amount will cover expenses and allow fishermen to make a living." Then he asks a question no one on the council wants to address. "Why does the Sustainable Fisheries Act allow such an unreasonably few years to rebuild the stocks?"

Two fishermen jump up at opposite sides of the room. "Let's answer that one, Joe," one yells.

"Show me why the fish is worth more than the fisherman," shouts the second man.

Paul Cohan rises from his chair and tries to calm the surge of voices erupting from the audience. He is an imposing figure, whose muscular frame and quiet authority command respect. He raises both arms. "Quiet, quiet," he says in a soothing voice. When the air is silent and the men have sat down, he looks over the crowd before speaking. "Let these people at the table make a decision. They're trying to work on our behalf. We can talk later."

He returns to his folding chair as Bill Amaru picks up on the moment when it is possible to speak directly to the fishermen. "Do you know the tightrope the council is working under?" He speaks fisherman to fisherman. "If this proposal is adopted, and we don't know whether or not we have the power to get it approved, you can't direct on cod. You must still target other species."

The meeting continues in a room where reality is only beginning to have some dominion. As the meeting comes to an end, the number "seven hundred" appears to be edging out the number "thirty." When the fishermen return to their homes, they find a letter in the mail informing them:

> . . . the Gulf of Maine (GOM) cod landing limit for vessels fishing under
> a multispecies day-at-sea (DAS) permit, and not fishing in the cod exemp-

tion program*, is reduced from 200 lb/DAS to *30 lb/DAS*, or any part of a DAS.

The asterisk refers to latitude and longitude points where exempt vessels are allowed to fish. Basically, the area stretches from Provincetown south along the outside of Cape Cod. The exempted areas do not include the areas where Kevin Scola, Kevin Shea, or Paul Vitale fish. The notice was in the mail as the meeting progressed.

As of July, nothing had changed. Bob MacKinnon put his boat up for sale. In January he began driving a limousine to earn enough money to put food on the table for his family while allowing him the time to attend meetings up and down the coast. Kevin Shea, while fishing for dogfish, is finding upwards of 1,500 pounds of mature cod in his nets. When he releases them, he hopes they are not food for the dogfish. The Gloucester draggers are experiencing the same abundance of cod, dead on deck, and equally dead when they are thrown back into the water. Fishermen in both ports are using the terms "sickening" and "just a shame" when referring to having to kill so many fish without being allowed to sell them.

In Gloucester, Paul Vitale and his father prefer to leave the F/V *Angela and Rose* tied at the pier instead of being a part of what they consider to be a travesty that is ruining the resource while wiping out the fisherman's ability to earn a living. The secretary of commerce is reported to be waiting for a recommendation from the National Marine Fisheries Service before deciding between "seven hundred" and "thirty."

Teri Frady, in the public relations department of the National Marine Fisheries Service, is quoted in an interview as saying, "We're considering the request." No urgency when she collects her paycheck. In the same interview, she allows that the Fisheries Service is basing their estimates of cod stocks on 1997 (two-year-old) statistics. "It's the overall mortality of the cod that's the greatest concern," Frady states, with seemingly little sense of the disconnect that sentence presents.[14]

"Mortality" is a pivotal word in the context of fisheries regulation. And it speaks volumes depending on who uses it and in what context. The *Review of Northeast Fishery Stock Assessments* issued by the National Research Council uses the term "fishing mortality" to refer to fish caught by commercial fishermen. Fish caught for recreational purposes, though equally dead, are not counted.[15] Cod brought to shore alive by Cape Cod hook fishermen are considered as part of the landings, and included in the numbers used to determine "overall mortality." To a fisherman, the only reason to kill a fish is to provide income. To kill a fish for the sake of killing a fish is unethical, and inherently stupid. To kill an endangered species, then throw it away, is insanity.

At a fisheries trade show hosted in Providence, Rhode Island, seventeen months after the May 1999 council meeting, the executive director of the New England Fishery Management Council together with Dr. Steven Murawski from the Northeast Fisheries Science Center at Woods Hole released the latest numbers for what they refer to as VPA (virtual population assessment) for nineteen species monitored. When asked about the disparity between what the fishermen were seeing and what the assessment showed for Gulf of Maine cod, Thomas Hill, the new chairman for the New England Fishery Management Council, answered, "The perception of cod biomass is distorted because cod used to cover a larger area." Chairman Hill expressed his belief that the area where cod live has now shrunk to a small area, a phenomenon he likened to the situation in Newfoundland before the collapse of the Canadian cod fisheries. Dr. Murawski, following the same tack, suggested that the fishermen's sightings might be "parochial," and not indicative of the larger picture. Basically, Dr. Murawski and Mr. Hill were telling the fishermen that if they saw a lot of cod or caught a lot of cod as bycatch in any one area such as the Gulf of Maine, it really meant that there were fewer cod overall than if the fishermen had neither seen nor caught cod. Most fishermen are too practical to put much stock in the "emperor's new clothes" explanation if a naked man walks down the street.

The thirty-pound limit on cod remained in effect through August 2, 1999. Then it was adjusted to one hundred pounds per day until January 5, 2000, when it was increased to four hundred pounds per day. As of May 1, 2002, the landings for cod and other fish species were regulated first one way and then another by U.S. district court Judge Kessler. In her mediated settlement agreement, the judge set a Gulf of Maine cod limit of five hundred pounds per day beginning August 1, 2002.

On June 2, 2001, the *New York Times* ran an article titled "Maine and the Lobster Catch." The article reports that Maine lobstermen harvested 56.7 million pounds of lobsters in the year 2000. That number is three times the lobster catch reported for the mid-1980s. The author attributes the change to "sound conservation of a limited resource."[16] Could it also be that lobsters benefit from all the dead cod lying on the ocean floor as a result of regulations that limited the cod catch to thirty pounds? And is it "sound conservation of a limited resource" to require the fisherman to kill cod and donate them as food for the lobsters instead of landing them and earning a decent living? Is it ethical to feed a protein source to lobsters, whose price is off-limits to many, instead of allowing it to be fed to those who cannot afford lobster?

6

SAVING THE FISH, SAVING THE FISHERMAN

Scientific research has added much to the knowledge of the fisheries, yet where the mackerel come from in the spring, where they go late in the fall and spend the winter, why they are found in great abundance off the New England Coast for a series of years, and perhaps the next year in the Gulf of St. Lawrence, remains as much mystery and matter of theory [today] as one hundred years ago.

—W. A. Wilcox, *The Fishing Industry*, 1887

High on a bluff facing northeast, with a view the length and breadth of Cape Cod Bay, sits a weathered clapboard house, surrounded by beach plum, honeysuckle, and shadbushes. In the fall, the prevailing northwest winds guide young ovenbirds, magnolia warblers, hummingbirds, and other migratory birds to the berries of these bushes, which the birds eat before continuing on down the coast.

For a period of up to two weeks, the ovenbirds will eat during the day in preparation for a night flight, when the air is cooler and predators are likely to be asleep. Many of these birds are only two to three months old and will be migrating for the first time, without the guidance or direction of an adult. The forces that guide them are still not totally understood.

The house on the bluff was formerly the summer home to a pair of bird banders. Now, thanks to their generosity, it is home for the Manomet Center for Conservation Sciences. Next door, in a newer building, Chris Glass occupies a small office on the second floor, with a window, one wall of bookcases bulging with scientific reports, and another wall supporting a work surface for his computer.

In Scotland, Chris trained as a marine biologist with a particular interest in animal behavior. At Manomet, he is the senior fisheries scientist and director of the Marine Conservation Division. He studies the natural behavior of the various species of groundfish harvested by Paul Vitale, Kevin Shea, and Tony Lemmi.

For fourteen years before he came to Manomet, Chris worked for the Agriculture, Environment, and Fisheries Department, a large government laboratory in Scotland. There as here, he researches methods for reducing bycatch. When he speaks, a Scotsman's voice mingles with a scientist's approach. "By studying the natural behavior patterns of the target species, we hope to see if there is any way we can use those natural behavior patterns to expel some species while keeping other species in the net."

One way that Chris "observes" fish behavior is to attach a moving video camera to a dragger's net in order to record how fish behave when near a trawl net. By experimenting with video cameras, Chris has learned that fish will tend to face the net as it approaches them. Then, as the sides of the net come alongside, most fish will turn and swim with the same speed and in the same direction as the net. When they become exhausted, they will suddenly turn and face the back of the net to be swept into the cod end, the part of a trawl net that traps the fish.

"In Aberdeen, in Scotland, we devised a means to sit on a fishing boat towing a net, fly the camera around the net underwater, and go inside and outside the net to actually look at the reactions of the fish in their habitat."

The video camera allows Chris and other scientists to see not only general patterns of fish behavior around a net, but also behavior specific to particular species. Haddock will almost always rise several feet as they turn; flatfish and cod will not rise but rather will enter the net at a lower level, leading Chris to conclude, "Such consistent differences in behavior can be exploited by designing nets in which different species can be shunted into separate cod ends, or unwanted species allowed to escape."

Linda Leddy, president of the Manomet Center for Conservation Sciences, will consider the Manomet Bycatch Reduction Project a success "if resulting gear changes for one fishery reduce bycatch by at least 40 percent while maintaining at least 90 percent of the marketable catch.

We hope another, less tangible, marker of our success will be increased cooperation among diverse interest groups—demonstrating again the importance of collaboration in finding answers to complex environmental questions."[1]

Her words are a welcome departure from the simplistic assumption that if there are too few fish, there must be too many boats. Unlike the science based on fish counts, Chris and Steve Kennelly, an Australian biologist, are asking why. When Steve arrived at the Manomet Center for Conservation Sciences, he first looked at four years of data collected in New England by the National Marine Fisheries Service. He then assessed the catch rates and the bycatch rates from a sampling of approximately ten thousand trawls. His findings: 47 percent of the whole New England catch was discarded.

"No fisherman likes to throw fish over the side," Chris says, "either because of regulations or because there's no market for them."

As coinvestigator together with Arne Carr and others at the Massachusetts Division of Marine Fisheries, Chris is conducting experiments with a net referred to as a "trouser trawl," named for its two openings narrowing into two distinct "legs" and feeding into two separate cod ends. Findings from the video camera show that different species react differently to a standard net. Thus Chris works with fishermen in varying the stimuli in each of the two legs to see if potential bycatch (the undersize cod or yellowtail flounder) can be induced to swim away from the net and back to sea. Different species tend to swim at different levels. Taking advantage of that information, the trouser trawl, with the addition of a separating panel, can separate haddock into one cod end and still permit the cod or other nontargeted species to swim into the other cod end and, if desired, back to sea. The aim is to reduce bycatch through use of selective gear.

Chris, Steve, and other scientists used to collect data using the alternate tow method, where trawling takes place with one net, then later with a net of a different-size mesh. The results of the two trawls were then compared. The inherent weakness in that method is that the area, and thus the number of fish being sampled, could be different with each tow. With the trouser trawl, the mesh size or configuration of one side can be different from the mesh size or configuration of the other leg, but both are pulled through the water at the same time and in the same general area. Thus, the selectivity of two different cod ends can be tested. By using one sample, the experiment overcomes the previous criticism, and provides a direct comparison of the selective efficiency of the two configurations, with the added advantage of requiring only one tow.

Frank Mirarchi has been one of the New England fishermen to ex-

188 | *Vanishing Species*

periment with the trouser trawl and its successor, the covered cod end, seen on the stern of the F/V *Christopher Andrew*. Frank trawls Middle Bank, beside Kevin, Joey, and Paul fishing on the F/V *Endeavor*. On the *Christopher Andrew*, Chris has wrapped one side of the trouser trawl with a dark canvas to simulate the inside of a large fish's open mouth in order to determine if that scares the small flounder from entering the net. By experimenting with different types and sizes of nets, Chris hopes he can eventually produce a means for fishermen like Kevin, Joey, and Paul to fish for regulation-size flounder while not disturbing the small spawning flounders.

When Chris mentions Frank, respect is in his voice. "Frank is a wonderful voice for the industry. He knows there are problems in the fishery, and he knows something can be done about it. He feels passionately about his work, that it's not all gloom and doom. His goal is to preserve a fishery for his son and his grandchildren to continue working in the future. He knows that it's in his blood and in his children's blood. Frank wants the stocks to be there for the future. And that's what we're all trying to do."

Instead of the computer-modeling techniques employed by the government scientists involved in fisheries management studies, the Manomet program is based on working with commercial fishermen on commercial fishing boats using some experimental fishing gear, collecting and measuring samples brought up in the gear, and then analyzing that data. Chris says, "If we are going to be successful, we have to have the fishermen involved in the research with us right from the start." To that end, Manomet has put together a stakeholders' council composed of members of the industry with a stake in the sustainability of the fisheries. One member of this committee is Frank Mirarchi. Another is Bill Amaru.

"Many fishermen are less able or less willing than Frank and Bill to put something back into the industry," Chris points out. "With people like the two of them around, the outcome is good because they go to all the meetings, they keep abreast of the scientific findings, and they really believe something can be done."

Not all scientists, environmentalists, and regulators believe that the answer lies in closing areas to fishing, such as the closures taking place on Middle Bank (also known as Stellwagen Bank). An article in the magazine of the Manomet Center for Conservation Sciences quotes Steve Kennelly: "The problem with that is while it reduces the discards and bycatch to zero in those areas, it also stops any fishing going on, thus depriving fishermen of their livelihood. Most of the successful stories in bycatch reduction around the world have occurred by coming up with more selective gear designs."[2]

Arnold (Arne) Carr is a senior marine fisheries biologist with the Massachusetts Division of Marine Fisheries, where he is project leader of the Conservation Engineering Program. Arne's work was originally conceived as a means to boost the efficiency of marine fishing in the Northeast. That was in the early 1980s, in the days when government was trying to promote the harvesting of its marine resources. Arne admits to being too successful in his efforts. "The efficiency got too efficient." In the past six to seven years, Arne's work has shifted from finding means to exploit the resource to finding ways to preserve the resource.

The video work Chris performs with the trouser-trawl experiment is done using cameras provided by Arne's group. The experiment is a collaborative effort between Chris's group at the Manomet Center for Conservation Sciences and Arne's group at the Massachusetts Division of Marine Fisheries. Arne combines his work as a marine biologist with his role as partner in American Underwater Search and Survey Ltd., a company specializing in high-resolution bottom surveys. Two of his company's most highly publicized contracts were for the search and recovery work for TWA flight 800 and for a *NOVA* program in search of the Loch Ness "monster." Arne grew up on Martha's Vineyard, and began scuba diving in the Sounds of Martha's Vineyard and Nantucket from the time he was twelve. A fascination with underwater equipment has guided his work since the days of his boyhood scuba diving.

Arne divides into three groups the equipment used in his underwater survey work. The first is your basic camcorder attached to four lines, spread-eagle, and clipped to the net at an angle where it will provide the desired footage, yet still be out of harm's way. The basic system, with housing to protect it from water leakage, costs approximately two thousand dollars (one thousand for the camcorder and one thousand for housing). A digital hookup brings the cost closer to five thousand dollars. This system is especially useful in the often-murky inshore waters of the Northeast. Use of the underwater camcorder began in the late 1980s and is employed today by both scientists and fishermen. Frank Avila, a New Bedford fisherman and Rodney's first cousin, uses it to check on the efficiency of his gear. It is light, portable, and relatively inexpensive, but can pick up only what swims across the lens.

The second of Arne's equipment groups consists of a hardwired camera connected by cable to a monitor in the vessel's wheelhouse. It sells for approximately ten thousand dollars. Two thousand to five thousand dollars extra provides a tilt/swivel mechanism similar to that used in surveillance and high-security operations. This system works better than the camcorder in deeper water and can be upgraded to provide clearer images at greater depths, but still has a range limited to the scope of its swivel/tilt mechanism and underwater visibility. Often the visibility range is reduced by fine sediment held in suspension after a storm or other disruption to the ocean bottom.

Arne's third group, the Cadillac of the underwater equipment available today, is what Chris used in Scotland. It consists of a hardwired robotic platform towing a high-resolution underwater camera. The camera is connected by cable to a video monitor in the wheelhouse. Rotating cylinders permit the camera to turn and "fly around the net," as Chris describes it. This system allows a marine biologist to observe minute changes in fish behavior as a school of fish swims in, out, or around a net. Its cost is in the range of $200,000. The knowledge and understanding it provides of fish behavior is invaluable, and has never before been available, except in the form of assumptions. Arne wishes it were available here.

Les Watling, Elliott Norse, and Page Valentine are three scientists actively working to prohibit use of the so-called rock hopper gear used by some draggers to comb the bottom for fish.

Watling and Norse are both Pew fellows, each funded by three-year grants of $150,000. Elliott Norse, Ph.D., is president of the Marine Conservation Biology Institute, which he founded in 1996. Les Watling, Ph.D., is a professor of oceanography at the University of Maine. He first gained public attention when he lowered himself and an underwater camera to the seabed in the Gulf of Maine, where he photographed portions of the bottom before and after trawling. Similar underwater scenes from a video made by Paul Parker and the Cape Cod Commercial Hook Fishermen's Association show a sandy sea bottom, swept clean of sea urchins, sand dollars, starfish, and marine flora after a commercial scallop dragger has fished over the area. Papers and talks given by these four scientists have received significant media coverage not because a large market exists for starfish, but because of the assumption that these damaged areas are the spawning areas of many of the groundfish whose species are dwindling.

Chris has also looked at what he refers to as "this bottom impact issue." From the many scientific meetings he has attended on the subject, together with information shared by some of his colleagues in Aberdeen, Chris has determined that "the scientific community really isn't certain at the moment if there is a cause and effect here." He refers to an article by a friend and colleague, Michael J. Kaiser, who states, "Bottom fishing in the world's oceans has been compared to clear-felling of forest habitats. This implies that fishermen systematically sweep entire areas of the seabed in order to maximize their catch. If this were true, fishermen would have become extinct years ago." Dr. Kaiser predicates his thinking on the fact that young sole and plaice have increased in numbers in the North Sea since the 1960s. He points out that these increases in the fish population "have been attributed to an increased food supply for these flatfish, possibly associated with a change in the fauna due to trawling."[3]

"Mike's work involves a fairly complex population argument," Chris explains. "If you have a standard population that's unfished, you've got a number of large fish, a number of small fish, and most of the population is in the middle. As we know, the big fish eat the little fish. So you get better recruitment [growth from birth to a stage where capture is possible] overall if you remove all the big fish and you leave all the fresh spawners. If you can keep a population right on that first peak, the spawning mass is improved by culling the top. But also, by capturing other things and removing predators out of the area, you permit the population to expand and spread."

To the marine biology community, this is a fairly well-known effect of fisheries, and it can often lead to changes in population distribution resulting in a larger biomass. Given this well-understood phenomenon, Chris believes that Dr. Kaiser's paper, in response to the position taken by Les Watling, is "very well written, very balanced, asking people to consider all of the potential effects."

Patty Lemmi in Provincetown has trouble accepting the fragmentation of the industry resulting from the hook fishermen's contention that the draggers are destroying the habitat. "In my heart of hearts," she says, "I believe that if every boat hook-fished, from the ninety-foot dragger to a boat the size of the *Patricia Ann II*, there'd be enough fish to walk on. But on the other hand, I feel that with the existing regulations, if they're given a chance, the fish will come back." From her position, Patty believes that the boats of 120 feet or more in length are the ones that should be most strongly regulated in order to rebuild the resource. "Those boats need a thirty-thousand-pound day to make a living. I could live about eight months off that. I do feel the bigger boats damage the bottom, but I don't feel the owner of a small dragger with a family to support should be prohibited from earning a living."

Patty receives her information from friends who dive for lobsters, and who report to her that a dragger will go through an area where they have been diving for months, and the next day they see the same area as ". . . just plowed. Everything that was growing and living is gone." Patty points out that the Cape Cod Commercial Hook Fishermen's Association has never said, " 'Don't fish.' It was more 'Stay off fragile areas. Don't take spawning fish.' " Her voice rises in contained frustration as she adds, "They [draggers] will take the whole school."

"I think it depends a lot on where you are coming from," Chris responds. "Whether you want to believe it's bad or you want to believe it's not bad. What I think we have to do is to shift the discussion to the middle, where we really get all the information we can and try to be balanced about it."

In the United States, that balance is perhaps more difficult to achieve because of three factors: the power of the press, the fear of litigation, and the importance placed on short-term economic policies. Each month, the National Marine Fisheries Service sends out press releases to the news media defending its need to protect the fish population and stressing the dramatic declines in the biomass of various species. The newspapers and magazines then print articles decrying the extremes of the situation.

The position taken by the National Marine Fisheries Service has been bolstered by the many lawsuits brought against it by various environmental groups. The economics include the fact that those same environmental organizations raise money by showing some accomplishments in their efforts to protect the fish populations for future generations. The simplest explanation for the decline in fish stocks is to blame the fishing community. And so, to the public reading the daily newspaper, the fisherman becomes the sole cause of the problem.

"From the engineering view of a biologist and a fisheries person who has spent a number of years trying to develop new fishing gear and techniques," Chris says, "I think we can do a lot in developing new gear to help reduce the impact. But it's not helped by the debate as it stands at the moment because that debate moved away from considering whether we can improve what we've got to talking about whether we should have it at all." Chris concludes, "And that seems to me to be the wrong approach right now.

"At Manomet, we are trying to involve the industry in being part of the solution. They are certainly the people who are aware of where the fish are. And the fish are there. By bringing the industry and everyone else along with us, we are more likely to add to the implementation of the results of our research, because everybody will have been involved in the development of it."

Rodney Avila agrees. "I believe it's time the whole industry unites and comes together, and figures out what we have to do that's best. Not what's best for ourselves, but what's best for the industry. What we need is a stable industry, with stable regulations, and we do need a rebuildable resource out there. We need to catch fish. We need to be fishing. But we don't need to destroy the resource to do it."

Over the last twenty years, both horsepower and vessel size have increased. Increased horsepower allows a fishing vessel to fish harder bottoms and around wrecks where the nets would previously have hung up the boat. Now, if a net is caught, the engine is strong enough to pull the boat off. A good twine man can be repairing the net while a second or third net permits the vessel to continue fishing.

Chris is convinced that "if you spoke to any fisherman, he would tell you that if he could stop fishing for two years and let stocks get to a certain level, then go back with sensible fishing practices, everything would be fine." But he agrees that the problem arises in trying to find a way to allow the fisherman to fish "over that painful period required to get enough large fish to support the fisheries. What we're trying to do is get to that point and still allow fishermen to operate in the interim."

As of August of 2002, regulations for commercial fishermen limit the cod catch to five hundred pounds per commercial fishing trip. This is better than thirty pounds, but by now everyone agrees that cod stocks have risen dramatically. Thanks to federal regulations, bycatch has risen at an even more dramatic rate. By tightening the restrictions on cod landings, the regulations have forced the fishermen to throw more and more dead cod to the lobsters. But no one in a regulatory position appears to have learned anything from the disasters of the past six years. Instead, a federal judge ruled for a suit brought by the Conservation Law Foundation, based on stock assessments taken two years prior to the ruling. As a result of the ruling, the National Marine Fisheries Service has been given a green light to strangle the fisheries.

The product brought ashore is only a small portion of the economic picture. To eliminate the fisherman is also to remove all the businesses servicing the fishing industry such as boatbuilders, rigging companies, ice companies like Gloucester's Cape Pond Ice, and ship chandleries like the New Bedford Ship Supply Company.

Below the cliff supporting the buildings of the Manomet Center for Conservation Sciences, a colony numbering close to five hundred seals occupies the rocks and the tidal pools beside the beach. As they jockey for mating positions and frolic in the sea, their barks ricochet up the cliff. They have no natural predators and, unless something changes, little competition for the fish they consume.

A scientific study analyzing the stomach content of seals indicates that 13 percent of their diet is Atlantic cod. Most of the cod eaten by the seals sampled were smaller than the minimum acceptable commercial size, and most had just reached spawning age.[4]

In the year 2002, local fishermen, who once competed for the cod in Cape Cod Bay, have been removed from the equation. A significant experiment that might eliminate not just fishing but fishing communities is being conducted to control nature's natural balance. It is too early to measure the consequences, and it seems clear that the men and women responsible for laying down the ground rules for the experiment—and also supplying the working capital to conduct the experiment—may not fully understand its ramifications.

Each man or woman involved in trying to preserve fish stocks for future generations is working for the perceived good of a larger cause. The environmentalists believe in saving the environment. The fisherman believes in saving the fish, thus enabling his children to maintain his way of life. The managers believe in the efficacy of the regulations. The issue has become so complex, and so many people involved have a financial stake in one small aspect, that the battle is being lost to special interests.

Frank Mirarchi, in Scituate, tries to make sense of the whole situation. He first says there are still too many boats. Then he qualifies his remark. "Most people left in the business are there because they want to be, not because they have to be." He slowly draws the fingers of his left hand through his hair as he pauses to think about what he has just said. "And I don't know what you do about that. I mean, it seems heartless to say we should draw straws and the short third are out." Frank and every other person knowledgeable about fisheries regulations agree that if the terms for rebuilding the stocks were extended beyond 2009, the fishermen could continue to fish and make a decent living while the biomass was being rebuilt.

He allows that another year like 1999, 2000, and 2001 is going to put a lot of fishermen out of business. "I can't recall the exact numbers," he says, "but I believe that in the fifteen months going from February first, 2000, through May first the following year, we have had seven months of closures. We're closed down almost fifty percent of the time. People can't withstand that for very long. Plus we've had the thirty-pound limit on codfish, and who knows what restrictions we're about to see for yellowtail, plaice, and hake?"

As Frank speaks, dogfish account for 50 percent of the fish being landed in Scituate, and the need to regulate dogfish is on the agenda at most meetings of the New England Fishery Management Council. Frank echoes Paul Vitale's comments in Gloucester. "I mean, you barely get back on your feet from one management action when the next one hits you. People just can't continue to bounce back for much longer."

The groundfish closure is scheduled to end on May 1, after the peak season for catching groundfish. The season for dogfish opens May 30. If the grounds for dogfish are closed, as anticipated, it will not pay to put fuel in the tank of a fishing vessel. In Scituate, few boats are being maintained properly. Bare hulls are visible through the scraped paint. None of the wooden boats have been hauled all year. Frank asks the rhetorical question: "How many years can you go without hauling and painting a wooden boat before it's no good?" He answers, "Not many. A couple of years and they're all done for." He speaks of one of the Scituate gillnetters with three small children. "There is no way that man can provide for a family with a business that used to run twelve months a year. Now it runs eight months a year. He might be allowed to land a hundred pounds of cod, might be allowed to land thirty pounds of cod, might be able to land dogfish, might not be able to land dogs. What does he tell his wife at the end of the week when the paycheck is twenty-nine dollars and ninety-five cents for the whole week?" Frank shakes his head and raises his eyebrows. "She naturally says 'Get a job, you idiot, before we all end up living in the street.' And rightly so," Frank adds. "You need some family stability. You can't just go on saying, 'Well, I'm a fisherman and I'm just going to tough this out. So what if we're living in a tent?' Not many people can do that."

Conversely, those who are profiting from efforts to shut down the New England fishing communities are not people who are "living in tents." The spiny dogfish is the most recent example of how money is raised at the fisherman's expense in order to support the men and women working in some areas of marine conservation. A full-page advertisement appearing in the Sunday *New York Times Magazine* solicits interest and, more subtly, contributions to continue efforts to prohibit commercial fishing for shark—including the spiny dogfish.[5] According to *Fishes of the Gulf of Maine* (the book cited by the National Marine Fisheries Service as the source for cod migratory routes), "In the Gulf of Maine, large sharks and the spiny dogfish are the worst enemy of the adult cod."[6] Quite obviously, any effort to rebuild groundfish stocks benefits from a winnowing of the predators of the young fish whose stocks are in danger. Yet, the advertisement prefers to ignore that aspect of conservation. By the year 2000, a federal ruling prohibited local fishermen from catching dogfish in Massachusetts Bay and the Gulf of Maine.

Frank allows that unless he had been able to diversify and use the *Christopher Andrew* for environmental research in the last few years, he would no longer be in business. In 1999, 50 percent of his income and his son Christopher's income came from research, the other half from fishing. Since then, the research portion of his income has increased; the fishing portion has decreased. Frank points out the importance of a strong economy. "If Legal Sea Foods couldn't charge twenty-one dollars for a fish dinner, we wouldn't be selling fish off the boat for a dollar fifty a pound. We'd be selling fish for fifty cents.

"The government has grossly mismanaged the fisheries," Frank says in accord with the rest of the fishing community. "They're like every other government agency. They've got tunnel vision. They're given a mission, and they just charge ahead with the full might and authority of a government agency to do what they think is the appropriate way to discharge their mission. And if they trample a lot of people in the mud and dust in the process, they're not too concerned about it."

On September 3, 1999, a much-publicized conference was hosted by the New England Aquarium. At the conference, Vice President Al Gore announced a $5 million federal disaster-relief program promising to pay $1,500 to fishermen such as Kevin Shea and Bob MacKinnon for each day their fishing grounds were closed by regulators between February and May. "For too long, we acted as if the ocean's resources were infinite, and we must help those who are now paying the price," he announced in a statement prepared by his staff in advance of the meeting. One unspoken flaw in the Gore Plan: the vice president had no new money to give. This was the same money that had been promised in February by Senators Kerry and Kennedy. And no fisherman had yet seen a dime of it.

To add further insult and additional damage to the fishermen's image, advance publicity heralding the vice president's appearance indicated to the public that its tax dollars were being spent to compensate fishermen who were somehow responsible for damaging the environment. No fishermen, save Bill Amaru and Eric Anderson, were allowed to attend the conference. And those two fishermen were there in the role of council members—not as fishermen.

That day, Tony Lemmi was fishing off Provincetown when he heard the "Gore Plan" for the fisheries announced on his radio. Until he spoke to Patty, he believed along with many other fishermen that an additional five million dollars was being allocated to help the fishing community.

"It's a cruel joke!" Patty says angrily. "I went all winter to the original tristate meetings in New Hampshire." It was a long ride, and the fishermen all worked on a plan with representatives from the National Marine Fisheries Service. "At the end, when the plan was finalized, the representatives from the Fisheries Service who had sat there for seven meetings announced that *they*," she emphasizes, "had the money and weren't allowed to distribute it according to the plan. It was the most frustrating thing!"

To Patty's knowledge, the money earmarked as disaster relief for the February, March, and April 1999 closures was disbursed in April to the National Marine Fisheries Service, where it remains. No one appears to know if it earns interest or, if it does, what is happening to that interest. "You're talking about guys who couldn't pay their mortgages, and our government gives the National Marine Fisheries Service the money." The disgust in Patty's voice is palpable. "It's like giving the fox the key, then saying, 'Here's the hen house,'" she mimics. "'You hold the key for us.'"

One thing for sure, the National Marine Fisheries Service is not parting with the money easily or with haste. By the first week of the year 2000, almost a year from when Kevin, Paul, Joey, and Bob MacKinnon were first prohibited from fishing, none of them had received any compensation, nor had they been recruited for research. Bob, along with 107 other vessel owners in Massachusetts, received a notice in October stating he would receive $1,500 per day for twenty-one days. He is to divide the money with his crew members.

Kevin, Paul, Joey, and *Endeavor* are not so fortunate, though they were equally impacted by the February, March, and April closures. A technicality rules. Prior to the closures, Kevin listed the areas he fished in terms of the blocks or quadrants established by the National Marine Fisheries Service to indicate which areas were closed, which open, and which were regulated for the catch of a particular amount for a particular species. The Fisheries Service accepted Kevin's log each trip he fished. Now, it maintains it will compensate only those fishermen who listed the area where they fished on the basis of latitude and longitude rather than block or quadrant numbers. "Personally, I doubt Kevin will see a penny of the money due him," Bob speculates, "even though two and a half million dollars is still in the hands of NMFS, and no one has any idea of what they are doing with it."

Rodney Avila, who was not effected by the closures, takes a sanguine approach: "The National Marine Fisheries Service has so much on their plate, and it's so overwhelming, that they can't concentrate on any issue, 'cause they're getting hit by environmentalists, they're getting hit by fishermen, they're getting hit by politicians."

Rodney's words might be the only sensible way to explain the events of a meeting of the groundfish committee of the New England Fishery Management Council held on November 1, 1999, at a site serving to reinforce the surrealism of the proceedings. The Sheraton Ferncroft Resort is located in the midst of five hundred acres of lawn and woods in Danvers, Massachusetts, halfway between the ports of Portsmouth, New Hampshire, and Boston, Massachusetts, but nowhere near the water. Its facilities include an eighteen-hole golf course designed by Robert Trent Jones, an indoor pool, outdoor pool, and spa. The interior is twenty-first-century medieval. The effect is baronial kitsch. Ancestral portraits of men and women in period costume line the paneled walls across from a fireplace where heraldic symbols have been cast into a stone surround.

On the lower level, inside a three-story windowless meeting room, Steve Correia, chairman of the New England Fishery Management Council's multispecies monitoring committee, is presenting view graphs accompanied by the arcane jargon used in such meetings. B_{msy} (representing the biomass that produces maximum sustainable yield or MSY), F_{msmc}, $F_{o.1}$, and F_{max} are a few of the symbols that appear in the scientific modeling Mr. Correia and other scientists have used in preparing the accompanying report on stock assessment and fishery evaluation. The questions posed by Paul Cohan, Carl Bouchard, and other fishermen in the audience indicate that the fishermen have not only learned to decipher this language, but have become experts at reading between the lines.

The purpose of the meeting is to review the stock assessment results presented by Steve Correia to determine the regulations that will comprise Framework 33 for the 2000 fishing year.

Prior to this meeting, Paul Howard, a retired Coast Guard commander and now executive director of the New England Fishery Management Council, put out a request to the fishing community for proposals relevant to the crafting of Framework 33. Five proposals were submitted. Of those five, all but one were from regular players who have a representative at each of the council meetings. The fifth was from Jimmy Bramante. And it is clear that neither the chairman of the groundfish committee nor anyone else seated at the table reserved for the committee members knows what to do with a Boston fisherman. It may be safe to say that the whole fishing effort out of Boston is no longer registering in the consciousness of the decision makers at the New England Fishery Management Council. It may also be safe to say that the few boats and boat owners left in Boston are not unhappy with this situation.

The irony that New England's largest deepwater port, the site of what once defined both commerce and personal wealth in New England, is being regulated by a local council that today relegates it to a position lower than that of a bit player makes the strong statement that a lot has been and is being lost under the present system. No other family fishing commercially in New England waters owns and operates an industry with greater vertical capabilities than does the Bramante family. Together the family owns boats that catch groundfish; it owns a company that processes, distributes, packs, and ships groundfish; and it owns a restaurant that prepares and serves groundfish. In addition, Bernie and

Danny are the auctioneers at what is left of the Boston Fish Pier auction. If the family businesses were in any industry other than fishing, they might be receiving incentives from the Department of Commerce. Instead, an arm of the Department of Commerce is placing severe regulations on them to curb their business.

As Jimmy Bramante points out, "We [the New England fishing industry] generate more revenues than either the Patriots or the Red Sox, and we've never asked for anything in return."

Jimmy Bramante was a member of the council for one year in the 1980s, but he found it impossible to attend the various meetings and support his family in a responsible manner while still being fair to the council. In his proposal, Jimmy points out that under the present regulations, a split-permit vessel (a charter boat, scalloper with a multispecies license, or amateur recreational boat) is allowed the same eighty-eight days of fishing for groundfish as is a commercial boat with only a multispecies groundfish license.

When Jonathan Mayhew, Jim Morgan, and Tom Phaneuf in Menemsha describe the situation with fluke in Vineyard Sound, what they say echoes the concerns Jimmy Bramante has about groundfish in the Gulf of Maine. Jimmy maintains that more boats are allowed to fish for groundfish than fished for groundfish before the boat buyout program went into effect. He describes commercial vessels with split-permit licenses that fish the days they are allowed to fish in their regions, normally south of New England, then head north to New England waters to fish an additional eighty-eight days during the summer months when fluke come inshore and when the F/V *Unicorn*, the F/V *Captain Mano*, and the F/V *Mattia-C* are required to be tied at the dock. To many, it is yet another case of the present regulations squandering instead of conserving the fish stocks.

In his letter, Jimmy requests that the qualification criteria be changed to permit fewer boats to fish for groundfish, and to thus allow those with commercial groundfish licenses to remain in business. This category would include just about all of the boats presently docked at the Boston Fish Pier. Jimmy also suggests that "effective conservation objectives" could be met while conserving a community of fishermen in New England if a ten-year goal was set starting in the year 2000 as opposed to the shorter time frame required by the Sustainable Fisheries Act.

After summarizing the contents of Jimmy's letter, council member Philip Haring tells the other council members that he telephoned "this gentleman and recommended to him that his proposal was more appropriate to Amendment 13." Issue dismissed.

A letter from Raymond J. Brown, chief law enforcement officer for the U.S. Coast Guard, follows Jimmy's letter, and begs for limiting the complexity of Fishery Management Plans. The Coast Guard, whose job involves protecting both the fisherman and the fish, admits to being shorthanded and "shortchanged" in its mandate to protect the ground-fish stocks.

In 1997, the year following the introduction of the Sustainable Fisheries Act, funding for the operating expenses of the Coast Guard earmarked for domestic fisheries and marine sanctuaries enforcement was cut from $455.9 million to $387.4 million.[7] For the corresponding period, the Coast Guard estimates that the inshore closed areas requiring patrolling increased by a factor of nine. In short, as the requirements of the job significantly increased, the money to fund the Coast Guard decreased. To make an impossible job even more impossible, Congress passed legislation to shut down Coast Guard stations and to eliminate the jobs of the men and women who manned those stations. An article in *Ocean Navigator* calculates the legislative results as a reduction of four thousand active-duty Coast Guard personnel and three thousand reservists, thus returning the U.S. Coast Guard to the size it was in 1967, long before the results of September 11, 2001, or the complex fisheries regulations that require the degree of Coast Guard enforcement necessary today.[8]

The Scituate Coast Guard Station, which operated at the same location on Scituate Harbor for sixty-two years, is now the management office for the Stellwagen Bank National Marine Sanctuary, another agency under the umbrella of NOAA and the U.S. Department of Commerce.

Judy Ramos echoes the feelings of the fishing industry when she says, "We get upset with the Coast Guard, 'cause they're law enforcement. They're policemen. You get upset with a policeman if he pulls you over and gives you a speeding ticket. But the same policeman stops a mugger that's just getting ready to attack you, you want to kiss that man on the lips. We're the same. We need these guys. We need the Coast Guard. And all the cutbacks have created a safety hazard for the fisherman."

The will of the electorate, which has chosen the members of Congress, appears to be to limit the budget and manpower of the Coast Guard. Yet the scope of its duties has not been limited. Since September 11, 2001, even more pressure has been applied to the agency. Given the dictates of the overwhelming task it has been given, together with its limited budget, the U.S. Coast Guard would naturally prefer to be responsible for monitoring a few large fishing boats instead of a lot of smaller boats. The present system pits economic efficiency against employment. And the Coast Guard is in the middle.

A commercial fisherman knows how to fish very well. This is part of the problem. The fisherman has combined his skills with the aids provided by new electronics and new gear to enable him to catch a lot of fish. But what is a better alternative? Is anything gained by eliminating a community of skilled fishermen who support themselves, their families, and various ancillary industries in their communities? Many of the men and women in the wholesale and retail side of the fisheries are concerned that when the stocks are rebuilt, as is hoped will result from all the regulations, no fisherman will be left to harvest the fish and to provide fresh fish for the table. Will a lot of unskilled people buy boats and head to sea, or will factory trawlers replace the fishing communities?

To Niaz Dorry, factory trawlers are still the greatest, largely unrecognized, threat to the fisheries. In a 1995 award-winning article appearing in *National Geographic*, an "expert" with the US. National Marine Fisheries Service is quoted: "Many of the small mom-and-pop operations are going to be left behind. The trend is going toward fewer, bigger, more efficient boats." Michael Parfit, author of the article, then adds, "The *Alaska Ocean* [an artist's rendering of this vessel accompanies the article] could be a flagship for this new era of industrial fishing. Based in Anacortes, Washington, the ship can process more than 600 metric tons of pollock a day. At 376 feet it is one of the largest factory trawlers in the world."[9]

The *National Geographic* article could help galvanize the thinking of many diverse groups such as Greenpeace, the New England fishing communities, and local fishermen, who all fear the scenario described might be the direction in which we are heading with our present management policies.

According to Greenpeace literature, a factory trawler similar to the *Alaska Ocean* can catch 400 tons of fish per tow and process 50 to 80 tons per day of the fish paste used in surimi, the imitation crab often found in seafood salad.[10] The remaining 320 to 350 tons of fish are discarded. Within the hull of a factory trawler, after the half-mile-long net is spooled, the fish are weighed, gutted, cleaned, and processed. The resultant fish paste or fillets are frozen, packed, and stored, ready to be shipped to the consumer.

Provisions for the crew of 125 on the *Alaska Ocean* include a separate deck for living quarters, a gymnasium, and cafeteria along with TV/video capabilities in most cabins. In some cases, supplies are provided to the crew by smaller vessels that can turn around and transport the fish product to any port in the world. Thus, the larger vessel can fish for months without returning to port. This process may be "efficient" for the owners of the ships, but it is wasteful of the natural resources we all share, and it returns little or nothing to local fishing communities.

The assumption many Americans have is that the large industrial fishing vessels similar to the *Alaska Ocean* disappeared from U.S. waters when the two-hundred-mile limit was enacted. On the East Coast, this is temporarily the case. On the West Coast, the temptation from the Alaska pollock fishery induced Congress to guarantee close to $65 million in low-interest loans to finance construction of ten factory trawlers. By 1988, the number of U.S.–owned vessels qualifying as factory trawlers jumped to forty-three, worth approximately $520 million. Estimates put the financing of these vessels through low-interest U.S.–guaranteed loans at around 80 percent. Much of that money has gone to foreign shipyards, where the cost to build the vessels is lower than it would be in the United States.[11]

In 1991, this overcapitalized and overfinanced fleet of fifty U.S.–owned vessels caught and processed 70 percent of the pollock landed in Alaska, though they accounted for only 2 or 3 percent of the entire U.S. fishing fleet. In 1994, the fleet of sixty U.S.–owned factory trawlers was estimated to have discarded 581 million tons of bycatch, more than the total weight of groundfish landed in the Northeast that year.[12]

The year 1994 was pivotal for the Alaskan pollock factory trawler. A number of factors hit the fleet simultaneously. The market for surimi fell from more than two dollars per pound to less than one dollar per pound; the efficiency of the fleet had significantly reduced the pollock stocks; and quotas instituted too late by the National Marine Fisheries Service prohibited the factory trawlers from catching enough to cover their overhead. For every seven U.S. factory trawlers fishing, one was in bankruptcy proceedings.[13]

More than one of the owners of these large nomadic vessels began to seek other fish stocks in other areas. The owners of *Atlantic Star*, a 369-foot, thirteen-thousand-horsepower fish harvester and processor, looked toward the Northeast Coast of the United States and saw that Gloucester was still harvesting herring. The Dutch owners of the vessel were aware that the Magnuson-Stevens Act prohibited foreign-owned vessels from fishing within the two-hundred-mile Exclusive Economic Zone. To comply, they proposed joint ventures to several Gloucester-based corporations. The plan floated by the consortium of foreign owners was for an "internal waters processing" agreement whereby U.S. fishermen would catch herring and mackerel and deliver them to the *Atlantic Star* for processing within a three-mile boundary as stipulated by the Commonwealth of Massachusetts.

Gloucester fishermen voiced concern that such a large increase in herring catches would place too much fishing effort on the stocks to maintain a healthy biomass. In addition, no one has yet determined to what extent herring provide the food fish for larger species whose numbers are dwindling. Paul Vitale, after having watched one vessel throw forty thousand pounds of cod—both juveniles and adults—over the side as bycatch, says, "I think at least for one year observers should be on all herring vessels each trip to see how they're working."

As the Gloucester community looked more closely into the proposed venture, it discovered local investment in the *Atlantic Star* venture to be only 2 percent, not 51 percent as claimed. And it discovered that the Dutch company planned to bring in its own trawlers to fish. As a result of the new findings, the Commonwealth of Massachusetts rejected the joint venture, but only at the last minute. The U.S. Congress followed suit by passing legislation to prohibit entry of the *Atlantic Star* and similar vessels into U.S. waters. But the fight is not over. The *Atlantic Star's* owners brought suit against both the Commonwealth of Massachusetts and the National Marine Fisheries Service on the basis of being denied due process of law. And they appear to be targeting mackerel through a joint contract in Nova Scotia.[14]

Frank Mirarchi in Scituate thinks the whole issue has been blown way out of proportion. "I totally disagree with this idea that the government has an agenda to replace the small, local fisherman with a few large factory trawlers. It's an easy charge to make. Sure, on the West Coast, you've got American Sea Foods and Tyson Chicken buying up the quota shares. But they're going nowhere as far as I can see. They're not even making any money on the vessel operations. They're making money on selling the food because they're vertically integrated corporations."

Patty Lemmi, a fisherman and member of the Massachusetts Fishing Partnership, would like to believe Frank's theory, but she tells the story of attending a recent meeting of the partnership where the speaker was Sebastian O'Kelly, the ombudsman recently appointed by NOAA for the Department of Commerce. Patty reports that someone in the audience asked Mr. O'Kelly if the government would like to get rid of the small fisherman. "And he actually never said no. He never said, 'What a ridiculous idea!' " Instead, Patty relates, Mr. O'Kelly turned the discussion to the subject of the moratorium on individual quotas scheduled to be lifted in the year 2000, subsequently delayed. Patty and other fishermen in the audience know that, unless policy changes, the lifting of quotas means large corporations will be given the opportunity to buy up individual quotas. No one in the audience of fishermen left the meeting with a secure feeling.

Perhaps the most basic way to gain an understanding of the situation facing the fishing community is to focus on the dollar. Regulating the fisheries has become a substantial business employing an ever growing body of earnest men and women financed by either public grant money or private contributions. The former is generated by taxes garnered from the public. The latter (often tax-deductible) comes indirectly from the public or is given freely as charitable contributions or through a foundation, usually set up by wealthy individuals and families who choose to support causes related to what they perceive as a way of improving the overall quality of life. Instead of paying taxes to a general pool to be administered by others, they are thus able to exert a substantial influence and control as to how their money is spent. "Saving the planet" has become a favorite avenue for foundation money.

Through the money contributed to causes relating to marine ecosystems, jobs are created for environmentalists, biologists, and a host of scientists hired to study and monitor the condition of the fisheries. Consider the number of universities that today offer both undergraduate and graduate degrees in some area of environmental science, and you begin to see that the graduates of those programs are going to find a way to create jobs for themselves—or change careers. Many scientists and university administrators see the twenty-first century as the era of the environment. Alison Richard, Yale University's provost, is quoted in *Nature* as saying, "Environmental issues have gone from having faddish, tree-hugger status to center stage, viewed now as serious and valued."[15] Universities help by writing grants to support their students and their departments. So-called soft money (money received from government sources to support the research of a grant written by a scientist in order to support his or her research plus a staff, necessary hardware, and students) drives the science on which fisheries regulations are based.

Funding for cooperative research between scientists and fishermen is rapidly changing the dynamic of fishery research. In 1999 funding was made available to support joint research on the recovery of the sea scallop population on Georges Bank. As fisheries regulators viewed the success of the sea scallop venture, relative to the gulf between scientific research and the fishermen's firsthand accounts of groundfish populations, the obvious answer appeared to be to fund joint research on groundfish. The results are beginning to provide a way for a fisherman like Frank Mirarchi to continue fishing in a sustainable way.

The fisherman provides an existing market with the produce it desires. If he needs a fishing vessel, he must personally pay for it. Conversely, if an institution involved in regulating the fisheries needs a research vessel, it must find public money to pay for it. As taxpayers, we have a stake in that vessel and that research. The fisherman's vessel is his responsibility, as is paying for the accompanying boat mortgage. When that fisherman is pitted against the publicly supported establishment, the cards are stacked against him—until the public realizes what it might lose with the disappearance of the fisherman and the access to fresh fish that he or she provides.

Few would say that previously frozen fish brought to port weeks after it was caught tastes "better" than the fish recently swimming in the sea, any more than they would say that a hothouse tomato tastes better than a tomato ripened on the vine in the summer sun. Yet we are limiting our future ability to savor fresh fish, and few are protesting.

Protests are being staged instead by organizations such as the People for the Ethical Treatment of Animals, who are urging legislators to levy taxes on meat, poultry, and fish. Steve Lustgarten, in a publication titled *EarthSave*, suggests, "Replacing fish on your menu with nutritious whole foods of plant origin is a direct and vital way of helping protect and restore beleaguered aquatic environments, both freshwater and marine. Another albeit less-obvious way is by reducing your consumption of all animal products."[16]

A better solution is not to expect people to forgo eating fish or to do away with the fisherman, but to learn from the works of men and women like biologist Chris Glass or conservation biologist David Wiley, who begin by studying fish behavior. Step two is to devise ways, based on the behavior of the animal, to harvest only that which is necessary in order to provide a small livelihood for the existing fishermen while permitting the stocks to grow to sustainable levels.

By allowing the local fisherman to harvest just enough fish to stay on the water, we will not create an economic incentive to induce others to enter the industry. Hopefully, we will not repeat the mistake made by the government when it previously created incentives for unskilled people to buy boats and "become" fishermen. Of course, this plan would take time and money to implement, but possibly far less than is being lost in the process of wiping out the economies of fishery-dependent coastal communities.

In some ways, little has changed from the days of Captain Sylvanus Smith. Gear has changed a little; technology has changed a lot; but New England groundfishing is still dependent on individual men and women who work in harsh and dangerous conditions to harvest a live resource for consumption by an ever growing population. We want to protect fish stocks for future generations. Yet we are drafting regulations that encourage the killing of fish. And we are drafting regulations that may modify the genetic makeup of groundfish. Species survive through adaptation. Fish are no different. As the required mesh size for fishing nets has increased, the small fish have had an easier time escaping. Thus they have been artificially selected to spawn at a younger age because the older, larger spawning fish are no longer around to continue the species. The same regulations that are creating havoc with the fish stocks are also eliminating the small fisherman, the one who often embodies generations of knowledge about fish and fishing. There has to be a better way.

Mark Plotkin, the ethnobotanist seen by Jimmy Bramante on the Discovery Channel, could be speaking of fishing when he says, "For through our ignorance, [and] greed . . . , we have set off a chain of events that is destroying both the ecosystem and the only cultures that know how to preserve it."[17]

"I feel that there is now an agenda or an atmosphere in Washington to end commercial fishing. I think they want to make the fishing grounds into a park," Harriet Didriksen states, only half in jest.

Harriet's remarks anticipated a two-day scientific workshop hosted by the New England Aquarium in March of 1999. There, Page Valentine, a geologist with the U.S. Geological Survey in Woods Hole, Massachusetts, and one of the opponents of dragger gear, proposed setting up thirty-six carefully delineated areas in and around Georges Bank and the Gulf of Maine as Marine Protected Areas where fishing would be prohibited. The proposed areas to be protected would include 29 percent of the ocean floor between New England and New Brunswick and 25 percent of the open ocean beyond the tip of Cape Cod—in short, the bulk of the prime New England fishing grounds.

Elliott Norse, founder of the Marine Conservation Biology Institute, organized the meeting. To many in the fishing community, it was another example of protecting property versus protecting people. But others asked the question: could a modified version of Valentine's marine park concept be the answer to conserve both the fish and the fisherman?

Nearly two thousand miles south of the meeting, 110 feet below the surface of the waters surrounding a tiny, five-square-mile volcanic island, two black eyes can be discerned looking up out of the sandy bottom. Suddenly a few grains of sand shift slightly, then a mass of sand measuring almost five feet across begins to move, transforming itself into the ethereal figure of a stingray that slowly flaps its "wings" and floats off through the water. Nearby, under a rocky outcropping, another eye is visible in a bed of sand. This one lacks the translucent protective membrane of most fish eyes. When seen against a sandy bottom, its most prominent feature is a black slit surrounded by the coarse sandpaper skin of a nurse shark temporarily in a docile state. Fifteen feet or so above the shark, an endangered hawksbill turtle slowly paddles by, seemingly oblivious to the ocean's other inhabitants. Fish of all colors and species swim in and around antlers of staghorn coral. This is the Saba Marine Park, the world's first financially self-sufficient marine sanctuary, funded by joint grants from the Netherlands World Wildlife Fund and the Prince Bernhard Fund in 1986 and officially designated a marine park in 1987.

Boats are not allowed to anchor here, and five moorings provide a night's shelter for the first five cruising vessels fortunate enough to tie up to them. The dive boats plying the area tie up to the same type of moorings placed strategically so as not to harm the existing underwater habitat. The Saba Marine Park is a no-fishing zone. An annual fish census indicates that since 1993 the fish in the park have been found to be larger than the fish sampled outside the park, and that the fish population at the edge of the park where fishing is permitted has increased.[18] Corroborating the evidence from Saba, fishermen report catches in waters adjacent to nearby St. Lucia rose 46 to 90 percent five years after a marine park was established.[19]

The island of Saba was formed some 500,000 years ago when molten lava pushed up through the crust beneath the sea to reach the air, where it dribbled down the edges of the newly created landmass to solidify as it met the sea. Over the years, the paths created by that lava have provided fertile conditions for the growth of many different types and shapes of coral. Today, sponges, sea anemones, sea fans, and purple, red, pink, and green coralline algae grow over and around the coral. These same formations provide both nourishment and sheltered hiding places for the many fish inhabiting the marine park.

During the retreat of the glaciers between eighteen thousand and fifteen thousand years ago, Saba remained relatively unchanged. Conversely, in the Northeast, twenty-five nautical miles east of Boston and twelve nautical miles south of Gloucester, a deposit of sand, gravel, and silt formed a plateau in the Atlantic Ocean stretching to within six nautical miles north-northwest of Race Point in Provincetown. This underwater plateau is roughly 18.75 miles long and 6.25 miles wide.[20]

As tidal currents move in and out of Massachusetts Bay, they bring nutrients up over this relatively shallow sand, where exposure to light from the sun transforms the nutrients into more than 675 species of phytoplankton. Both northern right whales and small capelin feed on the phytoplankton. The capelin in turn provide food for cod, flounder, sole, and the other groundfish harvested by Kevin Shea, Frank Mirarchi, Paul Vitale, and all the other inshore fishermen who fish in the Gulf of Maine.

This is Stellwagen Bank, named for Captain Henry Stellwagen, a U.S. Navy hydrographer credited with the discovery of the shallow underwater plateau in 1854 when he realized that the bank's shallow depth could be useful in navigation to indicate the entrance to Massachusetts Bay. In 1992, Stellwagen Bank, nearby Tillies Bank, and a portion of Jeffries Ledge, a combined area of 638 square nautical miles, was officially designated the Stellwagen Bank Marine Sanctuary. It later became the Gerry E. Studds Stellwagen Bank Marine Sanctuary in honor of the Democratic congressman from Massachusetts who advocated creation of the nation's eleventh marine park on Stellwagen Bank.

In 1990 (the year documented for the sanctuary's environmental impact study), over 280 commercial fishing vessels regularly fished within the boundaries of the sanctuary. The estimated value of fish landed by those vessels for the same year was in excess of fifteen million dollars (excluding bluefin tuna).[21] Today that number would be significantly lower due to the present regulations limiting days at sea, but it would be partially offset by the higher price paid for landed fish. In a study of seventy-six protected marine areas throughout the world, 69 percent of the reserves indicated the density of fish had increased since the area had been set aside as a reserve; 88 percent reported larger fish; and 92 percent reported greater fish biomass.[22]

What has yet to be quantified, but appears to exist, is the assumed increase in both size and abundance of fish in the areas where fishing is permitted around the perimeters of the sanctuaries. Until those numbers have been documented, the fishing community may not warm to Drs. Valentine and Norse's proposal of prohibiting fishing within marine protected areas. At present, fishing in the Stellwagen Bank Marine Sanctuary is governed by regulations mandated by the National Marine Fisheries Service and ultimately by the secretary of commerce. Formulation of these regulations is not dictated by the confines of the sanctuary, but rather by the scientific studies of stock biomass in New England waters.

Despite the recent increase in fish stocks, many fishermen wonder if prohibiting fishing in the Stellwagen Bank Marine Sanctuary is going to provide the "lasting protection" for the marine environment envisioned by Executive Order 13158 (the federal regulation providing for protected marine areas). Unlike Saba, whose steep cliffs and relatively small size have combined to limit coastal development, the towns surrounding Massachusetts Bay are some of the most densely populated in the nation. Effluents and various other pollutants are carried by rainstorms into Massachusetts Bay and out to the waters surrounding Stellwagen Bank. In addition, on September 6, 2000, as part of the cleanup of Boston Harbor, a $400 million system began discharging 360 million gallons per day of treated effluents close to this delicate ecosystem.

Few would argue that man is not capable of causing great, possibly irreversible damage to the environment. In a 1992 study, *Consumer Reports* analyzed the makeup of fish sold for human consumption. Almost half the fish tested were contaminated by bacteria from human or animal feces, and some of the fish tested contained PCBs and mercury.[23] A more dire result could be assumed if we consider that the fish tested may exemplify survival of the fittest and not give a complete picture of the extent of devastation to the fish population from human pollution. The point is brought home when we realize cod used to spawn in a small area off Boston Lighthouse and north to Bakers Island between Marblehead and Manchester-by-the-Sea. By the 1990s, few if any breeding fish had been seen in the area for many years, probably because of the pollution in Boston Harbor. Now that Boston Harbor is cleaner, Tom Phaneuf talks about seeing an abundance of spawning-age cod when he fishes in the area.

In England, scientists have analyzed the health of fish in eight rivers downstream from sewage treatment plants. The results disclosed male fish born with ovaries and eggs instead of sperm ducts. Researchers investigating the causes of the hormone-altering phenomenon note that sewage treatment plants routinely release combinations of pesticides, dioxin, plastics, detergents, and other industrial compounds into rivers and streams. The scientists involved in this research have come to believe that many of the ingredients in the effluents of the treatment plants either replicate the effects of estrogen or block production of testosterone, thus inhibiting the sexual development that aquatic animals require in order to reproduce.[24]

"You know where the dam stream goes up under Cunningham Bridge?" Charlie Butman asks as he recounts one of his stories. "Well, I can remember years ago, when I was a kid, the codfish coming in there so thick, so thick you could walk across that stream on 'em. They were goin' up Little Harbor to get the sea worms. See, the sea worms at a certain time they breed, they come out of the sand. Now how the hell do the codfish know this?" he asks out of curiosity. "I don't know, but I do know that's what they were after, the sea worms."

His eyes have that look of seeing something no longer there. "My Uncle Earle was working on the big house belonging to Dr. Chute, and we would look down over the water from the porch on the hill, and we could see great big pods of codfish, just like birds, you know, the way they fly in formation. And they were heading up the stream. And I've seen the pollock in there, tons 'n' tons of 'em. And they're going up for the same reason. You don't see that nowadays."

Cod and pollock no longer swim up Cohasset's Little Harbor in pursuit of the sea worms, the way they did in Charlie Butman's day. Water that used to nourish the sea worms still flows under the bridge, across the tidal flats, and into Little Harbor, but only an occasional blue heron or egret waits in the stream to devour the random eel.[25] There must not be enough minnows, eels, or sea worms flowing into Little Harbor from the streams to attract predators. But why?

To best protect marine resources, it is necessary to first understand what might be causing the degradation of the environment required for the spawning and healthy growth of groundfish and their food sources. Nutrients are essential for growth, but excess levels of nutrients in the water are harmful. Nitrogen is required for marine growth, but excess nitrogen has the adverse effect. Estuarine water must be clear enough to allow sunlight to penetrate to the bottom, where aquatic grasses, such as eelgrass, grow. These grasses produce oxygen and provide shelter for small marine animals. Higher levels of nitrogen and phosphorous, used in lawn fertilizers, increase algae growth on the surface. As the algae flourish, they block sunlight from reaching the eelgrass below. Without sunlight, eelgrass no longer produces oxygen. Algae have a short life span. As they die, they settle to the bottom and begin to decay, consuming additional oxygen in the water and encouraging the growth of bacteria such as *Pfiesteria*.

When grasses are prevented from producing the oxygen required for marine life in coastal estuaries (the breeding grounds for small marine animals), the fish either die or suffer enough stress to keep them from reproducing. A study recently conducted by the National Academy of Sciences concludes that the problem of coastal pollution is severe enough to warrant federal aid to stem it.

In the early spring, lawns abutting Little Harbor are dotted with small yellow flags stating "Pesticide Application. May be harmful to dogs and other small pets." In May of 1997, three separate applications of fertilized loam, spread on the lawn of one home, were washed down into Little Harbor by the spring rains. If such pesticides are harmful to an animal the size of a dog, it is hard to believe they are not fatal to a small minnow, sand eel, or capelin.

No environmental police, regional councils, or other regulatory bodies prohibit such runoff from reaching estuarine waters. Yet this runoff could be destroying a portion of the food supply for the groundfish population. In 1999, faced with a lawsuit from the Commonwealth of Massachusetts, the Town of Cohasset funded a study by local students and the engineering firm of Camp Dresser & McKee. The aim: to survey and monitor the water quality in Little Harbor. Results of the study indicate that after a rainstorm, as the contents of septic tanks and lawn fertilizer are carried into the harbor, the levels of both bacteria and nutrients increase significantly. Around Inner Little Harbor, where Charlie previously observed schools of spawning fish, residential septic tanks are the primary contributor of nitrogen, with lawn fertilizers contributing the remaining 30 percent. Two water samples taken from Little Harbor four hours after a rainstorm yielded the following results: sample A, a human coliform count of 540 colonies per hundred milliliters; sample B, 1,041. The maximum count allowed before beaches are closed to swimming in Massachusetts is 200 colonies per hundred milliliters; before they are closed to clamming, 14.

Instead of earmarking more money for scientists to study why fish no longer swim in close to shore looking for food, we allocate money to police the top of the food chain, namely, the fisherman. And we blindly accept that the problem lies solely with the fisherman.

Not all countries relegate the fisherman to the status of "fish killer." On the south coast of Brittany, France's maritime province, the walled town of Concarneau beckons tourists to visit an active fishing port and to pay homage to the world of traditional fishing. Families on holiday flock to Concarneau's granite ramparts to buy replicas of the blue and white-striped Breton sweaters worn by the local fishermen. Parents pay the equivalent of thirty-five dollars or more to purchase wall charts to show their children the different types of fish together with the particular fishing boats and gear used to catch them. And they come to Concarneau to explore the Musée de la Pêche, a museum devoted entirely to the history and tradition of fishing.

The museum is housed in the old arsenal, once a school to train fishermen in the art of fishing. Outside the stone entrance, the ubiquitous notes of a Peruvian flute mingle with a concertina of local design to produce sounds resembling sea chanteys. Inside the museum, vertical dioramas have been created to skillfully and lovingly depict scaled-down versions of different techniques for fishing. In sculpted elevations, traditional trawlers, gillnetters, and hook liners are depicted with their nets as they would be in operation under the sea. Delicate knots are tied to show a miniature seine net as it could have appeared in the eighteenth century. Outside the walls of the museum, stairs lead to the F/V *Hemerica*, a trawler decommissioned in 1981 and today affording the tourist a chance to walk aboard to better appreciate the life at sea of an offshore fisherman.

France produces what are arguably the finest cheeses in the world. French chickens from the area of Bresse are renowned for their flavor. French ice cream served in the evening is made fresh that same morning, and will be discarded that night if not consumed. But nowhere is it still possible to get fish fresher than on our New England coasts. So why are we destroying the fisherman in an attempt to save the resource?

How sad that in Massachusetts, where we are closest to the richest fishing grounds on the planet, and where fishing is so much a part of our history, no museum exists to equal Concarneau's. The New England Fish Exchange could have been the perfect setting for such a museum. Instead it provides office space for executives who could easily be in offices in the Financial District. Where we should take pride in our fishing heritage and teach our children to know and respect the work of the fishermen, we instead pit the fisherman against laudable, but perhaps ineffective, efforts to save the environment.

Harriet Didriksen suggests, "Because fishing people understand about dwindling fish populations, we fished with mesh the size we use. We could have fished with burlap and caught everything, had we been as greedy as many of the American people like to think we are. People who know how to fish know how to fish wisely. If we were to use up all of the shared reserves of fish, we would obviously have no livelihood."

If we seek a better understanding of what motivates and what degrades fish behavior, and thus begin to understand if fish stocks are dwindling for reasons other than overfishing, we will be a lot closer both to protecting the species that need protection and to continuing the existence of the fisherman and his community. The answer to why there are so few fish appears to be more complex than "too many boats." Yet we are closing down our fishing communities without pursuing answers to some of the questions we should answer before permitting generations of local knowledge and intact communities to disappear.

There are fewer flounder, dabs, halibut, and cod than there have been at other times. There are also fewer fishermen. Paul Vitale, Tom Phaneuf, and all the other men and women who still fish for a living are fishing because they love it. They are fishing responsibly, the way their fathers, grandfathers, or neighbors taught them to fish. The risk is high, the pay is low, and the stress is mounting. Yet, for them, it is still the best possible way of life.

7

EPITAPH FOR A WAY OF LIFE

I missed the dawn light and the sunrise, the suspense of every haul,
the calloused hands; I missed the smell and feel of boats and I
missed the water.

—Peter Matthiessen, *Men's Lives*

LATITUDE 40.43.39 NORTH
LONGITUDE 72.46.44 WEST
13:44, NOVEMBER 6, 1998

The F/V *Captain Sam*, U.S. documentation no. 604472,
was sunk in seventy-one feet of water two miles off
Moriches Inlet on the south side of Long Island. She went down bow-
first after a struggle lasting three and one-half hours. Prior to the sinking,
Paula Jerman and other divers from the Moriches Offshore Reef Project,
which financed the towing, had gone down to prepare a mooring to
anchor her to the spot where she will help form a reef to attract fish. A
salvage boat had used a blowtorch to cut holes in her hull to permit
water to enter; her seacocks, the through-hull openings, had all been
opened to allow water to flow through; and the compartment where the
engine had been mounted was open to the sea. Five members of the
Coast Guard sprayed water over, around, and through her hull in an

effort to sink her. Then they gunned the engines on the Coast Guard utility boat and careened around her port side to create a wave to wash over *Captain Sam*. She still would not give up.

The blue paint on her hull was only two years old. Her new engine had been installed at a cost of ninety thousand dollars two years before, and had neither a scratch nor rust on it when it was removed a week before her sinking. To those on board the ten pleasure boats assembled to witness the outcome, the white letters of her name against the blue of her hull proclaimed her dignity and reinforced the injustice of her demise.

For ten months, Mike Barry paid to dock *Captain Sam* at the Boston Fish Pier while he tried to find a buyer. Jim O'Brien expressed an interest in purchasing *Captain Sam* and creating a dinner cruise in conjunction with Jake's Restaurant; a boat owner offered to purchase her and bring her to the African coast; fishermen with older boats at the fish pier spoke about buying her to replace their own boats. The National Marine Fisheries Service stipulates in its buyout agreement that a fishing vessel once accepted into the program may remain on the water only if it is purchased by a nonprofit organization. The two options open to Mike were to sell *Captain Sam* to the reef project managed by the New York State Department of Environmental Conservation, Bureau of Marine Resources, or to see her sold for scrap metal to a firm in New Bedford. He chose the former.

The Moriches Offshore Reef Project exists to attract fish, to attract divers, and to create an artificial fish habitat in an effort to restore the fisheries. By July of the year 2000, this man-made reef consisted of the *Jean Elizabeth*, a 195-foot steel barge sunk in 1995; an 80-foot steel barge sunk in 1996; eight army tanks sunk in 1997; twenty armored personnel carriers plus the F/V *Niagara Falls*, a 90-foot fishing trawler, and *Captain Sam*, all sunk in 1998; another 80-foot steel barge and the F/V *St. George* sunk in 1999; *Cape Fear*, a 112-foot clam dredge sunk in March 2000; and 115 cement pipes totaling 250 tons.

On the morning of the sinking of *Captain Sam*, Jim, Mike's youngest brother, is the only one of the four owners who is here to witness her last hours before she becomes home to reef fish and recreational divers. Mike Barry is undergoing previously scheduled surgery; Steve Barry's newly acquired general store is opening today; and Bob Butman is at his job as engineer for a line of Boston Harbor commuter boats. Salvio Licata, the former cook on *Captain Sam*, is at sea.

A member of the reef project has made his 45-foot Bertram pleasure boat available to transport Jim Barry, his family, and various members of the press to the site. Jim stands in the stern. He rocks his year-old son Brian to sleep on his shoulder as he watches five members of the Coast Guard attempt to sink *Captain Sam*. Jim has not fished for three years. He decided to quit in August of 1995, the year Alicia, his youngest daughter, was born.

Several months before Alicia's birth, Jim was aboard *Captain Sam* trawling for fish alongside the F/V *Italian Gold*, an 80-foot stern trawler out of Gloucester. A gale was forecast. Mike and his crew decided to head back to port. *Italian Gold* continued out to sea. She never returned. All hands were lost. The boat was eventually located on the bottom approximately 150 miles east of Boston.

Jim never went to sea after that. Instead, he has chosen to raise his four children while his wife Sandy works as a computer programmer to support the family. He has no regrets about his decision to quit. "I took my bunk off the boat and brought it to my basement when we were stripping her," he says. "Someone had written Quit Smoking below the bunk above mine. When I lay in the bunk after I got it to my house, I saw where I had crossed out Smoking and written Fishing."

Tom Wright, owner of the Senix Marina, organizers of the sinking for the reef project, asks Jim if he plans to fish. "Not commercially," he answers. "But I'm going to take my son Brandon fishing for the first time next summer." He smiles at his nine-year-old son as he adds, "He's never been fishing, and I'm going to bring him to fish right here, where *Captain Sam* is."

Asked if he would encourage Brandon to become a fisherman, Jim looks surprised that anyone would ask the question. "He's too smart," he answers. "He hates fishing. When I used to pull out of the driveway to leave to go offshore for ten days, I would look toward the house and see Brandon and his sister Amanda [now six] crying at the window."

It is 13:41. *Captain Sam*'s name is underwater for the first time since Jimmy Bramante first launched her in 1979. The stern slowly rises out of the water, much as a whale would breach, and her bow slowly heads to the bottom. Then she stops. She is 87 feet long—16 feet longer than the water is deep. The vessel that will not sink is still visible. Tears are running down Jim's face. Sandy's face is also wet as she looks from her husband to the reminder of all they have shared and the dreams they had in 1986 when they bought into fishing as their way of life.

As the Bertram turns to bring its crew back to shore, *Captain Sam*'s stern slowly recedes into the sea. Jim takes Amanda's hand and leads her and Brandon to the starboard side of the boat, where the three of them throw coins into the Bertram's wake, toward the spot where *Captain Sam* went down. When asked about the significance of the coins, Jim explains that it is a longtime ritual he performed whenever he went to sea. "I'd do that for good luck, so I'd bring back more money than I threw into the water." He adds wistfully, "It always worked."[1]

In Gloucester, Paul Vitale reads about the sinking of the F/V *Captain Sam*, and he laments, "*Captain Sam* was a beautiful boat, a beautiful boat. They destroyed a lot of nice boats." Then, in a more strident voice, "The stupid thing about this buyback is that when the government agrees to buy a boat, it tells the owners they can only sell it if the boat won't be used for fishing. They say it's because they have to get rid of the fishing power. Well, guess what, that boat's not the power. It's the guy who takes the boat out who is the power." Paul's dark eyes flash anger and resentment as he says, "That buyback provision was just plain stupid. A simple clause could have been put into each sale agreement stating, 'this boat cannot ever be used to fish in New England waters.' If the boat ever came up here, the permit number would show it was illegal, and it would be confiscated. But that way, it could be bought by someone in another part of the world, and still be afloat somewhere."

Judy Ramos points out that in Portugal "they don't just scrap the boats the way we do here, and then say, 'That's it. Go find another way to earn a living.' They buy your vessel and let you build a new vessel, but with lesser engine power, a little bit smaller, so you can still fish— not with the power that you did, but with a brand new little boat. Portugal allows the people to earn a living." Judy adds that Portugal is a much smaller country, but the main diet of the country is fish.

The fishing schooner *Adventure* is now off the ways in Gloucester, undergoing work to restore its interior to permit it to serve as a museum and classroom on the water. Charlie's *Orca* still fishes out of Gloucester; *Captain Mano*, out of Boston. *Captain Sam*, the newest, the best equipped, probably the safest, is resting on the bottom. For Tom Wright and Paula Jerman, she represents a new beginning; for Charlie Butman, it is heartbreaking.

Charlie died two years later on Thanksgiving Day. He was seventy-four years old and had fished for forty years of his life. Unless a lot changes, there will not be another Charlie. His expansive personality and unbridled honesty required more space and more individual freedom than a man is allowed today. And we are all the poorer for it.

AFTERWORD

And so time and time again nature lovers launch earnest efforts to "save" from human depredation landscapes or wildlife populations that are nothing but the recent and unnatural creations of man's "interference" of a kind that in truth has shaped and perpetuated for millenniums the nature they love.

—Stephen Budiansky, *Nature's Keepers*

07:43, JANUARY 3, 2001

This morning I am on board the F/V *Christopher Andrew II*, U.S. documentation no. 576190, the 60-foot stern trawler belonging to Frank Mirarchi and his son Andrew. Our location is several miles off Duxbury Beach, close to the spot where I sailed through a sea of mackerel in 1969, as described in the preface to *Vanishing Species*. Today, instead of an abundance of mackerel, we are struggling to avoid an abundance of Gulf of Maine cod.

As for the numbers of fish, we have come full circle. During the time I have been writing this manuscript, the fish have begun to recover; the fishermen have not. For the ten years between 1976 to 1986, this vessel supported three families. Today it cannot support even one. The *Chris-*

topher Andrew II is not allowed to land fish today. Fishermen, other than those fishing for exempted species such as scallops, are not allowed to fish in Cape Cod Bay in January, February, March, and April. Nor are they allowed to fish in Cape Cod Bay in October and November. December, the one winter month when fishing is allowed, has just come and gone.

We are permitted to be here thanks to a piece of paper allowing Frank to participate in a research project conducted by the Manomet Center for Conservation Sciences and funded by the "crisis money" allocated to help fishermen survive the closures. The project was supposed to have been completed in December, when fishing was allowed in Cape Cod Bay. The permit to conduct the experiment was not received until December 23, two days before Christmas and eight days before the end of the allowable fishing days, which coincidentally left about two days in December when the weather was calm enough to permit the experiment to be successfully conducted. Special permission has been given to this one vessel to be fishing today, but live fish must be thrown back after being counted, weighed, and measured.

On board conducting the experiment are Tim Feehan and Gregg Morris, two biologists employed by Manomet. With them is Yoshiki Matsushita, a fishing technologist on a one-year scientific exchange program from the Japanese National Research Institute of Fisheries Engineering near Tokyo. They are paid out of a $6 million grant awarded to a group of three universities and the Woods Hole Oceanographic Institution. Collectively these institutions make up the Northeast Consortium, the organization formed to distribute and coordinate the efforts funded by the disaster relief money now allocated for research. Also on board is Dave Martins, conducting a separate tagging experiment for the University of Massachusetts at Dartmouth, and working with Bob Mac-Kinnon, who has been hired for six months as coordinator for the tagging experiment. Today, Bob is on another vessel.

Frank and Andrew Mirarchi are the only two fishermen being directly compensated by today's Manomet project. Chris Glass, principal investigator for the research, will be at the dock when the *Christopher Andrew* returns to Scituate, and he is in touch with Gregg via telephone throughout the day. Chris will review all data collected today and for the duration of the project. At completion, he will present the findings to Arne Carr at the Massachusetts Department of Marine Fisheries and co-PI (principal investigator) for the research being conducted.

Today is the third day on the water for the experiment. For the scientists on board, yesterday's work netted some unexpected results—results *not* unexpected for Paul Vitale, Kevin Shea, David Goethel, Bill

Amaru, or any of the other fishermen who have repeatedly spoken out at council meetings and written letters in an effort to make the men and women managing the fisheries understand that Gulf of Maine cod are abundant along the Northeast Coast. After stressing that this experiment is designed "to determine catch effort" as opposed to measure fish population, Gregg states, "What we are seeing is a revelation, and we think it would be worthwhile to share our data with some of the people managing the fisheries." Whether the fact of abundant fish will improve the lot of the small community-based fishermen remains to be seen.

The critical component of the experiment is basically hardware. It partially consists of a standard six-inch diamond-mesh cod end. This is the regulation fishing net used on the *Christopher Andrew* and other New England stern trawlers. Overlaying that cod end is a two-inch diamond-mesh cover net supported by a plastic frame. The immediate aim: to see how many fish, and of what weight and size, escape through the larger openings of the cod end to be caught in the outer net's smaller mesh.

A square mesh pattern tends to catch cod and other round fish; a diamond mesh pattern tends to catch flounder and other flatfish while allowing the cod to swim through it and back to sea. For the two last tows, the men switch to a six-and-one-half-inch square-mesh cod end overlaid by the same two-inch diamond-mesh cover net and plastic frame. This experiment also attempts to discover the best combination net to permit a species with a low catch limit to escape while permitting the fisherman to catch a species with a larger catch limit, thus reducing regulatory bycatch or the need to kill fish without being allowed to land them.

A sky streaked red at the horizon is slowly mellowing to lavenders and peaches, blending to fill the lower third of the sky and mitigating the telltale morning red of a predicted snowstorm. The water is a sharp blue-green against the sky—choppy, but without whitecaps. Gregg and Andrew ready the nets for the trawl as Frank moves rapidly back and forth from the wheelhouse to the stern. Yoshiki and Tim work with duct tape and WD-40 to fix the housing for the video camera that will be used in two of the five tows planned for today.

By 8:12 the sun breaks through the increasing cloud cover as the nets are slowly lowered into the sea, green mesh flowing out behind the boat. *Christopher Andrew* is trawling in sixteen fathoms (ninety-six feet) of water and moving at three knots. Frank is attempting to stay at this relatively shallow depth so the fish will not suffer from too rapid a change in depth when the net is hauled. Gregg hopes to avoid the schools of cod that hampered yesterday's work, and instead to net flounder and other flatfish. We are still a quarter mile from the site of yesterday's experiment.

At 8:26 the otter boards are lowered and the net pays out. Seagulls arrive to float on the surface in anticipation of the haulback. Ten minutes after the boards are lowered, Frank begins to winch in the net. He rapidly moves from port-side winch to starboard winch; then forward to the pilothouse, where, after jumping over Yoshiki and Tim, he checks to make certain we are not heading toward an unforeseen obstacle; then back to the winches. Clearly, for the fisherman, these scientific experiments bring with them a high level of stress. But Frank and Andrew are not complaining, not when the option is to stay home without pay. The larger of the green nets surfaces to the squeals of the spools. Rubber rollers and aluminum floats begin to attach themselves to the spool as they are wound up and around. Andrew hauls the net aboard and grabs the ever useful mallet. With one whack he flips open the closure, and the fish that would have been caught by a fisherman fishing with regulation mesh fall onto the deck. Skate, winter flounder, and a few Gulf of Maine cod intermingle with the trash fish large enough to be caught by the six-inch mesh.

Yoshiki, Tim, and Gregg move quickly to set up their measuring boards, hinged pieces of wood that open to reveal a waterproof rule marked off in centimeters up to seventy-four (thirty inches), with a metal piece projecting at a 90-degree angle to the board. Each of the three men picks up a fish, then quickly snubs its nose against the metal projection, flattens its tail to determine its length, and makes a pencil mark on the board at the tail level. Then he places it in a tub of salt water as he picks up the next fish. Cod, the more fragile of the species, are placed in a larger tub constantly being replenished by a hose shooting a stream of aerated salt water to revive the fish. Gregg scoops them up one by one to measure them before placing them in another tub of aerated salt water for Dave, who is also measuring them prior to tagging each cod and releasing it to the sea.

While the biologists measure the larger-mesh take, Andrew and Frank are bringing in the two-inch-mesh net. Whack! The mallet releases a far greater number of fish than were in the cod end. Crab, striped sculpin, cod, skate, winter flounder, and other flatfish together with the occasional scallop fall into a space partitioned off for the catch. The men jump to separate the commercial fish from the trash fish, which are not included in the experiment. Then they begin to count and measure. Undersize or juvenile fish too small to be commercially acceptable are weighed and then released. Adult cod, after being measured by Gregg,

Yoshiki, and Tim, are placed in baths of swirling salt water for Dave to tag.

Dave scoops up a cod from the swirling water in the bucket. He grabs it in gloved hands, places it on the narrow measuring board with its nose against the metal plate, and attempts to flatten the fish's tail against the rule as the fish squirms to get away. With his right hand, he grabs the pencil to write the fish's length on his clipboard. Then, holding the squirming fish with his left hand, he reaches with his right hand for the plastic gun that he previously loaded with sequentially numbered tags, much like the tags put on clothing in a department store. Still holding the fish with his left hand, he places the gun at the top of the cod's dorsal fin and pulls the trigger. The fish is still vigorously squirming. Dave quickly rises while holding the fish in both hands and moves to the side of the boat, where he lifts the cod over the side to the sea, all the while trying to keep the fish away from the beak of a hungry seagull. Then back to scoop up another cod from the bucket of water.

Each man moves with speed and efficiency. By 4:25 P.M. the sun is only half visible over the silhouette of Duxbury Beach and the Miles Standish Monument beyond. The *Christopher Andrew* has made five hauls. Dave has measured, notated, tagged, and released 237 Gulf of Maine cod ranging in length from twelve to twenty-five inches. In addition, he has had to retag 21 of that number when the first tag didn't hold. The previous trip he tagged close to 500.

Yoshiki, Tim, and Gregg have weighed, measured, and released 476 pounds of winter flounder, 76 pounds of yellowtail flounder, and 1,771 pounds of Gulf of Maine cod. In three tows utilizing the six-inch diamond-mesh cod end, 30.5 pounds of winter flounder were caught in the six-inch cod end; 287 pounds of winter flounder escaped through the regulation-size cod end into the two-inch net. One yellowtail flounder was caught in the cod end, 19 pounds in the two-inch net. Eighty-five pounds of cod were in the cod end, 690 pounds in the two-inch net. Two tows utilizing the six-and-one-half-inch square-mesh cod end netted 13 pounds of winter flounder, 146 pounds in the two-inch net. Twenty-four pounds of yellowtail flounder were caught in the cod end, 32 in the two-inch net. Twenty-one pounds of cod were in the cod end, 975 in the two-inch net. In addition, the three men have taken videos of the action in the net and videotaped action on deck. Frank takes the wheel, and we head home to Scituate.

The public's money has been well spent. The wealth of data collected today seems all the more impressive when you compare this experiment to the data collection conducted by the National Marine Fisheries Service, which, twice a year, makes one tow in each block of one hundred square nautical miles. Yet the official stock assessments are still determined by the data collected from those twice-yearly tows, together with fishermen's landings, which reflect sharply curtailed days at sea, catch limits, and only what is caught in a six-inch diamond-mesh net (which was increased to a six-and-a-half-inch net as of May 1, 2002). And those same assessments determine how few days a fisherman may fish and what areas are to be closed to fishing. Is it any wonder the fishermen protest the methods by which their industry is regulated?

Frank leans on the wheel of the *Christopher Andrew II* as he laments that the science being used is "just too light on data points. And that's the science that management has used to determine regulations." The Sustainable Fisheries Act requires that regulations be based on the best available science. "Available" is the key word.

"The three things we need to come up with," Gregg replies, "are conservation engineering, improved stock assessment, and innovative management." The fisherman may not last long enough to see the last component.

Unlike many other fishermen interviewed for *Vanishing Species*, Frank is a firm believer in the benefits of quota management of some sort. He feels that eliminating the common property concept in favor of privatizing fishing will create wealth for the fishermen and conserve the resource by matching the harvesting capacity to the resource and by eliminating the negative aspects of pulse fishing for one species while another is protected. Asked about the potential for the fishing quotas to end up in the hands of a few large corporations, Frank points out that in order to work, rules would have to be set up whereby quotas could not be sold on the open market but would revert back to the fisherman's community, such as the community of the CCCHFA. "Common pool property management hasn't worked for years," he states. "We have to be talking about what formula should be used to allocate quotas. For instance, quotas should be issued on the basis of points earned not just for how many fish a boat has caught, but for what measures the captain has taken to conserve the fish."

Andrew carefully repositions the hose to help revitalize a twenty-three-inch Gulf of Maine cod that somehow made its way through the six-inch mesh. Dave leans out over the boat to try to protect a fish from the beak of a seagull to allow the fish to swim away. I watch them and am reminded that the fisherman has a lot more in common with the scientist than with the men and women attempting to regulate the fisheries.

Frank Mirarchi has dedicated his life to promoting sustainable fishing.

He attends meetings whenever he thinks he can make a difference; he serves on committees and organizational boards if he thinks it will help the industry; he makes himself available for interviews where he is able to present the fisherman's perspective; and he is providing a means for his son Andrew to continue to fish. Bill Amaru is as committed to promoting sustainable fishing as Frank, and now fishes with his son Jason on the F/V *Joanne A.* Paul and Leo Vitale still fish together on the F/V *Angela and Rose*, and Paul represents the younger generation at both council and alliance meetings. Rodney Avila, whose life has been devoted to fishing and the fishing community, proudly tells me that his seven-year-old grandson wants to be a fisherman. One of Rodney's two sons is captain and co-owner with Rodney of the F/V *Trident.* Fishing is his career.

The same search for a better way that drives a scientist prompted Bob MacKinnon to dye his nets different colors to see if fish react differently to one color over another. It was also the force driving Luis Ribas (one of the fishermen who took part in the blockade of Boston Harbor) to experiment with nets he designs in an attempt to catch fewer cod and thus less regulatory bycatch. And it caused Provincetown fisherman Henry Souza to design the "raised foot rope trawl" to permit fishermen to catch whiting while avoiding lobsters and flatfish. And, aided by the monies allocated for "disaster relief," it is driving New England fishermen to collaborate with scientists in cooperative research programs similar to the experiments being conducted on the *Christopher Andrew* today.

Gregg Morris sums up the scientist's position when he states, "I love what I do. If you can make a difference in a positive way, that's what it's all about, right?" His words could easily be those of Paul Vitale, Bob MacKinnon, Kevin Shea, Paul Parker, or any of the other men and women who fish commercially and fish responsibly. Those values shared by the fisherman and the scientist together with a sense of stewardship may be what will save the fisheries. But time is short, and the health of both the fishing community and the ancillary industries that it supports is fragile. Frank Mirarchi tells the story of a Scituate dragger that came to the dock with a two-thousand-pound load of fresh fish, and no way to get the fish to market. The trucks that used to be at the dock to transport cleaned, iced fish to the dealer could no longer justify showing up in Scituate, because there had not been enough business on a daily basis. The fishermen were not allowed to fish enough days to keep the trucks in business. Fishermen are the most resilient and inventive human beings on this planet. They have to be. This particular fisherman managed to find a series of pickup trucks, and he and his friends transported the fish to Foley & Sons in New Bedford. But that is not the best way to preserve the quality of the fish.

When I first began to write *Vanishing Species*, Charlie Butman was working on our barn and telling me stories of the heyday of fishing. Bobby Butman was still fishing. Bobby's fishing stories were tales of government regulations shutting down the fisheries, putting our fishermen out of work, and siphoning off a valuable part of the economies of coastal communities.

At that time, I was certain that if the public saw the fishermen in terms of individuals instead of clichés it would react by working to protect the small fisherman while protecting the resource. And I was certain that we would demand a different system of managing the resource— one that was not encouraging the slaughter of one endangered species of fish in order to protect another.

After more than five years of interviewing fishermen, attending various meetings of the New England Fishery Management Council and ancillary committees, and reading whatever I could relating to the management of fisheries, I have come to believe that the picture of the fisherman presented to the public is often inaccurate. I was somewhat skeptical when Harriet Didriksen first told me that government policies would "eliminate the small fisherman." Five years later, I have come to respect her prescience. I have also come to realize that many people find it convenient to balance their desire to eat fish with their desire to protect the environment by designating the fisherman the scapegoat. Sadly, many of those people are in positions of regulating the lives of fishermen and the resulting lives of coastal communities.

I hope that Paul Parker, Bill Amaru, Frank Mirarchi, Bob Mac-Kinnon, and Niaz Dorry, together with organizations like the Manomet Center for Conservation Sciences and the School of Marine Science at the University of Massachusetts at Dartmouth, can work together to educate the public and devise new means to permit the small fisherman to fish while preserving the sustainability of the resource. But it is a gargantuan effort in the face of press releases issued by the National Marine Fisheries Service and regularly turned into articles in local newspapers where the biases still remain.

On December 28, 2001, U.S. District Judge Gladys Kessler ruled in favor of a lawsuit brought by the Conservation Law Foundation, the Ocean Conservancy, the National Audubon Society, and the Natural Resources Defense Council against the secretary of commerce, NOAA, and the National Marine Fisheries Service. Judge Kessler subsequently allowed input from various organizations to help her formulate interim fishing regulations for the 2002–2003 fishing season.

On March 6, 2002, in response to Judge Kessler's December ruling, Angela Sanfilippo, Andrew Giacalone, Paul Cohan, Paul Vitale, Bill Crossen, Bud Fernandes from Maine, Bob MacKinnon from Scituate, David Goethel from New Hampshire, Al Cottone, Joe Orlando, Bill Crosby, Vito Giacalone, and other second-and third-generation Gloucester fishermen travel to Room 222 at the Massachusetts State House in Boston, a room with dentil moldings, plaster acanthus-leaf cornice detailing, carved cherry bookcases with fluted pillars, and a marble fireplace. They arrive with the hope of communicating the message to the public that the scientific numbers from the National Marine Fisheries Service being used to shut down the fisheries are flawed and are being incorrectly interpreted.

The gathering was designed as a press conference and an opportunity for the fishing community to present its story, which many believe had been overlooked by Judge Kessler. In advance, the mayor's office in Gloucester had notified the press of the time and date of the meeting in hopes that the fishermen's story would be reported by local newspapers. In particular, Mayor Bell wanted to reach readers of the *Boston Globe*, which had just published an editorial based on old stock assessments and favoring a recommended limit of just twenty-two days at sea. The editorial writer seemed unconcerned that no one can support a family by working only twenty-two days per year, and apparently there was little interest on the part of the newspaper (at that time) in learning the truth about fish stocks.[1]

The mayor of Gloucester is angry. And rightfully so. Until he speaks, he gives the impression of a gentle patriarch, a thoughtful patrician. Now, in Room 222, he rises from his seat at the front table facing the audience. "This suit is crazy!" The way he elongates the letter *r* signals his passion for Gloucester and for his fishing community. To Mayor Bell, that fishing community defines 350 years of Gloucester tradition. And he will not let it be destroyed. He has argued long and hard for the forty million dollars of federal funding for studies and completion of a new fishing pier in Gloucester, and he is not about to look at an empty, underutilized pier. "The mission of coastal New England is to provide food for the world," he states simply. "And we aim to complete our mission!"

Next to the mayor, Ann Margaret Ferrante, the daughter of a Gloucester fishing family, looks tired. She is co-counsel for the Northeast Seafood Coalition, an alliance of fishermen from different New England ports who have united in an attempt to combat the latest threat, this one stemming from the federal ruling. For the last five days, Ann Margaret has been at meetings throughout the day and night as she attempted to draft a rebuttal in response to Judge Kessler's ruling, a ruling that could close down New England's fishing industry and destroy the remnants of the infrastructure that provide fresh New England fish to the public.

Steve Ouellette, outside counsel for the coalition, looks worried. He addresses the fishermen. First he tells them that the regulations being considered by Judge Kessler, who admits to knowing little about the fisheries, violate at least nine if not all of the National Standards set forth in the Magnuson Act. He then refers to one plaintiff, the Conservation Law Foundation: "By bringing this suit, they are playing around with more than fish stocks. They're playing around with your lives." He warns the fishermen that, "the Conservation Law Foundation hires its own PR firms and it hires people to put you out of business."

The irony here is that the suit in question does not directly address the fishing community. Yet the fishermen are the victims. As Bob MacKinnon sees it, "This suit has nothing to do with fish. It has nothing to do with whales. It has nothing to do with porpoises. It is all about money." Translated, that means that the Conservation Law Foundation exists only by raising money to fight causes. If it is not visible, it does not receive funds. And right now it is very visible at the expense of fishermen and coastal communities. And the public is not aware of what might be lost as a result.

Paul Howard, executive director of the New England Fishery Management Council, moves to an overhead projector. He places a series of transparencies on the projector, and the audience sees bar graphs and flow charts showing the rapid recovery of a majority of the groundfish stocks in both the Gulf of Maine and at a slightly lower level on Georges Bank. These transparencies are a product of the NMFS's Center for Scientific Studies at Woods Hole, the same group of national scientists responsible for the studies used by the Conservation Law Foundation in its suit *against* the National Marine Fisheries Service. But the transparencies show recent and relevant data—data not considered in the judge's ruling.

Paul Howard is followed by David Lincoln, a scientist from Gloucester, who also uses the federal government's scientific findings to show that stocks are recovering, and have recovered at remarkable rates— rates of recovery causing Frank Mirarchi in Scituate to say, "I never would have believed I would see these stocks returned to the levels of my childhood, and so quickly." Frank adds that it is the sacrifices of the fishermen that have made the rebuilding possible.

Paul Cohan, president of the Gulf of Maine Fishermen's Alliance, moves to a microphone set up for audience participation. He speaks with eloquence as he describes the many ways fishermen have been "tightening their belts" for ten years to help rebuild the stocks. Then he asks why they are "pawns in an eco-political drama."

Vito Giacalone, whose family has fished out of Gloucester for three generations, describes the conditions New England fishermen must fish under today: most are fishing alone on boats that used to fish with four to five men. Then he adds, "We're the true conservationists."

Paul Vitale speaks of the importance of safety at sea as it was stressed in his training at the Massachusetts Maritime Academy. He explains that present regulations place the fisherman in danger each time he goes out on the water. He points out that if Judge Kessler decides to accept proposed regulations that will close down the fisheries, she will also be closing down the 6.5 jobs ashore that each fisherman sustains by the nature of the work.

Paul Diodati, the man who replaced Phil Coates as director of the Division of Marine Fisheries for the Commonwealth of Massachusetts, is here in Room 222, in support of the fishermen. Staff members for Governor Jane Swift and U.S. Representative Barney Frank are present, as are two tireless advocates for the fisherman—Massachusetts state senator Bruce Tarr, who chairs the meeting, and Vito Calomo, executive director of the Massachusetts Fisheries Recovery Commission. Noticeably absent are representatives from Senator Kerry's office, Senator Kennedy's office, and the *Boston Globe*, which chose to send its reporter for the fisheries to Pawtucket, Rhode Island, to cover another issue being tackled by the Conservation Law Foundation.

The men and women sitting in chairs or standing with their backs against cherry bookcases are the elite cadre of the Gloucester fishing community. These people are not your guys who hang around the dock with nothing better to do than hop onto a fishing boat. They are not your nomadic spare hands on a swordfishing boat. These men and women grew up with fathers, grandfathers, and great-grandfathers who fished out of Gloucester. And before that their great-great-grandfathers fished in the waters off the coast of Sicily. As children, they attended the wakes and funerals of fishermen at Our Lady of Good Voyage, Gloucester's church atop the hill facing the sea. They are the survivors, and up until now they have come back from every storm. But they have never before encountered a threat quite like this lawsuit before Judge Kessler—

a lawsuit that has dramatically shifted and redefined alliances in the fishing debate, a lawsuit that may focus attention on how science is being distorted by special interests.

A line has been drawn using scientific tools such as stock assessments, computer models, and the numerical assumptions required in any effort at scientific evaluation. Those numbers, computer models, and assumptions could be meaningful to the scientist trying to better understand where the fish go, why and where they spawn, and why there are more or less of them at different times. Unfortunately, those numbers, computer models, and assumptions are being put to a very unscientific use. One interpretation of those numbers and assumptions is being taken as fact and used to establish whether men and women may work or not work, whether coastal communities will survive or not survive, and also whether the public will be able or not be able to eat fresh native fish. That interpretation of numbers and assumptions may also result in the least sustainable means of catching fish, the factory trawlers, replacing the true conservationist—the small fisherman.

Two weeks after the meeting at the State House in Boston, a group of Chatham hook fishermen met at the headquarters of the Cape Cod Commercial Hook Fishermen's Association for a presentation of the position Judge Kessler had just heard from the scientists working for the National Marine Fisheries Service in Woods Hole.

Outside, thirty- to forty-knot winds were blowing sleet and freezing rain against the windows. Inside, Steven Murawski, the evening's guest speaker and chief of the Population Dynamics branch of the Northeast Fisheries Science Center, was wearing a short-sleeved Hawaiian shirt and jeans. And that was not his only disconnect. He began his talk by showing a slide of himself with a giant marlin he had caught in his earlier years. The audience was not impressed. Dr. Murawski then showed a series of slides similar to those shown by Paul Howard and David Lincoln in Boston. Dr. Murawski's slides, however, pointed to a drastically different interpretation. In the slides shown in Chatham, and in the bar graphs presented to Judge Kessler, the target for sustainable fishing has been raised to a higher level than that previously required by the Sustainable Fisheries Act. Thus the increase in fish stocks shown in all three slide presentations appears to be well below the required target numbers, even though the actual numbers indicate a remarkable rebuilding of the fish stocks, an increase of 150 percent since 1990.

For the audience of fishermen, Dr. Murawski's new approach to fisheries management will mandate even fewer days at sea, lower catch limits, and fewer boats on the water. It basically eliminates commercial fishing for the men and women whose livelihood is dependent on the numbers and interpretations presented.

"We're going to push the limits," Dr. Murawski states.

"Are you saying we're all part of an experiment?" a fisherman asks.

"It's just 'adaptive management.' "

Another fishermen points out that what he had just been shown is "bullshit" to him.

Call it what you like, but the whimsical material presented in Chatham has no basis for determining how or when the men in this room can work, or how many fish or what kinds of fish they should be catching.

When Brian Rothschild, dean of the Graduate School of Marine Sciences and Technology for the University of Massachusetts, heard about the Chatham meeting, he emphatically stated, "What you have to do is look at the law of the land, and that's how we govern. And I don't interpret the Sustainable Fisheries Act as saying that we do experiments with fishermen's lives." He added for clarification, "There's ten national standards [inherent in the SFA] and there's the 'best science available' requirement. It [the SFA] doesn't say that you do an experiment and that experiment is the best science available."

In Chatham, as the meeting was ending, a fisherman in a plaid shirt seated in the middle of the room asked why science and the government aren't doing more for the fisherman. He wanted to know why habitat degradation isn't being studied and why the take of herring and other food fish for the cod isn't being analyzed better as possible threats to the cod stocks. His questions remain unanswered.

Brian Rothschild is possibly the best qualified person to answer questions relating to the fisheries. His father was an obstetrician at a time when medical doctors had their offices attached to their homes. In that atmosphere, the young Brian had opportunity to observe tropical fish in the fish tank in his father's waiting room. And he had access to a microscope. Ever since, he has worked with fish, either in academic or government jobs. He has held professorships and studied fish at the University of Maryland and the University of Washington. He has been either a visiting professor or faculty advisor at the University of Hawaii, Scripps Institution of Oceanography, Woods Hole Oceanographic Institution and Harvard University, to name a few. His government employment includes work with the Department of Commerce. He has served as senior policy advisor to NOAA, director of the Southwest Fisheries Science Center, LaJolla, and deputy director of the Northwest and

Alaska Fisheries Science Center, Seattle. Along with Senator Magnuson, he helped organize the Magnuson Fishery Management and Conservation Act.

From his perspective in helping to craft the Magnuson Act, Dr. Rothschild is not happy with the way he sees the provisions of that act being distorted. By the time Brian Rothschild and I met in his office, Judge Kessler had produced two separate orders imposing restrictive fishing regulations on the grundfish community. The first order would have allowed Paul Vitale in Gloucester to fish twenty-two days out of a year; the second might allow him to fish sixty-six or seventy days of the year, but the actual requirements of the latter ruling are so unclear that fishermen like Paul in Gloucester and Frank Mirarchi in Scituate are trying to work in June, 2002 under regulations that won't be clarified until August—two months in the future. And the Coast Guard, which President Bush has targeted for "homeland security," has no spare recruits to either interpret the new rules or police the fisheries.

"My view is that both Judge Kessler's first remedy and the compromise remedy are far outside the intent, the notions and the ideas of the Sustainable Fisheries Act," Brian Rothschild says, "especially with regards to its legislative history as the Fishery Management and Conservation Act of 1976. So I think the whole thing is really out of hand, particularly from the point of view of equity." He leans back in his chair as he explains, "A group sues the government for not doing its job. Everybody agrees the government isn't doing its job, so the government should pay, but it's not the government who is paying. It's the fishing industry. And, in fact it's the component of the fishing industry that can least afford to cut back on their days at sea." Dr. Rothschild occupies a corner office about a quarter mile from where Judy Ramos lives overlooking New Bedford Harbor. As he looks out the window in that direction, he says, "I really feel sorry for the people who have their lives invested in the fisheries and are being held to a standard that I think is much too hard. I just don't think it's right, and," he adds, "if you're saying this is conservation, it isn't!"

Basically all problems with fisheries regulations reduce themselves to problems with stock assessment. And stock assessments, specifically stock assessments for cod, are imprecise because they involve a lot of steps using precise data, much that has yet to be collected. Everybody knows that the stocks of cod are at a relatively low historical level. "Whether or not they are overfished," Rothschild says, "that's something nobody knows because the definition of overfishing is not very clear, technically, and so people say that if a stock is low, that it is overfished. But [without realizing it, he recalls the words of the fisherman in Chatham] one reason it [the stock] could be low is the ocean environment."

Some fisheries scientists and environmentalists point to the collapse of the Newfoundland northern cod fishery as the rationale for demanding stringent regulations to protect the New England fisheries from the same type of collapse. And they often use that fishery as an example of why they are "protecting the stocks for fishermen." Brian Rothschild sees the causes for the Newfoundland fisheries collapse in different terms. "In most of these fisheries where the stock has collapsed, it's due to a combination of fishing and the environment. We tend to think of the natural environment, but we also have the anthropogenic environment [that caused by human degradation]." He explains, "I mean you can't separate now the changes in the ocean temperature completely from the changes in the atmosphere, and that's an oversimplification because a small change in the ocean temperature can have a very big change on the density structure of the ocean and thereby the ocean currents." His implication is that current changes can move fish, cause changes to the food formation for fish, and alter spawning. "You know, there's a lot we don't know," he reminds us.

As Dan McKiernan predicted, the fish are returning. And, as Dan predicted, no one has figured out the best way to deal with a recovering resource. Kevin Shea described a day in December 2001 when he was allowed to fish, but allowed to land only 400 pounds of cod. He was fishing alone because he could no longer afford to pay Paul or Joey. The first day, he made four sets and hauled up 1,400 pounds of cod in three hundred feet of water. One thousand pounds had to be thrown back, all market-size cod and all dead due to the depths of water where he was fishing for winter flounder. The next day, he decided to set only three nets in an effort to avoid catching so much cod. Again, he caught 1,400 pounds of cod. He was allowed to land only 400. The remainder would be food for dogfish, lobsters, and other scavengers. "It was sickening," Kevin related.

Through January, February, March, and April, Kevin watched the charter boats return with coolers full of fish and no regulations on the catch, except for an additional limit of two more inches on the minimum size for cod. Kevin was not allowed to fish from January through April, but the charter boats were. He thought of the old phrase, "If you can't beat 'em, join 'em." And he used the time to study and qualify for a captain's license to enable him to take recreational charters out on *Endeavor*. He joked that his captain's license was a "license to steal." But not for long! Kevin successfully captained two charter party trips. Then the National Marine Fisheries Service effectively clamped down on the commercial fishermen's advantage in chartering while the fishing grounds were closed to them. A new ruling permits a commercial fisherman to take charters out for pay only on the condition that the captain-fisherman not fish commercially for three months after a charter. The regular charter boats continue to leave the dock, and their paying guests return with the usual coolers full of an unlimited amount of cleaned, iced fish.[2]

Scituate Harbor in 2002 is a sad contrast to Scituate Harbor when Charlie Butman fished on board *Orca*. Today, only three draggers and three gillnetters are left in the harbor. The draggers cannot find crew, for no one can earn a living based on the minuscule catch allowed by the regulations, together with the uncertainties of changing regulations. And the gillnetters or day boats cannot earn a living because they are not allowed to fish in the areas within a radius that allows them to return home at night. Kevin Shea took *Endeavor* out to Nauset and anchored there overnight during the Scituate closures so that he would be able to fish. This is an area exposed to pounding seas and rolling waves. It is also where deep-sea divers find the remains of many an eighteenth-century vessel. Fortunately for Kevin, it was a mild winter with few storms.

There is something wrong with regulations that force men and women into life-threatening situations, just as there is something wrong with regulations that require the killing and discarding of a valuable resource. There is something wrong with closing down small, independent businesses that provide jobs and support communities in a way that attracts more business to the area and enriches the larger community. And there is something wrong with regulations made by men and women who are in the position of making philosophical decisions to regulate others' lives but who are not directly affected by the decisions they make.

Harriet Didriksen and other fishermen speak of fishing as a privilege. One reason they fish is because they feel privileged to be able to be outside on the ocean. Harriet echoes the sentiments of many traditional fishermen: "I do not feel I own the fish. My family used to fish offshore from Hatteras to Canada—steaming twenty-four hours out of New Bedford before reaching the fishing grounds. Now, we don't go that far because you run into the various boundaries, either the two-hundred-mile boundary or the Hague Line or one of the boundaries marking a protected area." Harriet points out, "Our people were willing to go to sea when others weren't. It's a hard life, a miserable life. But, it's a life where people who are not highly schooled have been able to make a good living—if they are willing to do the work. And that's been the type of people who have gone fishing and stayed with it. If it were not for the people who took the risk, there wouldn't be much of a fishing industry in this country."

Bob MacKinnon is a fisherman who has worked tirelessly to keep his community on the ocean. In a meeting at the Manomet Center for Conservation Sciences in February 2001, Chris Glass outlined the many ways the attending fishermen could get funding for cooperative research projects between scientists and the fishing industry. Chris was being supported by a grant stemming from the same research project that took place while I was on board the *Christopher Andrew II*. The fishermen attending the meeting were there on their own time to learn more about how each could participate in future research projects.

The fishermen know Chris and trust him. This trust enabled him to solicit ideas for research projects from the audience, and it stimulated a flow of creative responses from the fishermen in attendance. Bob MacKinnon was one of those fishermen. At the close of the meeting, Chris suggested that each of the men there should think about thanking Senators Kerry and Kennedy and any other politicians responsible for the lobbying required to secure the twenty million dollars now available to fund the planned scientific research. Somehow, no one thought to thank Bob MacKinnon, who has been beating on the doors of both Kerry and Kennedy, sitting outside the offices of William Delahunt, U.S. congressman from Massachusetts, and traveling to meetings up and down the coast to speak for the fishermen. Bob's efforts on behalf of the fishing community have brought to the various elected officials a portrait of specific individuals not allowed to earn a living—one being Bob's son, who just left the industry. Without Bob MacKinnon's efforts, money might not be available to purchase the computers used to tally numbers of fish or to pay the salaries of the scientists involved in the research or to pay for the fuel to take the *Christopher Andrew II* from the dock to the fishing grounds where the experiments are being conducted.

A beige trailer sits in the parking lot alongside the building housing the labs and offices of the Graduate School of Marine Sciences and Technology for the University of Massachusetts, where Brian Rothschild is dean. This trailer houses the computers, records, and all the data generated by the cod-tagging experiment coordinated by Bob MacKinnon and previously employing Dave Martins, who is now in Alaska. Bob's tagging experiment is beginning to show results that reinforce the fishermen's first-hand accounts of the behavior of what the scientific community now labels "Gulf of Maine Cod."

Brian Rothschild unequivocally speaks of the tagging experiment as a "great success," and he points out that it reconfirms that cod swim

234 | Vanishing Species

from the Gulf of Maine to Georges Bank and from Georges Bank to Browns Bank off Nova Scotia. "From a stock assessment point of view," he says, "the immigration [or movement] of cod can exaggerate mortality rates." One reason the National Marine Fisheries Service stock assessments show such a high mortality rate for Gulf of Maine cod is that they don't take into consideration that the cod swim out of the area. Cod don't recognize national boundaries, and when they are caught in Canada, they don't count with NMFS as fish being landed from the same stock—even though they may be sold by Frank Patania in Boston and served in a Boston restaurant. Brian Rothschild uses the term "change of abundance" to explain what the stock assessments from NMFS are measuring. The stock assessments used to establish the Gulf of Maine cod TAC (totall allowable catch), the same stock assessments that are putting the inshore fisherman out of business, do not take into consideration that cod move.

In most cases, if you subtract natural mortality from abundance, you get fishing mortality. "But, in this particular case," Dr. Rothschild says, referring to cod, "there is a third component, which is immigration. So if you don't include cod immigration, then you consider natural mortality fixed and you over-estimate fishing mortality."

What Bob MacKinnon is seeing is one stock that travels from the Gulf of Maine south to Georges Bank, not two separate stocks as is indicated in the stock assessment surveys prepared by the National Marine Fisheries Service. And the cod-tagging experiment is providing some precise data that previously was not available. Brian Rothschild describes the tags as being "like clocks that record the ocillation and pressure wave that goes over a cod as it swims. If I see that a codfish was picked up at three-thirty in the afternoon of August 14," he explains, "I can check my tide table and see when it was high tide. And I can then tell you where that cod was and I can plot the track of that cod."

The pressure placed on the National Marine Fisheries Service by some extreme environmental groups has caused NMFS to tighten regulations on the fishing communities to the point where the inshore fisherman fishing for groundfish is being put out of business on the pretext that the "best available science" is being used. Yet at this time the data being collected by Bob MacKinnon, Frank and Andrew Mirarchi, Dave Martins, and others is not being considered in formulating fishing regulations, even though it might reverse the movement to eliminate our inshore groundfishing communities in New England.

To make matters worse, the type of science being employed to regulate fishermen's lives may be flawed at best and inaccurate at the least. Matthew Stommel, a fisherman from Woods Hole, Massachusetts, is the son of a distinguished oceanographer and scientist. Matt grew up learning that if you are using a statistical sampling to measure something, you should be accurate, and that inaccuracies can have disastrous results. In February 2000, he happened to see the cables for the NOAA research vessel *Albatross IV* being calibrated, and he noted that each of the two cables was being measured separately and incorrectly.

Matt Stommel realized that the cables being measured would be pulling the bottom trawl used to estimate fish populations, the same trawl that would eventually determine how many days he would be allowed to work each year and how many fish he would be allowed to catch. He contacted the National Marine Fisheries Service and asked them to check the lengths of the cables before the spring population survey began. The cables needed to be of equal length in order to keep the net open to incoming fish. Regulators chose to do nothing about the unequal cables. Prior to Judge Kessler's decision, Matt Stommel again asked NMFS to check the calibration of the two cables, a difference estimated to be as great as six feet and enough to significantly low the estimated biomass of groundfish stocks.

Two-and-one-half years later, 1,700 tows later, and one judge's decision later, the issue of uneven cables on the primary vessel used by federal scientists to regulate the fisheries was finally addressed. The number of fish needlessly thrown overboard dead in that two-and-one-half-year time span, and the resulting hardships endured by fishermen and their families, remain to be calculated.

Bob MacKinnon could have left the fishery when he was forced to sell his boat. Instead, he chose to work at odd jobs that permitted him to continue to work for his community. As a result, he was available for the job as coordinator of the cod-tagging experiment when it came along. Fortunately, Bob loves the water and wants to find a sustainable way to enable him and the other men and women in his industry to get back doing what they do best.

And that's what *Vanishing Species* is about. It's about finding something you love and working to protect it. It's also about fairness and respect—respect for other species, respect for a unique way of life, and respect for the integrity of coastal communities. It's about protecting fragile ecosystems, including the men and women who are a part of that balance. It's also about belonging to something larger than yourself. And it's about the importance of feeling good about what you do every day as well as what makes you a contributing member of a larger community. Yes, it's about more than catching fish.

Notes

1 New England Groundfishing (pp. 1–42)

1. On February 22, 2002, the *Boston Globe* reported, "Officials at the Massachusetts Port Authority agreed yesterday to negotiate new leases . . . that could extend into 2027" (Mac Daniel, "Boston Fish Pier Tenants Get New Deal, Development Fears Persist at Prime Site," p. B3).

2. From a World Wildlife Fund ad in *Time*, international edition, July 20, 1998.

3. As cited by Haberstroh, "Scuttled But . . . ," p. A7.

4. Bigelow, *Narrative History of Cohasset*, p. 404.

5. Captain Sylvanus Smith, *Fisheries of Cape Ann* (Gloucester: Press of Gloucester Times Co., 1915), p. 88.

6. Ibid., p. 90.

7. Ibid., p. 91.

8. Johnston, *New England Fisheries*, p. ix.

9. Garland, *Down to the Sea*, p. 17.

10. Oaks, *Gloucester Fishermen's Institute*, p. 12.

11. Garland, *Down to the Sea*, pp. 17–18.

12. As quoted by Rob Jogodzinski, "Shooting Dice with the Devil," *National Fisherman*, April 1998, p. 29.

13. Ibid., p. 29

14. Church, *American Fishermen*, p. 28.

15. Smith, *Fisheries of Cape Ann*, p. 198.

16. Jensen, *Cod*, p. 128.

17. See Warner, *Distant Waters*.

18. From a graph showing commercial landings prepared by the Northeast Fisheries Science Center, and included in the National Research Council, *Review of Northeast Fishery Stock Assessments*.

19. Moss and Terkla Doeringer, *New England Fishing Economy*, p. 20.

20. Ibid., p. 17.

2 The Regulations versus the Regulated (pp. 43–89)

1. Bigelow and Schroeder, *Fishes of the Gulf of Maine*, p. 192.

2. Ibid.

237

3. One technical difference exists in that the gillnetter is charged for sixteen hours each time he or she leaves the dock, even if the vessel is only on the water for three hours. The rationale is that the extra hours make up for the fact that the nets remain in the water while the boat returns to port.

4. *New Bedford Standard Times*, March 1, 1994, p. A5.

5. National Research Council, *Review of Northeast Fishery Stock Assessments*, p. 62.

6. Paul K. Dayton, "Reversal of the Burden of Proof in Fisheries Management," *Science* 279 (6 February 1998): 821.

7. Associated Press article, "Fisheries Official Has Catch Seized," *Boston Globe*, May 23, 2001, p. B4.

8. Shrimp are considered a vector species in transmitting the *anisakis simplex* or cod worm. The dealer who buys cod from Frank Mirarchi and other local fishermen employs two to three workers to examine each cod to remove worms from the Gulf of Maine cod with tweezers before distributing the fish to retail markets and restaurants.

9. Charlie Ess, "Harboring Seals," *National Fisherman*, (January 2000), p. 24.

3 Are Regulations Destroying the Fish and Fisherman? (pp. 90–108)

1. "Philanthropy in America," p. 19.
2. Allen, "Bottoming Out," p. C1.
3. Safina, *Song for the Blue Ocean*, p. 43.

4 Demand Creates Supply (pp. 109–144)

1. As quoted by Scott Allen in an article entitled "Top New England Fishing Ground Collapses," p. A1.

2. The National Marine Fisheries Service semiannual trawl survey that provides what is referred to as a "relative abundance index" is also a component of stock assessments.

3. As reported by Riccardi, "Chilean Sea Bass?" pp. C3–C4.

4. On a winter menu for the Boston restaurant Icarus, one of the restaurant's fish suppliers was credited with catching the fish "with a hook and line."

5. Soares and Peterson, *Aquaculture Opportunities*, p. 4.

6. Goldberg and Triplett, *Murky Waters*, p. 7.

7. Soares and Peterson, *Aquaculture Opportunities*, p. 4.

8. "Status of World Aquaculture," p. 6.

9. Joshua N. Goldman, "Potential for Finfish Culture in Massachusetts," paper presented at the Symposium on the Potential for Development of Aquaculture in Massachusetts, Chatham/Edgartown/Dartmouth, Massachusetts, February 15–17, 1995, p. 13.

10. Goldberg and Triplett, *Murky Waters*, p. 9.

Bibliography

Ackerman, Edward A. *New England's Fishing Industry*. Chicago: University of Chicago Press, 1941.

Adams, Steve. "A Wave of Danger: New Rules Keep Fishermen out Longer in Unfamiliar Waters." *Patriot Ledger*, January 27, 1999, p. 9.

Allen, Scott. "Bottoming out: Biologists Say Huge Weighted Nets Are Diminishing the Food Chain on Seafloor off New England." *Boston Globe*, August 17, 1998, p. C1.

———. "A Top New England Fishing Ground Collapses, Codfish Stocks Drop in Gulf of Maine." *Boston Globe*, December 11, 1998, p. A1.

Archives Committee, City of Gloucester. *Deaths at Sea before 1873*. Addendum to Fishermen's Memorial & Record Book, 1995.

Barcott, Bruce. "Aquaculture's Troubled Harvest." *Mother Jones*, November–December 2001, pp. 38–45.

Bartlett, Kim. *The Finest Kind: The Fishermen Of Gloucester*. New York: W. W. Norton & Company, 1977.

Benson, Tom. "Finding the Right Balance: Local Fisherman Hopes Study Leads to Regulatory Relief." (Quincy, Mass.) *Patriot Ledger*, December 11, 2000, local p. 1.

Bigelow, E. Victor. *A Narrative History of the Town of Cohasset, Massachusetts*. Committee on Town History, 1898.

Bigelow, Henry B., and William G. Schroeder. *Fishes of the Gulf of Maine*. 1953. Reprint, Cambridge, Mass.: Woods Hole Oceanographic Institution and the Museum of Comparative Zoology, Harvard University, 1964.

Boesch, Donald, et al. "Factors in the Decline of Coastal Ecosystems" (Response to "Historical Overfishing and the Recent Collapse of Coastal Ecosystems). *Science* 293 (27 July 2001): 344.

Boreman, J., B. S. Nakashima, J. A. Wilson, and R. L. Kendall, editors. *Northwest Atlantic Groundfish: Perspectives on a Fishery Collapse*. Bethesda, Md.: American Fisheries Society, 1977.

Boston Cooking School. *The Boston Fish Pier Seafood Recipe Cookbook*. 1913. With an introduction by Jasper White. Reprint, Watertown, Mass.: Doyle Studio Press.

Bowers, George M. *Statistics of the Fisheries of the New England States for 1905*. Washington, D.C.: Government Printing Office, 1907.

Budiansky, Stephen. *Nature's Keepers: The New Science of Nature Management*. New York: Free Press, 1995.

Bunting, W. H., editor. *Steamers, Schooners, Cutters & Sloops: Marine Photographs of N. L. Stebbins Taken 1884 to 1907.* Boston: Society for the Preservation of New England Antiquities, 1974.

Carey, Richard Adams. *Against the Tide.* Boston: Houghton Mifflin Company, 1999.

Carr, H. Arnold. "Trawl Impacts Vary Depending on the Bottom." *Commercial Fisheries News*, February 1999, pp. 11B and 20B.

Castro, Carlos A., and Scott J. Soares, compilers and editors. *Proceedings of the Symposium on the Potential for Development of Aquaculture in Massachusetts.* NOAA Technical Memorandum NMFS-NE-109, U.S. Department of Commerce, National Oceanic and Atmospheric Administration, National Marine Fisheries Service, Northeast Region Northeast Fisheries Science Center, 1996.

Chapelle, Howard I. *The American Fishing Schooners, 1825–1935.* New York: W. W. Norton & Company, 1973.

Church, Albert Cook. *American Fishermen.* Text by James B. Connolly. New York: Bonanza Books, 1940.

Cone, Maria. "Pollutants Seen Feminizing Aquatic Life." *Los Angeles Times*, syndicated in *Boston Globe*, September 23, 1998.

Cordell, John, editor. *A Sea Of Small Boats.* Cambridge, Mass.: Cultural Survival, Inc., 1989.

Daley, Beth. "Report Advocates Marine Preserves, Seeks Park Regions in Gulf of Maine." *Boston Globe*, November 20, 2000, p. B1.

Dayton, Paul K. "Reversal of the Burden of Proof in Fisheries Management." *Science* 279 (6 February 1998): 821.

Dobbs, David. *The Great Gulf: Fishermen, Scientists, and the Struggle to Revive the World's Greatest Fishery.* Washington, D.C.: Island Press/Shearwater Press, 2000.

Doeringer, Moss and Terkla. *The New England Fishing Economy: Jobs, Income and Kinship.* Amherst: University of Massachusetts Press, 1986.

Edwards, William Churchill. *Historic Quincy, Massachusetts.* Quincy, Mass.: City of Quincy, 1945.

Ess, Charlie. "Harboring Seals." *National Fisherman*, January 2000.

Garland, Joseph. *Down to the Sea: The Fishing Schooners of Gloucester.* Boston: David R. Godine, 1983.

Garofalo, Lt. John (U.S. Coast Guard). "Protecting America's Fisheries." *Coast Guard* (Washington, D.C.), May 1998, insert.

Goldberg, Rebecca, and Tracy Triplett. *Murky Waters: Environmental Effects of Aquaculture in the United States.* Executive Summary. Washington, D.C.: Environmental Defense Fund Publications. 1997.

Greene, Katie. "Bigger Populations Needed for Sustainable Harvests." *Science* 296 (17 May 2002): 1229–1230.

Haberstroh, Joe. "Scuttled But. . . ." *Newsday*, November 15, 1998, pp. 7–8.

Harris, Michael. *Lament for an Ocean: The Collapse of the Atlantic Cod Fishery, a True Crime Story.* Toronto: McLelland & Stewart, 1998.

Highsmith, R. Tod. "The Sea's Unwanted Bounty." *Conservation Sciences*, fall 1997, pp. 8–13.

"Is Our Fish Fit to Eat?" *Consumer Reports*, February 1992, p. 103.

Jackson, Jeremy B. C., et al. "Historical Overfishing and the Recent Collapse of Coastal Ecosystems." *Science*, 293 (27 July 2001): 629–638.

Jegallian, Karin. "Plan Would Protect New England Coast." *Science* 284 (9 April 1999): 237.

Jensen, Albert C. *The Cod: A Saga of the Sea*. Inglis, Fla.: Deep Sea Press, 1984.

Johnston, Paul Forsyth. *The New England Fisheries: A Treasure Greater Than Gold*. Accompanying the Russell W. Knight Collection of New England Fishing Scenes. Salem, Mass.: Peabody Museum of Salem, 1984.

Kaiser, M. J., and J. W. Horwood. "Damage Limitation in the Deep." *New Scientist*, October 11, 1997, p. 55.

Kurlansky, Mark. *Cod: A Biography That Changed the World*. New York: Walker and Company, 1997.

Leddy, Linda. "A Cleaner Catch." Editorial. *Conservation Sciences*, fall 1997, p. 2.

Lustgarten, Steve. "Fish: What's the Catch?" *EarthSave*, February 21, 1999, p. 3.

Maggio, Theresa. *Mattanza: Love & Death in the Sea of Sicily*. Cambridge, Mass.: Perseus Publishing, 2000.

Main, J., and G. I. Sangster. "A Study of Bottom Trawling Gear on Both Sand and Hard Ground." Department of Agriculture and Fisheries for Scotland, Scottish Fisheries Research Report No. 14, 1979.

Matthiessen, Peter. *Men's Lives: The Surfmen and Baymen of the South Fork*. New York: Random House, 1986.

McCloskey, William. *Fishdecks: Seafarers of the North Atlantic*. New York: Paragon House, 1990.

Meade, Tom. "Fish Farming Industry Spawns Ecological Concerns." *Providence Journal-Bulletin*, February 13, 1994, p. 1A.

Morse, Dana L. "The Northeast Fisheries Assistance Program and Fishing Industry Grants." Paper presented at the Symposium on the Potential for Development of Aquaculture in Massachusetts, Chatham/Edgartown/Dartmouth, Massachusetts, February 15–17, 1995.

National Marine Fisheries Service. *Background Information: Stock Status of Gulf of Maine Cod*. Northeast Regional Office, Gloucester, Mass.: U.S. Department of Commerce, September 17, 1998.

National Marine Fisheries Service. Strategic Plan for Fisheries Research. Washington, D.C.: U.S. Department of Commerce, February 1998.

National Research Council. *Marine Protected Areas: Tools for Sustaining Ocean Ecosystems*. Washington, D.C.: National Academy Press, 2001.

———. *Review of Northeast Fishery Stock Assessments*. Contract No. 50-DKNA-6-90040 of the National Academy of Sciences and the National Oceanic and Atmospheric Administration. Washington, D.C.: National Academy Press, 1998.

Naylor, Rosamond L., Rebecca J. Goldburg, Jurgenne H. Primavera, Nils Kautsky, Malcolm C. M. Beveridge, Jason Clay, Carl Folke, Jane Lubchenco, Harold Mooney, and Maxz Troell. "Effect of Aquaculture on World Fish Supplies." *Nature* 405 (29 June 2000): 1017–1023.

New England Fishery Management Council. Northeast Multispecies (Groundfish) Stock Assessment and Fishery Evaluation (SAFE) Report. Saugus, Mass., 1999.

NOAA Foundation for Stewardship. "NOAA Fisheries Strategic Plan." Web page, May 1997.

Oaks, Martha. *The Gloucester Fishermen's Institute, 1891–1991: A Social Center for Men of the Sea.* Gloucester, Mass.: Gloucester Fishermen's Institute, 1991.

Orlean, Susan. *The Orchid Thief.* New York: Ballantine Publishing Group, 1998.

Ostrom, Elinor, Joanna Burger, Christopher B. Field, Richard B. Norgaard, and David Policansky. "Revisiting the Commons: Local Lessons, Global Challenges." *Science* 284 (9 April 1999): 278–282.

Parfit, Michael. "Diminishing Returns: Exploiting the Ocean's Bounty." *National Geographic,* 188, no. 5 (November 1995): 2–37.

Pauly, Christensen, Dalsgaard, Froese, and Torres. "Fishing down Marine Food Webs." *Science* 279 (6 February 1998): 860–863.

"Philosophy in America: The Gospel of Wealth." *The Economist,* May 30–June 5, 1998, p. 19.

"Pioneers of the Banks: Four Interviews." Compiled by Joseph D., Thomas, edited by Paul Cyr. *Spinner* 3: 90–119.

Plotkin, Mark J. *Tales of a Shaman's Apprentice: An Ethnobotanist Searches for New Medicines in the Amazon Rain Forest.* New York: Penguin Books, 1993.

Posewitz, Jim. *Beyond Fair Chase: The Ethic and Tradition of Hunting.* Helena, Mont.: Falcon Press Publishing Co., in cooperation with Orion—The Hunters Institute and the United Conservation Alliance, 1994.

Prybot, Peter K. *White-Tipped Orange Masts.* Gloucester, Mass.: Curious Traveler Press, 1998.

Riccardi, Victoria Abbott. "Chilean Sea Bass? You Must Mean Patagonian Toothfish." *Boston Globe,* October 21, 1998, pp. C3–C4.

Robinson, Sue. "It Pays to Display." *National Fisherman,* February 1999, p. 18–19.

Safina, Carl. *Song for the Blue Ocean: Encounters along the World's Coasts and Beneath the Seas.* New York: Henry Holt and Company, 1997.

"The Sea Survey." *The Economist.* May 23, 1998, pp. 3–18.

Scheffer, Victor. *The Year of the Whale.* New York: Charles Scribners Sons, 1969.

Shillinger, Kurt. "In Africa, a New Idea for Sustainable Farming: Saltwater." *Boston Globe,* March 13, 2001, pp. C1–C3.

Soares, Scott, and Susan Peterson. *Aquaculture Opportunities: Handbook for Local Officials and Aquaculture Proponents.* Made possible by a grant through the Massachusetts Executive Office of Economic Affairs from the U.S. Economic Development Administration in collaboration with Ecological

Engineering Associates, Marion, Mass., and Trio Algarvio, New Bedford, Mass., 1996. Center for Marine Science, Environment and Technology, University of Massachusetts—Dartmouth, North Dartmouth, Mass.

"Status of World Aquaculture." *Aquaculture Magazine, Buyer's Guide '98 and Industry Directory*, 27th edition, 1998.

Story, Dana A. *The Shipbuilders of Essex: A Chronicle of Yankee Endeavor.* Gloucester, Mass.: Ten Pound Island Book Company, 1995.

Stump, Ken, and Dave Batker. *Sinking Fast: How Factory Trawlers Are Destroying U.S. Fisheries and Marine Ecosystems.* A Greenpeace Report. Washington, D.C.: Greenpeace, August 1996.

U.S. Coast Guard Fiscal Year 2000 Budget in Brief. Washington, D.C.: U.S. Coast Guard, 2000.

U.S. Department of Commerce, the National Oceanic and Atmospheric Administration, Sanctuaries and Reserves Division. *Stellwagen Bank National Marine Sanctuary, Final Environmental Impact Statement/Management Plan.* Volumes 1 and 2. Silver Spring, Md.: U.S. Department of Commerce, July 1993.

Walsh, Tom. "Survival Course: Project Aims to Keep Right Whales from Extinction." (Quincy, Mass.) *Patriot Ledger*, May 14, 1999.

Warner, William W. *Beautiful Swimmers.* Boston: Little Brown and Company, 1976.

———. *Distant Waters: The Fate of the North Atlantic Fisherman.* Boston: Little Brown and Company, 1983.

Watkins, Paul. *The Story of My Disappearance.* New York: Picador USA, 1998.

Watson Murphy, Martha. *A New England Fish Tale.* New York: Henry Holt & Co., 1997.

"Whale Protection Rules Are Finalized." Dateline Falmouth (AP). (Quincy, Mass.) *Patriot Ledger*, February 23, 1999, p. 13.

White, Donald J. *The New England Fishing Industry: A Study in Price and Wage Setting.* Cambridge, Mass.: Harvard University Press, 1954.

Whynott, Douglas. *Giant Bluefin.* New York: North Point Press, Farrar Straus and Giroux, 1995.

Wilcox, W. A. *The Fishing Industry: Annual Report of the American Fish Bureau.* Gloucester, Mass.: Robinson & Stephenson, February 1887.

Williams, Nigel. "Overfishing Disrupts Entire Ecosystem." *Science* 279 (6 February 1998): 809.

Williams, Wendy. "Dead Whales Underscore the Threat of Human Noise to Ocean World." *Boston Globe*, June 27, 2000.

Acknowledgments

In *Vanishing Species*, I have tried to paint a portrait of an industry. By including many different aspects of fishing, from the time the fish is swimming until it is served on a plate, I have attempted to show the reader the magnitude of the changes taking place. One segment of this story I hope I have adequately addressed is the scientific element. A large body of scientists are at work measuring and quantifying the disappearance of the fish stocks. Other scientists are at work looking at ways to increase spawning. Not many scientists are at work looking at the larger picture of *why* the fish might be disappearing. A special kind of scientist, the anthropologist, is studying the impact the disappearance of fish is having on the fishing community.

This book owes a debt to many of those scientists, notably Brian Rothschild, dean of the Graduate School of Marine Sciences and Technology, University of Massachusetts; Chris Glass and his colleagues at the Manomet Center for Conservation Sciences; and Arnold Carr, Michael Pol, and Dan McKiernan at the Commonwealth of Massachusetts, Division of Marine Fisheries. Stephen Murawski at the Northeast Fisheries Science Center at Woods Hole, a member of the Manomet stakeholders' committee, was kind enough to send me the *Review of Northeast Fishery Stock Assessments*, published in 1998 by the National Research Council, to which he contributed several years of research. I hope he will forgive my uncontrollable need to capture a scene.

I hope others in the scientific community will forgive the limited scope of the scientific material presented. For anyone who wishes to read some of the pertinent scientific papers on the subject, I recommend *Northwest Atlantic Groundfish: Perspectives on a Fishery Collapse*, edited by John Boreman, Brian S. Nakashima, James A. Wilson, and Robert L. Kendall.

I am grateful to Philip G. Coates, past director of the Massachusetts Division of Marine Fisheries, for allowing me to meet with him, and for sharing his views on the present state of groundfishing in New England. Special thanks go to Pat Fiorelli at the offices of the New England Fishery Management Council for her help and willingness to point me toward new sources. Bill Napolitano at the Southeastern Regional Plan-

ning & Economic Development District for the Commonwealth of
Massachusetts was instrumental in helping me track down various
publications and sources on the latest research into the potential for
aquaculture in New England.

Initially, I had intended to include the opinions of several men and
women involved in regulating the fisheries at the federal level. When I
telephoned them, I discovered a reluctance to talk to anyone writing a
book on groundfishing. Calls were never returned, and letters were ignored. After closer scrutiny, I learned that many of the men and women
whose work involves managing the fishing industry are fearful of being
quoted because of their concern about possible lawsuits. To me, that
tells its own story.

I have reported only what I saw or what was reported to me, and
what I have verified to have occurred. I am especially grateful to Lieutenant Commander Gwen Keenan in the Washington, D.C., office (most
recently in the Miami, Florida, office) of the U.S. Coast Guard for all
her help in providing information supporting my premise that the Coast
Guard's task is becoming increasingly difficult in an inverse relationship
to the size of its budget. I would particularly like to thank Lieutenant
Edward Sweeney of the New Bedford Coast Guard Station for his help
in permitting me to be on a boat for the Moriches Inlet reef-building
effort. I would also like to thank Lieutenant Williams, U.S. Coast Guard
Boston office, for his help in locating the F/V *Giannina G.*, formerly the
F/V *Orca*. Special thanks go to John Kelly, captain of the *Island Girl*,
for transporting me out to Moriches Reef—and back.

Thanks to Trevor Lloyd-Evans at the Manomet Center for Conservation Sciences, I was able to include much of the information on birds
appearing in the book. Because of Rich Canastra at New Bedford's
Whaling City Display Auction and Bruce Wheeler at the Portland Display Auction, I am able to provide the various statistics on fish landed
and fish sold through auction. Thanks to Amy O'Hearn at the Massachusetts Registry of Motor Vehicles, I was able to obtain the correct
numbers of environmental plates issued in Massachusetts. Thank you to
Linda Johnson at the Cape Ann Historical Museum for her help with
source materials.

Special thanks to Frank Mirarchi, who not only allowed me to interview him on several occasions and permitted me to go out on his F/V
Christopher Andrew II on a research trip, but also carefully read and
edited the complete manuscript for both factual information and stylistic
errors. There is no more gracious or informed man or woman on the
waterfront.

I owe a debt of gratitude to a number of writer friends who took time from their own writing not only to read my manuscript but also to edit, proofread, and reorganize some of the material. Thanks to Gail Bryan and Anne Moore, *Vanishing Species* is in the coherent shape you see before you. And thanks to Debby Tate, Evelyn and Geoffrey Farnum, and all the newspaper articles they sent me, I was able to stay in touch with the constantly changing landscape of fisheries regulations and developments. A special mention to Sally Weltman and David Replogle, who saw this book in print when others did not and encouraged me along the way to converting a larger audience.

For steering me through the intricacies of getting a book into print, I want to thank Phyllis Deutsch and Mary Crittendon at University Press of New England. Special thanks go to Will Hively, the best copy editor, who asked all the questions I should have asked myself.

This book would never have been completed without the aid of my husband and daughter. Richard's constant and unflagging encouragement, together with his scientific background, kept me writing, and kept me informed. He not only upgraded the computer system for me and reformatted the text but also acted as a scientific clipping agency, keeping me in touch with relevant articles and reports. And he made a map for me and for you. Whenever I could not find the perfect word, he supplied it. My daughter Lily spent most of a college break editing the material for style. She was a constant source for new material and always a reliable boost to my spirits.

Index

Many ship names are preceded by "F/V."